GW00777401

se for *War Torn*

"This is a wonderful book, exhilarating, poignant, tragic, heroic and above all full of courage. From the very first page I felt proud to follow in these women's footsteps."

—CHRISTIANE AMANPOUR, CNN correspondent

"*War Torn* is honest, heart-wrenching and laced with self-deprecating humor."

—*Los Angeles Times*

"*War Torn*—a book Bush should read."

—HELEN THOMAS, former UPI White House correspondent

"*War Torn* poignantly, though often with bittersweet overtones, documents [the reporters'] courage, compassion and professionalism. . . . an invaluable recollection of all that was and is Vietnam."

—*Rocky Mountain News*

"Timely . . . a refresher course in the wages of war."

—*The Des Moines Register*

"A powerful collection of memories by nine remarkable women . . . a terrific book, parts of which will rank with Michael Herr's *Dispatches* (1977) in capturing the atmosphere of the American experience in Vietnam."

—United Press International

"The nine chapters are as distinct as the women who wrote them. Each, in its own way, speaks to the will of the reporters to defy convention in pursuit of their personal and professional callings, and to the odd conjoining of joy and grief the experience exacted."

—*The Honolulu Advertiser*

"[The women] told the stories that weren't being told. They spoke about the children. They spoke about the soldiers. They spoke about the utter destruction. They taught us about the people of Vietnam, their history, their customs. . . . Their reporting was more complex, as was this war. . . . These intensely personal stories of war chronicle their heroic efforts to uncover the truth."

—*San Francisco Chronicle*

"Stories hammered out in foxholes under falling mortars. Hard drinking and sex for escape between assignments. If these sound like chest-thumping tales told by generations of male war correspondents, maybe that's the triumph of *War Torn*. . . . The stories satisfy the main question: what it was like for women to work and live in the most male environment of all, war. Hell. But they wouldn't have missed it for the world."

—*The Hartford Courant*

"For the women of *War Torn*, it was perversely, as Charles Dickens wrote of another conflict almost 200 years earlier, the best of times and the worst of times, a time of reason and a time of insanity. Their book is a fascinating, worthy tribute to a group of talented, courageous and stubborn women."

—*The Orlando Sentinel*

"[*War Torn*] offers compelling reasons why the news industry ought to encourage conflict reporting from both genders. . . . A refreshingly honest book."

—Associated Press

"Candid and introspective . . . full of the unexpected."

—*Stanford Magazine*

"None of the nine women who reminisce about covering the Vietnam War in this book went there because she was satisfied with the status quo. Instead, each leaned out to grab on to the defining moment of her generation, and each came up with her own version of the brass ring: some double dose of talent, courage, perseverance or perception that makes these reflections just plain gripping."

—*San Jose Mercury News*

"*War Torn* is, surprisingly, a love story, but the lover is more mercurial, volatile, and dangerous than any siren you'll find in Greek mythology. The lover is Vietnam. The story is the oscillating passion of nine women journalists who covered the war there and in Cambodia between 1966 and 1975. . . . They describe all of it with a language so beautiful, it can only come from seasoned writers who are stricken straight through the heart with love and pain."

—*Martha's Vineyard Times*

"Readers will be glad these reporters finally decided to probe their past. In *War Torn*, Vietnam becomes real again, the way it was during the 1960s, when it was vivid and live every night on the news."

—*Deseret News* (Salt Lake City)

"The writing here has almost uniform greatness; it's so vivid, so acute, so achingly and unflinchingly honest that it transports you across the years and miles. . . . Here's to nine female journalists who didn't have to go to war, but nonetheless put themselves in its path. . . . Thank you, all, for the solace you gave to your lovers and brothers, and now for adding one more volume to the classic literature of war."

—Bookreporter.com

"Path-breaking . . . Like the men who fought there, these women came of age in a terrible place, and their reminiscences ably complement an almost exclusively male literature. . . . [A] superb gathering of talent whose work presents an overlooked perspective on the war."

—*Kirkus Reviews* (starred review)

"Fascinating . . . vivid recollections of danger, loss, and anguish."

—*Booklist*

WAR TORN

Introduction by Gloria Emerson

Random House Trade Paperbacks · New York

Tad Bartimus

Denby Fawcett

Jurate Kazickas

Edith Lederer

Ann Bryan Mariano

Anne Morrissy Merick

Laura Palmer

Kate Webb

Tracy Wood

WAR TORN

The Personal Experiences
of Women Reporters
in the Vietnam War

2004 Random House Trade Paperback Edition

Copyright © 2002 by Denby Fawcett, Ann Bryan Mariano, Kate Webb, Anne Morrissy Merick, Jurate Kazickas, Edith Lederer, Tad Bartimus, Tracy Wood, Laura Palmer

Introduction copyright © 2002 by Gloria Emerson

Map copyright © 2002 by Anita Karl and Jim Kemp

This work was originally published in hardcover by Random House, an imprint of The Random House Publishing Group, a division of Random House, Inc., in 2002.

Library of Congress Cataloging-in-Publication Data
War torn: the personal experiences of women reporters in the Vietnam War/Denby Fawcett . . . [et al.]; introduction by Gloria Emerson.
    p. cm.
    ISBN 0-375-75782-1
  1. Vietnamese Conflict, 1961–1975—Personal narratives, American. 2. Vietnamese Conflict, 1961–1975—Journalists. 3. Women Journalists—United States. I. Fawcett, Denby.
DS559.5.W3677 2002   959.704'3'0922—dc21   2002069922

Title-page photo credits, *top row:* Horst Faas, Wide World Photos, personal collection of Jurate Kazickas, personal collection of Tad Bartimus; *center row: The Honolulu Advertiser* (Bob Jones), personal collection of Laura Palmer, personal collection of Tracy Wood, personal collection of Anne Morrissy Merick, UPI; *bottom row:* Neal Ulevich, ABC News, personal collection of Tad Bartimus, U.S. Air Force

Printed in the United States of America

Random House website address: www.atrandom.com

9 8 7 6 5 4 3 2 1

Book design by Mercedes Everett

We dedicate this book to those who went and those who waited,
and to those who did not live long enough to tell their own stories.

A Note to the Reader

This book is about our experiences as women reporters covering the Vietnam War from 1966 until the fall of Saigon in 1975. Each of us has written a chapter about what we saw and felt in Indochina—our adventures, fears, excitement, and the difficulties and loneliness.

Vietnam was a unique war for all journalists, because there was no censorship. The U.S. military provided extraordinary access to combat operations. We could fly on bombing missions, parachute into hostile territory with an airborne unit, spend a week with the Special Forces in the jungle, hitch a ride on a chopper and land amid rocket and artillery as a battle raged, or be taken prisoner like a soldier. This access gave women reporters a chance to show that they could cover combat bravely and honorably, holding their own even under the most frightening and stressful circumstances.

The idea to write our book came after a group of us was brought together by Christine Martin, the dean of the Perley Isaac Reed School of Journalism at West Virginia University. In April 2000, Chris invited us to speak at a symposium she organized called "On the Frontlines: The Women Who Covered the Vietnam War and Changed Journalism History." Chris was one of the first to believe our stories were valuable. It was her persistence that persuaded us to get together for the first time as a group. Until then, many of us had kept our thoughts about the war to ourselves. We owe her our enduring gratitude.

Once we started talking and thinking about Vietnam, it was hard to stop. The audience of students, faculty, and community members inundated us with questions about our Vietnam experiences. None of us expected to be caught off guard, but late into the evening a man stood up and asked, "Why have we never heard these stories before?" Everyone was silent for a moment. Then Tad Bartimus said simply, "Because no one ever asked us."

We did not realize it then, but that was the moment this book was born. In the weeks that followed, the energy and emotion we felt surprised us as we continued to reach out to one another, from one end of the country to the other, via e-mail and telephone. Our extended conversations helped us realize that our individual experiences could be collectively relevant and significant to others. Who better to tell our stories than ourselves?

Seven of us participated in that remarkable weekend in West Virginia: Tad Bartimus, Denby Fawcett, Jurate Kazickas, Edith Lederer, Anne Morrissy Merick, Laura Palmer, and Tracy Wood. To create as broad a picture as possible of a woman reporter's life in Vietnam, we invited other women to add their stories to ours. Happily, Ann Bryan Mariano and Kate Webb joined the project.

We wanted a book that would be deeply personal and brutally honest about our experiences. Thousands of books have been written about the war—generals, politicians, soldiers, historians, nurses, diplomats, and spies have all had their say. But there has never been a book like ours, a collection of intensely personal memoirs from women writing about the Vietnam War as they lived it.

Although most of us would never claim to have changed journalism history, things are dramatically different now for women who want to be war correspondents. By the time of the Gulf War in 1991, nearly every major news organization had women leading its coverage. Several years later, in Bosnia, almost half of the journalists were female. And in Afghanistan, it was routine to have women reporting for television, radio, and print on every aspect of the fighting and devastation. In the early days of the war in 2001, Maria Grazia Cutuli, a correspondent for an Italian magazine, was killed along with several male journalists.

Some of us went on to cover other wars, but there was never any other war quite like Vietnam. We are writing about Vietnam now because we feel it is important to keep those agonizing yet strangely exhilarating days alive, those dark days that changed us in ways we are still trying to understand. Many younger Americans know Vietnam only as an abstraction—a few paragraphs in a textbook, a documentary on the History Channel, or as thousands of names on a black granite wall in Washington, D.C. But for those who served and those who suffered, for those who fought and for those who watched it unfold on television, Vietnam will always be a part of us.

We hope this book adds to the historical record of America's longest and most controversial war and that it will inspire another generation of journalists and all those who dare to pursue their dreams wherever they may lead.

Acknowledgments

We would like to thank our agent, Esther Newberg, for her enthusiasm and commitment to this book. To our editor, Bob Loomis, our heartfelt thanks for his passionate faith in this project from the beginning. He remained totally unfazed by constant e-mails, phone calls, manuscripts, and photographs hurtling in from around the world (often late). All of us appreciate Dominique Troiano, his assistant, who managed, with a smile, to keep everything organized. Thanks also to Dennis Ambrose, our superb production editor, and to Mercedes Everett for so elegantly designing the book's interior. To Carol Schneider and her incomparable publicity team at Random House—Tom Perry and Elizabeth Fogarty—our sincere gratitude for their relentless efforts on our behalf. Many thanks to Andy Carpenter for his artistry in designing the cover we all love. Horst Faas, a walking encyclopedia on the Vietnam War, deserves a standing ovation for meticulously proofreading our chapters. And once again, our love and gratitude to Chris Martin, who knew before anyone else that a book about women reporters in Vietnam was both necessary and important.

This book could not have been written without the patience and support of our husbands, children, families, and friends. Their love and good humor helped us over the hard parts, and they never seemed to resent our long hours at the computer remembering and reliving a past that most had never shared with us.

All our thanks to: Anne Allen, Roger Altman, Peter Arnett, Jaak

Aulik, Evangeline Blood, William Broyles, Jr., the Bynum family, Nancy Collins, Cynthia Copple, Tom Corpora, Kris Dahl, Lt. Gen. Michael S. Davison, Jr., U.S. Army (Ret.), Philippe Debeusscher, Linda Deutsch, Lucille De View, Paisley Dodds, Do Van Kien, George Esper, Dr. Ed Feldman, Jolynne D'Ornano, Jr., Pam Dohrman, Annie Garcelon, William Gay, Sabrina Geer, Tony Goodman, Jean Gray, Jeanette Hermann, Don Hirst, Bob Jones, J. J. Keyser, Khe Sanh Vets, Nancy Lankford, Frieda Lederer, Dafna Linzer, Eva Kim McArthur, George McArthur, Carol Mann, Mai Mariano, Tony Mariano, Bob McKay, Lou Michael, Betty Southard Murphy, Eileen Murray, Ellen Nesselrode, Elizabeth Neuffer, Bryan and Paul Nguyen, Lou O'Rourke, John Perra, Karl Purnell, Richard Pyle, Paul Sanders, Paul Scanlon, Father Mark Shier, Ernie Spencer, Roger Steffens, Rev. Ray Stubbe, Steve Tice, Tran Mong Tu, Karen Vinacour, James Wallace, Dean Wariner, Cate Wood, and Audrey Woods.

Contents

Introduction

Remembering Women War Correspondents in Vietnam

Gloria Emerson

For many years after the war there was one question posed to me, over and over again, that I refused to answer because it was frivolous. What people kept asking me was this: "What was it like being a woman in Vietnam?" as if I might discuss a career opportunity. I wanted the harder questions. Recently, in a radio interview, I was asked it once more and said: "I don't know; I've never been a man." It seemed important for a number of years to talk about the war, and its dismal, awful history, especially to students. After one speech at a college, a young woman came up to me and solemnly said: "I'm so glad a woman was there to see it." Her remark so shocked me that I turned my back on her. It was as if she were dismissing all the Vietnamese women whose lives were deformed by the war, the many Vietnamese women in the South who risked torture and death in opposing the Americans and their Vietnamese allies, and the American nurses who cared for the wrecked soldiers. It would have been kinder to explain all this to the student, but I was not merciful in those days or sufficiently patient.

But I have at last changed my mind and think there might be much to learn from the accounts in this book of nine young women

GLORIA EMERSON, a correspondent in Vietnam for *The New York Times* from 1970 to 1972, won a George Polk Award for her reporting. Her book on the war and its effects on American society, *Winners & Losers*, won a National Book Award in 1978. She is the author, most recently, of a novel, *Loving Graham Greene*.

in the theater of war we will always call Vietnam. I was reluctant to complain about the tiny problems of being a female in a large male press corps when the lives of soldiers in all the armies were so unpromising and always wretched. Civilians in Vietnam were powerless to protect themselves. The war was old when I got to it, and it often seemed preposterous, since few believed we could win. The mood was sour, angry, defiant. The troops wore peace symbols, and *FTA*—Fuck the Army—was written on their helmets, on the tops of sheds, and on walls and inscribed in their hearts. Some of the troops were glad to see me, while others did not want to talk because the war had overwhelmed them. In the villages, the Vietnamese often had many things to say and, because I was without a weapon, they did not see me as a menacing figure. I did not frighten their babies or children. Sometimes there was confusion. "What is it?" a Vietnamese woman asked Nguyen Ngoc Luong, my brilliant interpreter. I am very tall and always wore loose civilian clothing. My hair was in the ponytail that many GIs preferred in their mutiny against haircuts. It was explained that I was an American female. The curious woman seemed unconvinced but was polite.

On one day in the war, I thought I knew what it felt like to be a Vietnamese woman. I had been doing interviews at a Special Forces camp and was boarding the chopper out of there. Then, trouble: one of the Green Berets appeared and began pulling me out. He was acting a little roughly, so I put up a fight and tried to hold on to the tiny ankles of a Vietnamese passenger to slow things down. The Vietnamese man looked horrified. There were empty seats on the aircraft, but the soldier was not concerned about the passenger load. Of course, he got me out and shoved me into the door gunner's seat on the outside of the chopper as if he knew how terrified I was of sitting there. Up until then, no man had ever grabbed or pushed or lifted me against my will, but this could not be said by Vietnamese women forced out of their villages by soldiers. I feared falling out and that my legs—too long and dangling—would be shot from below. The door gunner paid no attention; he was looking at the ground for targets. The noise of the rotor was too loud for me to talk, and I could only huddle against him in that small space. Perhaps it was just a diversion for the American to put me there, and in time it seemed more comical than cruel.

There have always been a few women—like those who tell you

their stories in these pages—who have flung themselves in a war for the adventure of the unknown. They usually are young, have spirit and stamina, a passion for the story, and the intent to be journalists, an easy profession to infiltrate if you wanted only to be a stringer. In his wonderful book *China Hands: The Adventures and Ordeals of the American Journalists Who Joined Forces with the Great Chinese Revolution,* Peter Rand writes of the inspired, brilliant Americans who wrote about China in its chaos and civil war. One of them was Barbara Stephens, who was twenty when she arrived in Chungking to work for the United States Office of War Information and eventually became a stringer for Agence France-Presse. She learned to speak Chinese fluently. A friend said of her: "She was at home in China as I would be at home in Chicago." She had great friends among the other journalists, who regularly fell in love with her. What they really liked to do together was talk, drink, and eat, Mr. Rand writes. Stephens was gathering material for a book and often made long, horrendous trips for her work. She was fearless. She was twenty-five when she began her perilous voyage alone to write about the abuse of the Sinkiang tribal people by the Nationalist government. She was aboard a Chinese air force plane when it crashed. Her friends buried her outside of Nanking; the American ambassador conducted the service. On a tall marble slab, written in Chinese characters, were these words: "She was young, brave, liked to talk, liked to drink. She had a husky voice. She is buried here." When Mao Zedong proclaimed the People's Republic of China on October 1, 1949, no American journalist was there to report it. The old China hands were not wanted.

The most famous woman war correspondent of the last century was the late Martha Gellhorn, who started her long career writing about the Spanish Civil War and whose reputation soared in World War II. She often wrote her articles with a poetic fury. When she came to Vietnam in 1967, she headed for a children's hospital to write a magazine article and found out everything. "American weapons are killing and wounding uncounted Vietnamese children. . . . This terrible fact is officially ignored; no Government agency keeps statistics on the civilians of all ages, from babies to the very old, killed and wounded in South Vietnam. I have witnessed modern war in nine countries, but I have never seen a war like the one in South Vietnam."

And she called it "a war of crime" to friends. In World War II, Gellhorn and other women, few as they were, could not cover combat, but her dispatches from the fighting in Italy seem to have been written just as the fighting stopped. She wrote about all of it: the refugees, the wounded, the Allied troops, the Russians, the Germans in defeat. Nothing was ever too hard for her, and she did not care for whiners or people who could not hold up. She was proud, funny, always generous, and often cranky, and she expected too much of people. When I asked why she never spoke about her marriage to Ernest Hemingway, or the man, she said: "It's my pride not to."

What was lodged in her heart all her life was the war in Spain, from 1936 to 1939. She waited until Franco died in 1975 to go back to the country she so much loved. In Madrid, the city where she had once lived, which had been so mercilessly shelled during the civil war, she stayed at the Palace Hotel, weighted by cruel memories. She wrote: "When I last visited the Palace it smelled of ether and cabbage and there was often blood on the marble steps. The Palace had been the largest military hospital in Madrid. . . .

"The clientele was very young then, though pain ages the face, and wore shabby pajamas, scraps of uniform," she wrote. "In the corridors, now deeply carpeted and discreetly lit, piles of used bandages collected on bare floors."

What had once been the old operating room was now a walnut-paneled television room, but she recognized the two cut-glass chandeliers and the stained-glass skylight. Gellhorn wrote on the day of Franco's funeral: "In this room, filled with Franco's devoted followers—old men wiping their eyes at the sight of the coffin, ladies sniffling into delicate hankerchiefs—soldiers of the Spanish Republic had pieces of steel cut from their bodies, had their legs and arms amputated."

Not just Gellhorn but many other women appeared during the war in Vietnam. Oriana Fallaci, already famous for her interviews with political figures, came and did a long interview with Nguyen Van Thieu, the president of South Vietnam, and another with General Vo Nguyen Giap, in Hanoi, both of them to appear in a collection of pieces, *Interview with History*. Frances FitzGerald visited South Vietnam in 1966, 1971, and 1973 and was acclaimed for her fine book *Fire in the Lake: The Vietnamese and the Americans in Vietnam*. Liz Trotta covered the war for NBC, only the second woman assigned by a network. Marlene

Sanders reported for ABC in the spring of 1966 but could stay only a month because of family obligations.

A small French combat photographer named Cathy Leroy, who lived and worked among American riflemen, soon became a legend in the sixties for her astonishing courage, tough tongue, and persistence. The troops loved her. She began by stringing for AP under the famous photo editor Horst Faas. Men still speak about Leroy. The other night in New York, Jack Laurence, who was a famous CBS correspondent in the war, remembered how during the 1968 Tet offensive and the fierce fighting in Hue, she had been captured for one day and released, then wounded and patched up. She stayed, covering the fighting in Hue until the end, and it lasted twenty-six days, Laurence said. In an old issue of *Newsweek* whose theme was "Americans at War," there is a famous Larry Burrows photograph. Four marines are rushing through elephant grass, carrying a body. He looks dead and his head is very close to the ground, but you cannot see his wounds, just the desperate faces of the men gripping his clothing and limbs. Off to the side, watching all of it, is the childlike figure of Leroy, a tight cap covering her blond hair, two cameras around her neck, tension on her face. Burrows, the greatest of all the talented photographers, was killed in 1971, and many were surprised that Leroy had managed to stay alive. Other women took photographs, but not the same as hers: Barbara Gluck and Nancy Moran, whose husbands were *New York Times* correspondents assigned to Vietnam, took softer photographs and learned to be very good.

In the huge international press corps, one of the toughest and most talented, intelligent reporters was Judith Coburn, who wrote for *The Village Voice* and broadcast for Pacifica Radio. Her reporting displeased the Vietnamese and American authorities, so, while in Hong Kong in June 1972, she was refused extension of her visa at the Vietnamese embassy. No reason was given; it never was. Unable to return to Saigon to collect her possessions and notebooks, the resourceful Coburn then went to Cambodia to write for the *Far Eastern Economic Review.* Kate Webb of UPI was there, filing the daily war story, which she did so well, and Elizabeth Becker, a stringer for *The Washington Post,* began her long involvement with that country's history and politics. In 1972, Cambodia was more dangerous than Vietnam.

Correspondents with big, powerful newspapers did not get blacklisted the way Coburn was because their expulsion would have caused an uproar. I was called in for warnings, once by a civilian at the U.S. embassy over lunch in his villa. He hoped to make my attitude more optimistic about the war. Slightly more pressure came from the managing editor of my own paper when he came to Saigon for a short trip. "You've done some good writing on what is wrong with the war, now tell us what is working," he said. I was astonished. There was no way to comply with his suggestion, so I promised nothing.

I had so much wanted to write about the war, and hammered at my newspaper to send me there. I had been in the country years before the Americans came in, and knew Vietnamese of many different political persuasions in Paris. Reading the stories of a young correspondent named Beverly Deepe, I hoped that I might do as well as this enterprising and smart reporter who covered politics and the fighting. She started out as a stringer for *Newsweek* in 1962 and worked in Vietnam for the *New York Herald Tribune* from 1962 to 1964 and for *The Christian Science Monitor* from 1967 to 1969. Most correspondents assigned to Vietnam put in eighteen months, but Deepe was there for seven years, a record. Her intelligent coverage and analysis of the political and military situation was first-rate.

It was at Khe Sanh, which so many feared would be our undoing, a Dien Bien Phu, that a young AP stringer named Jurate Kazickas was wounded. More than thirty years later, over lunch on Madison Avenue, she mentioned it nonchalantly. Outside the restaurant in the sunlight, I looked carefully at her face, but the surgeon who dug the metal bits out of her skin did such a lovely job that you cannot see the scars. She writes about those desperate days at Khe Sanh in this book.

During the long war, courage was not always useful, nor was prayer or lucky charms or any kind of juju. A good example of this was the death of the photographer Dicky Chapelle, who was on an operation with marines when a land mine exploded. In Henri Huet's photograph, we see her lying on her stomach on the ground, being given last rites by a kneeling Marine Corps chaplain. She looks very small, her face disfigured, and there is too much blood on her jacket. She wore, as usual, small pearl earrings, and there was a flower in the band of her bush hat. Nearby, two soldiers are staring, stunned by the sight of a dying American woman. She started out in World War II, was greatly accustomed to war, and reportedly said, as her last words: "I guess it was bound to happen."

It was believed that Kate Webb of UPI was dead after *The New*

York Times ran her obituary, but she survived her captivity and went on reporting, not in Vietnam but in Cambodia. There is no more harrowing account in this collection on what a woman journalist was forced to endure than what she has written. When we met in Phnom Penh, she was a very composed, good-looking woman with such a soft and low voice that the rest of us seemed to be shouting. I wanted to tell her to get out, that the risks in Cambodia were becoming too great, but there was an unspoken code among correspondents not to say that sort of thing.

Here is our first chance to read all sorts of stories by nine women who went to the war and were changed. I don't know if any of them would agree with this sentence by Ward Just, a novelist, who once covered the war in Vietnam and was wounded. He wrote: "It was a privilege to have been there." I wish I felt the same way, but I can't quite manage it.

CHINA

NORTH
VIETNAM

Hanoi

LAOS

Gulf of
Tonkin

HAINAN

Con
Thien

DMZ

LAOS

Rockpile

Khe Dong
Sanh Ha

Quang
Tri

DEMILITARIZED
ZONE (DMZ)

Hue

Da Nang

Que
Son

DakTo

THAILAND

Kontum

Bong Son

Pleiku

Qui Nhon

CAMBODIA

SOUTH

Mekong R.

Phnom
Penh

VIETNAM

Nha
Trang

Cu
Chi

An Loc

Bien Hoa

HIGHWAY
4

My
Tho

Saigon

South
China Sea

Can
Tho

Mekong
Delta

Gulf of
Thailand

Kms.

0   150

0   150

Miles

VIETNAM
circa 1970

The twelve years of official American fighting in Vietnam claimed the lives of 58,178 U.S. military men and women. Most of them (47,386) were killed directly in combat or died later of war-related injuries. The other 10,792 were victims of accidents or illness or died from other causes. There still are 1,948 listed as missing in action. More than 300,000 U.S. military men and women were wounded.

It's unknown how many millions of Vietnamese from both sides died between 1961 and 1972 directly or indirectly because of the war. An estimated 185,000 to 225,000 South Vietnamese military personnel were killed and 500,000 to 570,000 are believed to have been wounded.

North Vietnamese and Vietcong combat deaths are estimated at 900,000, with unknown thousands wounded. Civilian casualties are believed to exceed one million.

- 1858–1954
  French colonial government runs Vietnam.

- 1950
  France receives financial aid from the United States to fight the Vietminh, led by Ho Chi Minh; China supplies the Vietminh with weapons.

- 1954
  May 7, Vietminh forces, commanded by Gen. Vo Nguyen Giap, defeat the French at Dien Bien Phu.

  July 20, Geneva agreement ends French colonial rule in Indochina; Vietnam is divided into North and South at the 17th parallel, the so-called demilitarized zone (DMZ); Ho Chi Minh becomes president of North Vietnam.

- 1956
  June, sixteen members of the 14th Special Forces Operational Detachment (Green Berets) arrive in Vietnam to train South Vietnamese Special Forces

fighting opponents of President Ngo Dinh Diem's government; other small groups of advisers come later.

- 1961
December, President John F. Kennedy increases the number of U.S. military advisers in South Vietnam; Spc. 4 James Thomas Davis is first official U.S. casualty.

- 1962
Number of U.S. advisers in South Vietnam reaches 12,000.

- 1963
November 1, South Vietnamese military overthrows and assassinates President Diem.

November 22, President Kennedy assassinated in Dallas. Vice President Lyndon B. Johnson sworn in as president.

- 1964
March 26, first U.S. prisoner of war, army major Floyd J. Thompson, is captured when his observation plane crashes near Khe Sanh in South Vietnam. Thompson will be released in March 1973.

July 1, Lt. Gen. William C. Westmoreland is appointed U.S. military commander in Vietnam.

August 4, U.S. Navy jets strike North Vietnam in the wake of suspected attacks against the U.S. vessels *Maddox* and *Turner Joy* in the Gulf of Tonkin.

August 7, Congress passes the Tonkin Gulf Resolution, authorizing President Johnson to take all necessary measures to prevent attacks on U.S. forces in Vietnam.

November 1, Vietcong stage first attack aimed specifically at Americans, hitting Bien Hoa air base, just north of Saigon. Five U.S. soldiers are killed.

- 1965
February, U.S. begins air attacks against North Vietnam. The bombing will go on almost continuously for three years.

March 6, President Johnson sends marines, the first official U.S. combat troops, to Da Nang.

July 28, Johnson commits up to 125,000 U.S. combat troops; draft expands to 35,000 men per month.

October 23–November 20, battle of the Ia Drang valley, near Pleiku, Central Highlands, the first combat between U.S. forces and North Vietnamese army (NVA) regulars and the first time B-52s are used to support ground combat. It's the bloodiest battle of the war to date: 305 U.S. soldiers died and more than 3,560 North Vietnamese are killed. The high casualty toll leads officials on both sides to believe they can win waging a war of attrition.

- 1966

April 12, B-52 bombers used for first time against North Vietnam. U.S. military strength in Vietnam exceeds 385,000 by the end of the year; more than 5,000 U.S. troops killed.

- 1967

May 1, Ellsworth Bunker replaces Henry Cabot Lodge as U.S. ambassador.

November 3–December 1, battle of Dak To, along the Cambodian-Laotian border, the heaviest fighting since Ia Drang in 1965. 289 Americans are killed.

November 29, Robert S. McNamara resigns as secretary of defense. U.S. troop strength more than 485,000 by the end of the year; at least 9,300 Americans killed.

- 1968

January 20–March, siege of Khe Sanh.

January 30, Tet offensive begins; North Vietnamese attack more than thirty major South Vietnamese cities and towns.

March 16, My Lai massacre by soldiers of the U.S. 23rd Infantry (Americal) Division; more than 500 South Vietnamese civilians are killed. U.S. military covers up the killings.

March 31, President Johnson announces he will not seek reelection.

April 1–15, 1st Cavalry Division launches Operation Pegasus to relieve siege at Khe Sanh.

April 4, Martin Luther King, Jr., is assassinated in Memphis.

June 5, presidential candidate Robert Kennedy is assassinated in Los Angeles.

August 28, demonstrators, including those opposing the Vietnam War, chant "The whole world is watching" as Chicago police beat protesters at the Democratic National Convention.

November 1, U.S. halts bombing of North Vietnam in preparation for start of peace talks.

November 5, Richard M. Nixon elected president.

- 1969

January 25, first peace talks in Paris.

Spring, U.S. troop strength peaks at 543,000.

June, U.S. begins troop withdrawals.

September 2, Ho Chi Minh dies at age seventy-nine.

October 15, more than 1 million Americans participate in antiwar demonstrations across the U.S.

- 1970

  Paris peace talks are at a stalemate throughout most of the year.

  March 18, Gen. Lon Nol overthrows Prince Norodom Sihanouk as leader of Cambodia.

  April 29, U.S. and South Vietnam begin fighting the North Vietnamese and the Khmer Rouge in Cambodia to cut off supply lines and staging areas.

  May 4, four students at Kent State University in Ohio are shot and killed by National Guard troops during an antiwar demonstration. The killings lead to more antiwar demonstrations across the country.

- 1971

  January 30, ARVN troops supported by U.S. aircraft invade Laos in an attempt to cut the Ho Chi Minh Trail, North Vietnam's supply line to the south.

  May 3, at least 7,000 people are arrested by police and federal troops during antiwar demonstrations in Washington, D.C.

  November, U.S. troop strength drops to 156,800.

- 1972

  March 30, North Vietnam launches Easter offensive; U.S. resumes bombing of the North. South Vietnam never does regain all of the territory that is overrun.

  April 27, Paris peace talks resume.

  June 17, burglars break into Democratic Party offices at the Watergate complex in Washington, D.C.

  December, U.S. conducts eleven-day "Christmas bombing" of Hanoi.

- 1973

  January 23, President Nixon announces agreement reached with the North Vietnamese for "peace with honor."

  January 27, Vietnam cease-fire begins; hours before the cease-fire, Lt. Col. William B. Nolde, forty-three, is killed by an artillery shell near An Loc. He is the last official U.S. casualty of the Vietnam War.

  February 12, release begins of more than 590 U.S. POWs.

  March 29, last American POWs released from Hanoi; last U.S. combat troops leave South Vietnam.

  August 15, U.S. halts all B-52 strikes in Indochina. The action primarily affects Cambodia.

- 1974

  August 9, President Richard M. Nixon resigns in the Watergate scandal; Gerald R. Ford becomes president.

- 1975

  January 1, Khmer Rouge launch offensive in Cambodia.

  March, North Vietnam begins major offensive in the Central Highlands.

  April 17, Cambodia falls to the Communists.

  April 30, the fall of Saigon.

- 1976

  July 2, North and South Vietnam are unified.

  Sources: U.S. State Department, U.S. military, and other government documents; *Nam: The Vietnam Experience, 1965–75,* by Tim Page and John Pimlott (editors); *Vietnam: A History,* by Stanley Karnow; *Reporting Vietnam: American Journalism, 1959–1969,* compiled by the Library of America; *The Vietnam War Day by Day,* edited by John S. Bowman; *Encyclopaedia Britannica;* and news and eyewitness accounts.

WAR TORN

Denby Fawcett

Walking Point

Those were the days when all of us were young,
very pure, and very sincere.
—Bao Ninh
The Sorrow of War

One afternoon in the fall of 1966, I went to the Saigon Zoo. Walking past the cages of lethargic, dusty animals, I was drawn to a group of Vietnamese soldiers standing around a cement pit. They were watching two captive bears dancing on their hind legs, begging for candy and fruit. The soldiers threw the bears peanuts; then one of them casually tossed a lighted cigarette into a bear's mouth. The soldiers laughed as the bear struggled to cough up the burning cigarette.

In Vietnam, I tried hard not to dwell on the plight of the poor bears or think too long about the dramatic deaths of friends I expected to know forever. There was no forever there . . . just one surprise after another. You had to fortify yourself for what was coming next. Only now, so many years later, do images drift back with mighty and haunting force.

In the night when I can't sleep, I see the smiling face of my friend Riley Leroy Pitts, the handsome black army captain we called Pittsie Old Boy, a Medal of Honor winner. Pittsie threw himself on a grenade to save his men at Ap Dong, a dud Chinese grenade that failed to explode. After escaping death once, Pittsie got up off the ground and moved forward to kill the Vietcong machine gunners who had trapped his company in a jungle so thick, they could not fire

---

DENBY FAWCETT is a political reporter with KITV (ABC) television news. She lives in Honolulu with her husband, former NBC news correspondent Bob Jones.

back effectively. Pittsie Old Boy, dead at age thirty, mortally wounded while trying to prevent the Vietcong from shooting more of his men.

On other restless nights, I hear the voices of marines at the Rockpile near the demilitarized zone saying, "They must have paid you a fortune to come here." The truth is, I paid my own way to the war and initially made so little money, I had to carefully count what I spent for books, clothes, and rent.

Covering the Vietnam War was the pivotal event of my life. Yet in the years afterward, I never mentioned my days on helicopter assaults, my fear of getting shot in the face, or the heady social life in Saigon for the same reason most soldiers kept quiet. It was a "bad war." Nobody wanted to hear about it, and even if they did, they wouldn't understand.

I don't think any of us were prepared for what we would see in Vietnam. I went to the war in May 1966, as a merry explorer, a journalistic kind of person, plagued with a short attention span and an unstoppable curiosity. I was twenty-four years old, the oldest child of an artistic mother and a father in the advertising business, glamorous and brilliant people who loved me dearly. They urged me to always keep one step ahead of comfort, and from them I learned the benefits and perils of making friends with the untamed side of yourself.

I decided I must go to Vietnam when *The Honolulu Advertiser* sent my then boyfriend, and many years later husband, Bob Jones, to cover the war. The Honolulu morning paper wanted a reporter in Vietnam to do stories on Hawaii's 25th Infantry Division, a local unit deployed to Cu Chi between Saigon and the Cambodian border, and in Pleiku in the Central Highlands. Hawaii, with its large military population, had a focused interest in the war.

Just out of Columbia University, I was languishing as a reporter on the evening *Honolulu Star-Bulletin* women's page, assigned to write features and to help the paper's star society reporter cover Honolulu social events. I yearned to be part of Vietnam, the biggest news story of my generation. Yet I was stuck wearing a borrowed evening gown to cover the Junior League ball or busy taking endless notes at the Chinese Narcissus Festival. My single goal in heading for Saigon was to remake my destiny.

My *Star-Bulletin* editors thought I was joking when I asked them to free me from the society pages to cover the Vietnam War. They said it was out of the question, so I quit my $80-a-week job and I was ready to leave for Vietnam as a freelancer when, at the last minute, *Honolulu Advertiser* managing editor Buck Buchwach took a chance and hired me as one of his reporters. Buchwach told me I would have to pay my own way to Saigon but promised me a letter of accreditation and $35 for each article I wrote.

When I told my parents I was going to Vietnam, they were worried, but rather than try to discourage me, they kept their concerns to themselves. They were friendly extroverts who loved to throw parties on the lawn of our big Honolulu beach house. But between the parties they could be extremely sensitive. My mother read a book a night during the periods when she could concentrate, momentarily free of her episodes of manic depression, a disease that scared us and sometimes swept her away from us when we were children.

My father, a bookish man himself, loved British mystery stories and his volumes of Walt Whitman, lovingly preserved from his days as a Stanford University student. His own darkness was binge drinking—usually two-day-long spells he referred to as "toots"—confusing my brothers and me as we watched him bounce back from the alcoholic binges, miraculously transformed into the thoughtful and kind father he was before.

Both my mother and father were quietly withdrawn as I prepared to leave for the war. I remember the night before I departed walking into my father's dressing room on the first floor of our house to find him sitting in the twilight in boxer shorts, staring at the wall, the TV set across from him turned off. He brooded by himself, knowing there was nothing he could do to protect me from the danger ahead. The room was shadowy and silent, the only sound the waves crashing on the beach in front of our house.

I packed my suitcase with sundresses recently shortened to the appropriate 1960s mini length by my mother's Japanese dressmaker, sandals, pearls, dark glasses, and a bathing suit. I had no idea what to bring to a war.

When I arrived at Saigon's Tan Son Nhut airport, hundreds of soldiers were pouring out of planes—the American presence in Vietnam would double by the end of the year from two hundred thousand to four hundred thousand troops. The only other women in the airport were Vietnamese customs officials. Everyone stared at me. The American embassy listed 758 American women in South Vietnam at the time. Until then, I had spent my life happily unnoticed in the background. The constant attention was unnerving.

The *Honolulu Advertiser*'s Saigon bureau was in Bob's two-room apartment near An Quang Buddhist pagoda, the headquarters of the monk Thich Tri Quang, an outspoken critic of the Saigon government. I bought a Chinese bike for $20 to get around the city; the bike made me feel vulnerable and exposed if I happened to ride home at the same time that government troops were tear gassing our neighborhood to quell the pagoda's frequent antigovernment demonstrations. During the tear gassings, helpful Vietnamese bicyclists signaled me to follow them down side alleys and lanes to escape the acrid air.

Besides the tear gas, there were also blackouts. In a botched attempt to tame the rebellious monks at the pagoda, South Vietnamese officials cut off electricity to our neighborhood almost every night. The enforced darkness only strengthened the monks' resolve and, for us, heightened our sense of adventure and romance as we typed our news stories by candlelight.

The *Advertiser* promoted my presence in Vietnam as a reporter "specializing in color stories on Saigon and its environs." A story in the paper informed readers I would do "articles on men and women who are lending their teaching, building and medical skills to winning the peace." I was supposed to remain in the safety of Saigon writing features; Bob was to take care of the dangerous war coverage.

It was easy to find bizarre feature stories. One of my first pieces was on tourism in Vietnam, a report I later sold to the *Saturday Review* magazine. With a shooting war in full swing, the South Vietnamese government continued to spend money to promote tourism. The Vietnam National Tourist Bureau opened its doors each morning in a musty office next to the Majestic Hotel on the north bank of the Saigon River. Pamphlets on the counter proclaimed Saigon as "the Pearl of the Orient." My favorite pamphlet urged tourists to come to Vietnam . . . a hunter's paradise "with game filled areas 50 to 250 miles from Saigon." A red-lettered stamp across the top cautioned: "Temporarily suspended under the present situation."

Any American could visit Vietnam without a visa if he stayed for less than seven days. Pan American World Airways offered five flights a week to Saigon from Hawaii and the continental United States. Tourists did come, but not many. They were mostly hippies, druggies, or curiosity seekers such as the Dwight Folletts of Oak Park,

Illinois, a couple I interviewed for my piece. Dwight was the president of Follett Publishing Company. "We must be the only tourists here," he said as he and his wife sipped wine on an American friend's penthouse terrace. "We came because we wanted to see what was happening in Vietnam ourselves. In the United States everything we read is either black or white."

The Folletts' activities included watching Buddhist monks stage an antigovernment protest that broke up after the Saigon police sprayed the monks with tear gas and beat them with sticks. A few days later, the Folletts took a trip to the beach resort of Nha Trang, where they ate fresh lobster in a former French café. Follett told me, "I am coming out of this more a hawk than a dove. We must help these people."

Two months after I arrived in Saigon, Bob departed to take a new job with KGMB-TV, the CBS News affiliate in Hawaii. At age twenty-four, I became *The Honolulu Advertiser*'s chief Vietnam reporter. The paper made me a full-time staffer with weekly wages and a living allowance. I moved into the center of Saigon and began to do what I wanted to do in the first place, cover combat. But it wasn't as easy as I expected.

The main difficulty for women journalists in the early days of the American military escalation was talking your way into combat zones. Military commanders did not like the idea of male reporters getting killed, and they were even more horrified at the thought of a woman reporter getting shot. One of the first officers I asked for permission to go into a combat area turned me down, saying I reminded him of his daughter. I swallowed hard in frustration, knowing the same commander would never say to a male reporter, "You remind me of my son." Another time in the far north of South Vietnam, I was bumped from a helicopter dropping a long-range reconnaissance team into enemy territory because there was "too much weight." I weighed 110 pounds.

When I finally did get permission to go into a forward area, it came unexpectedly from the U.S. Marines, a group I had mistakenly stereotyped as sexist. I was so surprised, I did not even have the proper equipment. A redheaded marine private, Francis "Rani" Martin of San Francisco, had to loan me his boots, which were about three sizes too big. The marines flew me to the Rockpile, just south of the so-called demilitarized zone, at the time one of the bloodiest battlegrounds of the war. I was frightened speechless as I watched body bags filled with dead marines placed on the helicopter that delivered us.

The first words from one of the corporals as I got off the helicopter with Tom Corpora of United Press International and NBC's George Page were: "Hey, you had better dig yourself a hole. We have been mortared every night, and it usually starts about now."

When it got dark we could see the lamps of the North Vietnamese on the hill across from us moving fast as they got into position to mortar us. A marine captain told us not to smoke because he didn't want the North Vietnamese to target our lighted cigarettes. Desperate for a smoke and frightened, we disobeyed. We lighted up and then burned a hole in C ration boxes with the tips of our cigarettes and smoked with the lighted end hidden in the boxes. The taste was terrible, but the effect was calming. I felt slightly less jittery when I spotted the old marine sergeant in the foxhole next to us sneaking cigarettes by covering his head with his rain poncho. We waited, but the enemy mortars the captain expected didn't come.

That same night at the Rockpile, one of the marine radio operators asked me to call the coordinates for an air strike on the mountain across from us where the North Vietnamese had been firing on the Americans. He handed me a piece of paper: an exactly worded script to radio instructions to A-4 Skyhawks on where to drop the napalm, 250-pound bombs, and antipersonnel bombs on the North Vietnamese. The radio operator and other marines huddled close, waiting to hear the pilots' amazement when they heard an American woman giving them directions of where to bomb. I read from the paper and awaited an answer. "You are kidding," crackled the radio reply from the sky. "Hey, listen, the grunts have a girl down there. They are living good." That cracked up the corporal and his friends. Today, I am embarrassed to think how readily I agreed to become a participant in a story I was covering. But at the Rockpile, it seemed normal—a favor for the marines who helped me to get my start as a war reporter.

Field troops laughed a lot, especially in the most dangerous places. One night I tried to urinate discreetly, out of sight of the one hundred or so marines sleeping on the ground in the jungle in the heart of enemy territory. As I walked quietly to the edge of the encampment, seeking privacy, I accidentally set off the trip wire to a flare, illuminating myself like Mick Jagger in concert, waking up all the marines, who at first feared the bright flare light was a warning of an enemy attack.

If it wasn't others laughing at me, it was GIs laughing at the irony of their own situation, like the two army soldiers who had to get hurt to be saved. I was with Hawaii soldiers from the 25th Division on the biggest combat operation of the war, known as Junction City. We were on a patrol in a forest of defoliated trees in War Zone C, seventy miles northwest of Saigon, near the Cambodian border. When the Vietcong fired on us, American planes responding to a call for close air support bombed us instead of the enemy. We all fell on the ground. There were horrible screams and finally a chilling silence. Then minutes afterward, raucous laughter. Two soldiers in front of where I was ducking for cover had both been hit in the buttocks. They were laughing from the morphine the medics had given them and from the hope and excitement that these "million-dollar wounds" in the butt would be considered serious enough to get them sent home from the Vietnam War for good. They were carried out on stretchers as envious GIs flipped them the bird and cheered and yelled obscenities.

The Vietnamese had their own ways of getting a laugh, sometimes by testing you to see if you fit in, and were ready to indulge in some of their more peculiar customs. I went down to Vinh Long in the Mekong Delta to do stories on Lt. Col. Lou Michael, an adviser to the Vietnamese army. Maj. Luong Dinh Bay, the Vietnamese commander of Chau Thanh district, invited Michael and me to dinner at his house. He wanted to treat us to a regional dish he said we would love. His cook passed around beautifully presented platters of what appeared to be fried chicken. Major Bay told me the meat was frogs' legs. Everyone took pieces with their chopsticks. The meat was filled with tiny bones but tasted delicious in a light sauce of garlic and butter. After we finished and the maid brought out caramel custard for dessert, Major Bay told me the dish we had eaten was sautéed rat.

Rice-field rat is a delicacy in the Mekong Delta. Paddy rats are clean, country rodents living off rice. After the March harvest, villagers caught the rodents in traps. Often the rats were so bloated with rice, the farmers didn't need traps. They just chased the rats down, bopping them on their heads with sticks.

. . .

In any firefight, I had an irrational fear of getting my face shot off. I always flattened myself on the ground, pressing my head into the earth and ridiculously pulling my helmet over my head and face like a tent. Positioning my helmet into a shield for my face made me feel safer even though it was an illusion, like a snail retracting into its shell for protection when a huge human was ready to stomp on it. My elaborate face cover was uncomfortable and limited my vision. But once I saw something out of the side of my face shield so beautiful and disturbing, I still think about it today.

In December 1966, I accompanied Hawaii soldiers from the 2nd Battalion, 27th Infantry, the Wolfhounds, on a helicopter assault west of Cu Chi to search for a sergeant they had heard was captured by the Vietcong. When our helicopters swept down onto an empty field, enemy soldiers in the tree line ambushed us. As their bullets pinged off the sides of our helicopters, we jumped out before the skids touched the ground, throwing ourselves flat down into the elephant grass. I pulled my helmet over my face. While the Hawaii soldiers and the Vietcong were shooting at each other, still facedown, I looked sideways to see two yellow butterflies flutter past my eyes and then dart off through the grass, the sun shining on their wings, the butterflies fragile and perishable, going about their natural purpose, oblivious to the danger of the firefight. The humans screaming and shooting at each other, aberrant and temporal. Nature enduring. The disparity between the soaring butterflies and the destructive humans reminded me of Stein in Joseph Conrad's *Lord Jim*, transfixed by the beautiful, rare butterfly darting over the face of a man he had just killed. Stein could not believe his luck, coming across the priceless specimen he wanted to add to his extensive butterfly collection.

Combat could push you to test your own limits. I once asked to walk with the point squad, the most dangerous and exposed unit on a patrol. The point man at the very front of the unit is the most likely to walk into an enemy ambush, the most likely to trip a booby trap or step on a mine. I wanted to see what it would be like to be so vulnerable. As I moved slowly down the trail behind the point man, a Vietnamese peasant suddenly stepped out on the path. The point man shot and killed the man, not knowing if he was a Vietcong or an innocent farmer. I was as startled and scared as the point man and wondered if I would have done the same thing. There were soldiers who loved to walk point because of the adrenaline rush. I did that once and never asked to do it again.

As time went on, I stopped having trouble getting permission to cover combat. If a military commander tried to stop me, I usually gained his confidence by telling him I had been at the Rockpile, had walked behind a point man, and had lived through a direct air strike in War Zone C. I was working hard every day, and I was filing lots of stories.

Then, a chance meeting I had with Gen. William C. Westmoreland, commander of the U.S. armed forces in Vietnam, changed everything and resulted in what could have become an enormous setback not only for me, but for all the other women reporters covering the war. The incident showed how tenuous our hard-earned privileges were, how quickly they could be rescinded. In April 1967, I traveled out to Plei Djereng, a remote army base in the Central Highlands of South Vietnam, to cover a unit from Hawaii, the 1st Battalion, 8th Infantry of the 4th Infantry Division. The unit was nicknamed the "Pineapple Battalion" for its leader, Lt. Col. Harold H. "Pineapple" Lee. While I was there, Westmoreland helicoptered into the base unexpectedly to boost the morale of Pineapple's troops, who were jittery after losing sixty-four men to injuries and death in a face-to-face encounter with a reinforced North Vietnamese battalion near the Cambodian border.

Lee told Westmoreland what had happened and then led him to a display of enemy weapons captured during the battle. There were Russian AK-47 rifles, rocket launchers, a Chinese SKS light assault rifle, and a pile of Chinese grenades. Westmoreland looked down at the Chinese grenades and told Lee to have them destroyed. "They're dangerous. One might explode and hurt one of these lads."

A North Vietnamese "body snatcher" lay in the middle of the captured weapons on display. Westmoreland was fascinated by the small ivory hook on the end of a long wire, a tool the Americans assumed North Vietnamese used to retrieve their dead and wounded during and after battles to prevent Americans from counting them as enemy dead. Westmoreland eyed the body snatcher as a valuable prop to use in future briefings to explain how the North Vietnamese were successfully obscuring their losses by retrieving corpses of their soldiers with body snatchers. In Westmoreland's strategy of attrition, the goal was to kill more of the enemy soldiers than they could kill of ours to force the North Vietnamese to quit. An important measure for his strategy was the daily body count, the grisly scorecard in which large numbers of dead were supposed to mean victory and few enemy dead failure—a scorecard that in the end turned out to be meaningless.

"May I have it?" Westmoreland said as he looked at the body snatcher. Before anyone could answer, the general's aide leaned over and scooped up the war souvenir an infantry soldier had retrieved after the battle and probably hoped to keep for himself.

Westmoreland then walked forward to address the troops. "You men look like a bunch of Indians. You are tan, lean, and mean."

Many of the soldiers were still shirtless, their faces streaked red with dust. They sweated in the midday glare. Westmoreland's fatigue pants were neatly pressed with creases down the center, his jungle boots shined to a high polish. He did not sweat.

"Red, how many hot meals have you been getting a day?" he asked, pointing at a slim, shirtless blond whose hair had been reddened by the dust. "You, lad," he said, pointing again.

"Two, sir," the GI answered.

Before "Red" could continue, Westmoreland finished for him: "One hot meal in the morning and one in the evening, with C rations for lunch." Westmoreland was famous for asking questions to which he already knew the answers.

Then he launched into a Westy pep talk. "You see, Uncle Sam is taking care of you with chow, weapons, and equipment," he said as his eyes scanned the soldiers' faces. "You're the finest men we ever put into battle. The enemy is tough. His strategy is to discourage the folks at home, but the support at home grows. The world is beginning to realize that we're giving the South Vietnamese the freedom of choice so that they won't be taken over by the guerrillas, who are nothing but bandits, and by the North Vietnamese. By keeping pressure on them like you men have been doing, in due time they will realize that their strategy won't work. We are not like the French. We were invited here to help, I am proud of the job you are doing, and the American people can be proud. You are the finest soldiers America has ever had, and I take my hat off to you."

As he walked around talking to the troops, Westmoreland seemed surprised to see me. Back in Honolulu, the Westmorelands rented a house near my family's house. My mother played tennis with Westmoreland's wife, Kitsy. Westmoreland said hello and asked me how many days I had been at the forward base. I told him several, and then he moved on to talk with the soldiers.

Later, I found out this seemingly casual encounter caused Westmoreland to consider an order to prohibit women reporters from staying overnight in the field in South Vietnam. Westmoreland's directive would have made it almost impossible for women to cover the fighting. Reporters could not expect to go on a combat operation during the day and afterward demand a helicopter to take them out in the evening. There was no such special taxi service in and out of the war. ABC News producer Anne Morrissy (later Merick) and *Overseas Weekly* reporter Ann Bryan (later Mariano) organized the women reporters to fight the directive. Eventually Morrissy and Bryan lobbied the Pentagon and succeeded in keeping our battlefield access.

When the women reporters organized to fight the Westmoreland proposal, it was the first and last time we got together as a group. I never made an effort to be friends with other women reporters in Vietnam. I am not sure why. When I think back now, I am sad, knowing how much we had in common and how we could have supported and comforted one another. I felt closest to Kate Webb of UPI, but all that meant at the time was a nod of acknowledgment as we passed each other walking down Tu Do Street in Saigon.

Westmoreland's notion to prohibit women reporters from staying overnight in the field was prompted because he was concerned we might inconvenience and endanger soldiers who would rush to protect us in firefights. He also was worried that the women correspondents might collapse emotionally when faced with the horrors of combat.

The truth is, the human mind has an amazing ability to block out the full horror of war when it becomes too difficult to endure; of course, this ability to mentally withdraw is the same for men and women. The unbearable event takes a backseat, poised to return when you least expect it, but for the immediate horrific moment, it is buried.

I once walked through a field of American bodies, more dead people than I had ever seen, blocking them out completely as I focused on getting my story. I was covering the aftermath of a battle in

May 1967 between a North Vietnamese unit and two companies from the 4th Infantry Division fifty-five miles west of Pleiku in the Central Highlands.

After I arrived by helicopter, I passed through the field dotted with the American dead, their bodies half hidden by mud, some of them blond and red-haired soldiers, looking foreign and out of place, their white legs sticking out of the mud pools in odd angles. Eighteen had been killed and seventy-five wounded in a four-hour attack by the 66th Regiment of the North Vietnamese 1st, or Le Loi, Division.

Their company commander was at the other side of the field. As I got closer to him, I was prepared for him to tell me to get the hell out. I was a reporter coming from the outside, intruding on his grief, shaking him out of his shock with questions about the carnage. A stranger who did not know the tangle of dead and wounded men. When I reached him, the tall blond captain smiled. "Hi. Aren't you Denby Fawcett? I just saw a story about you in *Stars and Stripes*." We started chatting, never mentioning the mud lake of corpses, blocking it out. The captain so glad to see me. Thanking me for coming. Me, thanking him for letting me cover his unit. Cocktail party chatter. Many of the injured, still bleeding, waiting to be evacuated.

Our conversation stopped when soldiers on the other side of the mud field started screaming at a prisoner, a frail North Vietnamese who looked more like a fourteen-year-old boy than a grown man, holding his hands above his head. The Americans found him in the jungle, collapsed beside a fallen tree trunk. His leg injuries prevented him from keeping up with his North Vietnamese unit as it retreated to safety in Cambodia. He was led through jeering lines of battle-shocked troops.

"Show him the bodies, show him the bodies," a private sobbed. His platoon leader was dead. One of the men told me the private felt responsible for the lieutenant's death. Weeping, the private fell on the muddy corpse of his lieutenant and ripped off the nylon poncho covering his face. "Show him the body! Show him the body!" hoping the North Vietnamese prisoner would regret what had happened.

The two men pulled the sobbing private off the lieutenant's body, and the North Vietnamese soldier looked straight ahead, now trembling all over, barely able to keep his shaking hands lifted in surrender. The captain quickly grabbed the prisoner and shoved him into a deep foxhole to keep him out of sight of the angry Americans ready to tear him apart. In the hole, the prisoner shook uncontrollably, certain he was about to be shot or buried alive. Another private peered down into the hole and said, "If he don't stop that shaking, he's gonna kill himself of shock." Meanwhile, the dead were still in the mud, waiting to be removed. I was writing down notes, the rain splattering the ink on my notebook. Before leaving, I thanked the captain again for letting me come. He smiled and thanked me. Cocktail party conversation. Women just like men in the middle of the unbearable, unable to think about it. The human mind protecting itself. At least for the time being.

Westmoreland's concern about soldiers endangering themselves as they rushed to protect women reporters was unwarranted. In combat it was usually every man and woman for him- or herself. In September 1966, on a marine operation with the 1st Battalion, 9th Marines, in a village called Duc Ky, south of Da Nang, the loneliness of combat came home to me. Surrounded with people and bombarded by noise, I was essentially alone when the shooting started.

Looking for an easy and safe story, I asked the marines if I could go on a "county fair." That was the name for an operation in which an entire village was surrounded by American troops at dawn. The villagers were taken out of their huts and led into barbed-wire-enclosed tents, where they were screened to see if they were Vietcong, and if it was decided they were not, they were given candy, medical treatment, and lectures on the legitimacy of the South Vietnam government. Marines guarded the perimeter of the village so nobody could escape, while South Vietnamese soldiers helped the marines by searching the villagers' huts for hidden enemy soldiers and stockpiles of weapons. After the search, the villagers were allowed to return to their huts.

Instead of being peaceful, this county fair turned bad from the start. When the marines began to surround Duc Ky village, a marine engineer attempting to detonate a booby-trapped gate stepped on a land mine, cleverly set next to the gate. All that remained of the marine were tiny fragments of flesh the marines carefully collected and placed in four ponchos. As they carried off the sagging, bloody ponchos, one marine said: "Fucking shame. He was going to meet his wife in Hawaii in two weeks." Another marine carrying a poncho of the remains said, "He should have watched where he was stepping." It was difficult to think the sagging bags had ever been a "he."

Later that same day, Vietcong snipers shot at the marines' command post in the village, wounding a private named Fred Gunther. Gunther was taken out to a Buddhist shrine in a rice field to await evacuation by helicopter. I was out in the field with the marines. When the medevac helicopter swept in to pick up Gunther, the Vietcong in the trees around the shrine shot at us and the helicopter, hitting the helicopter twice even though it had a big red cross on its side. There was no place to go for cover. I was completely ignored as the marines fired back at the Vietcong, screaming "Fuck you!" and "Fucking assholes!" and flipping them the bird. It was as if I was not there. The shooting was intense and short lived, but for that brief time we were being attacked in the rice field, I was certain I would be shot. Later that day, when I got back to the Da Nang press center, I went straight to the bar to quickly drink two water glasses full of Scotch, and then I went to bed even though it was still afternoon.

You might wonder if women reporters expanded coverage of the Vietnam War by pursuing different kinds of stories from those sought by the male reporters. In my own case, I would have to say no. I made a point of covering exactly the same kinds of stories as my male colleagues, mainly because I never again wanted to be typecast as a women's-page reporter. But every now and then I would come across a tale out of the mainstream too interesting to resist. A story ignored by the male reporters in the foxholes.

Such was the story of Hank and Evangeline Blood, missionaries on a personal quest in the middle of a shooting war. I met the Bloods in June 1966, when they lived in Kontum in the Central Highlands. Hank and "Vange" were struggling in discomfort in the heart of Vietcong territory to raise their four young children and to translate the Bible into a mountain tribal language understood by only four thousand people.

They were with the Wycliffe Bible Translators, a Protestant group studying seventeen of Vietnam's forty-odd nonwritten tribal languages. After putting these languages into writing, Wycliffe linguists translated the Bible and taught the villagers how to read the Scriptures in their own languages. It was a long-term project. Most of the translators had come to Vietnam before the intensification of the war with the American troop buildup. Even though they were living dangerously, they stayed on in hostile enemy territory because they wanted to finish their translations.

Hank Blood told me: "We are not traditional missionaries. We

Personal collection

don't marry people, bury or baptize them. We believe in giving people the Word of the Lord through the Scriptures."

During the Tet offensive, a year and a half after my visit with the Bloods, North Vietnamese soldiers threw grenades into their house, wounding Vange and her youngest daughter, Cathy. Enemy troops killed six other missionaries in the attack. Vange and the children were spared, but Hank was taken prisoner, along with a missionary nurse named Betty Olsen and USAID worker Mike Benge. Six months later, Hank died of malnutrition and pneumonia in their captors' encampment along the Ho Chi Minh Trail. About three months later, Betty Olsen died of malnutrition and amoebic dysentery. Benge buried them in shallow graves.

Benge vowed to live. He survived his capture by his ingenuity and his ability to eat anything, including the small fish that feasted on his ulcerated and torn skin as he lay in streams to bathe. He scooped up the fish and ate them live, also small green frogs he swallowed whole while they were still kicking.

Vange Blood is now seventy-two and lives in Duncanville, Texas. She takes full comfort in her belief that God has a plan for each person. She told me, "The full effect of Hank's life will not be known until eternity."

. . .

Vietnam was a war of music. Music could help you forget the war, at least for the time being. Sometimes today to get in the mood to write about Vietnam, I listen to my old recordings, especially those of Aretha Franklin. I forgot how much I still love Aretha's songs, such as "I Never Loved a Man (the Way I Love You)," "The Weight," "People Get Ready," and "A Natural Woman."

American music was everywhere in Vietnam. Everybody had portable radios. You could hear American Forces Radio at the most remote battlefields, radios blaring country and western music beloved by southern soldiers, and, for the rest of us, rock and roll. And my own personal favorite, soul music, especially the songs by James Brown, the Supremes, or the Mamas and the Papas. Mama Cass was white, but she understood soul and the blues. I think this obsession with music is why so many Vietnam veterans appreciated the Robin Williams movie *Good Morning, Vietnam.*

Music was my own refuge. When I returned to Saigon, I would take a long shower under the single cold-water spigot, change into a freshly pressed dress, and put on my Supremes and Rolling Stones tapes.

I lived with a Vietnamese family above their souvenir store on Nguyen Van Thinh Street off Tu Do, the raunchy bar district. Nguyen Oanh's store on the first floor sold a strange mix of curios, including Vietnamese lacquer pictures of tigers and Jesus Christ, snakeskin belts, stuffed endangered animals, and tortoiseshell purses—exotic objects sometimes purchased by hapless GIs not really in search of souvenirs but sidetracked on their way to Tu Do Street to find bar girls.

The Oanh family's apartment was on the second floor, and my place was on the third floor across the open hallway from the single room used by their teenage son, Nguyen Phuc, known as Paul, now a hospital pharmacist in Fort Worth, Texas, but then a studious university student. Paul focused on his studies, never complaining about my late hours, my friends, the loud music. Our lives went on their separate but equally intense paths, Paul across the hall memorizing facts for his organic chemistry tests; I on the other side of the breeze-way writing news reports on the Formica kitchen table, pounding away on my Olivetti Lettera 32 portable typewriter, Armed Forces

Radio always blaring in the background, rock and roll, blues, sad country and western ballads.

My apartment was two rooms. The "kitchen" was a hot plate in the living room, my drinks chilled in a small refrigerator a Hawaiian soldier from the 25th Infantry Division at Cu Chi scrounged (stole) for me. My few dishes were washed in the bathroom sink.

I loved living with the Oanhs and their six children. They made me feel safe as they went about their business in their apartment and store, while upstairs a ceiling fan cooled my king-size bed, soft sunlight slanting through the potted palms on my balcony perched over the bar district, two resident lizards scampering across the ceiling upside down, chirping sweetly to each other. Outside, the noise from the street below was deafening, especially at night. Pimps and Saigon cowboys roaring by on their Honda scooters, a bar girl screaming, "You, GI, you numbah welve" (number twelve, the lowest). A drunk GI screaming back: "You fucking cunt!" I in my sanctuary above the crowded streets, Paul studying, the Oanhs' maids cooking dinner.

We all had our methods for blocking out the war. Writer Michael Herr says when he was in Saigon, he always went to sleep stoned. My own opiates were Scotch whiskey purchased cheaply from the PX, and sex. I was in love with my life and too selfish to be interested in a permanent relationship with anyone. My relaxation was friendly sex, made intense by the situation of war. My most memorable affair was with another reporter, our lives tightly bound for the moment by the incredible events we witnessed as we were seduced and terrified by combat. We once made love in the old Cham Sculpture Museum in Da Nang. The museum had no security; we just slipped in through the fence at night. We traveled together, doing stories in the field. He wore my hair ribbon in his hat for good luck, and it must have worked, because no harm came to him.

Once, another friend and I had sex on the banks of the murky, oil-spotted Da Nang River, outgoing artillery pounding in the background. My most unforgettable romantic night was on one of the thirty-foot sampans on the Perfume River in Hue.

It is normal for people in their twenties to be obsessed with sex; in Vietnam sex was like breathing good air, a stamp of gratitude for being alive. Aretha Franklin, in her famous spiritual "People Get Ready," promises redemption for the dead souls headed on the train to Jordan, but as for herself, she says, "Thank you because I am living." That's exactly how we felt, briefly, sexually in love, so glad to be living.

I wasn't a drug user, but that certainly wasn't for lack of opportunity. When I walked out of Nguyen Oanh's in the morning, I always stopped to visit an elderly Vietnamese woman selling secondhand paperback books from her street stand. The lady proudly showed me sealed packs of Marlboros, but the filtered cigarettes inside were marijuana joints, $.25 a stick, $2.50 a pack, and $25 a carton. Pedicab drivers asked GIs first if they wanted girls, then if they wanted pot. One army official told me, "We are fighting this war with flower power instead of firepower." A TV correspondent friend told me he smelled marijuana when he jumped into a bunker during a North Vietnamese shelling at Con Thien just south of the DMZ. When he asked the marines about it, they offered him a joint, which he gratefully accepted.

Reporters got stoned in the old French villas rented by news agencies for staffers. The most infamous was the villa on Bui Thi Xuan Street named "Frankie's House" by photographers Sean Flynn and Tim Page in honor of their Chinese houseboy, Frankie. The *Time* magazine and United Press reporters and photographers who lived in Frankie's House had their own opium purveyor they called Puff the Magic Dragon. Puff would come in the early evening by bicycle with his opium and pipes packed in a satchel and keep the pipe loaded and fired up for whoever wanted to smoke. Because of the curfew, Puff often stayed overnight, crawling under the stairs to sleep on a piece of cardboard. Puff, like most opium preparers, was an addict himself, smoking the dregs of whatever was left over after the Frankie's House residents finished.

One of the *Time* reporters was addicted to opium. His first words to anybody entering Frankie's were: "Want to smoke some opium?" He hated to smoke alone. Even though I was not a pot smoker, I yearned to try opium. I loved "Kubla Khan," the opium dream poem by Samuel Taylor Coleridge. Opium seemed romantic and Asian. One night, a *New York Times* reporter and his wife and my current lover and I kept the addicted *Time* writer and Puff company, smoking opium until we couldn't move. Puff lay on the floor, sucking in what remained in the pipe. We had to prop ourselves up against the wall, talking in slow motion; it seemed to take minutes to get out a single word. Opium left me feeling numb, as though I had a shot of Novocain in the brain that swept down to the tips of my toes. It was a slow and unpleasant feeling.

Fine dining was another way to escape the war. Even on combat patrols, I always took a bottle of Tabasco sauce and a fresh onion in my pack to enliven gray and greasy C ration entrées such as ham and lima beans; I also carried along a few cans of French Beaujolais. Associated Press photographer Horst Faas discovered Beaujolais in cans in a small Corsican market on Tu Do Street. As other reporters discovered it, we quickly depleted the store's supply. The canned wine comforted me. I figured if I died, my last meal might be salty and dry C ration beef stew, but at least it would be washed down with French wine shared with friends.

Sometimes, the farther forward you went on a combat operation, the better the food. Fresh meat and produce were sent to dangerous areas to boost morale. One night Capt. Michael Davison's Charlie Company, 5th Battalion/7th Cavalry, 1st Cavalry Division, in the Que Son valley, was served T-bone steaks hoisted down in tin canisters from a hovering helicopter and fresh nectarines from California still in their wooden crates. The next day when we moved out on patrol, I watched in disbelief as a sergeant with a hatchet crushed the remaining crates of nectarines. He told me he had to destroy the nectarines so the Vietcong would not eat them. Of course, that was a possibility: hungry Vietcong with nothing more than their usual rations of rice and slivers of dried fish, overjoyed to come across the nectarines. But the idea seemed odd. In later days, when I was scared and wanted to laugh, I would think of the Vietcong guerrillas in black pajamas setting down their AK-47s to slurp the expensive California nectarines, fruit skins stuck to their lips, nectarine juice rolling down their cheeks.

The Vietcong and American combat troops had little respite. Reporters could always return to the sleazy and seductive Saigon, alive by night, filled with wonderful cafés and restaurants. You could relax for a moment in a feeling of security, the city so close to the war, yet so far. There was always a sense of purpose in Saigon, be it the energetic enterprise of prostitutes and pimps and children begging in the streets or Vietnamese residents going about their daily business: the shopkeepers, hairdressers, and restaurant waiters.

After I filed my stories, I liked to go to Brodard's on Tu Do Street, a French-style coffee shop where we played "California

Dreamin' " on the jukebox and marveled at the large resident rat— the rodent sticking his head out of the wall like an actor coming on-stage, then running down the side of the bar in front of everyone, before scampering back up the wall again to disappear into his hole. The Vietnamese patrons paid no attention. "Funny, if it happened in a restaurant in any other part of the world, people would be mad, but here it doesn't even matter," said UPI photographer Dana Stone.

Before he got to Vietnam, Dana had been a mailman in Vermont, a logger, and a merchant seaman. He came to Vietnam working as a seaman on a commercial vessel. As he steamed toward the city, he worried the whole time that the war would end before he got there.

Dana is dead. On April 6, 1970, he and his best friend, Sean Flynn, son of the actor Errol Flynn, disappeared on Route 1 in the Parrot's Beak area of Cambodia. Photographer Tim Page has spent years trying to find out what happened to them. He says he has dis-covered from interviews with Cambodian peasants that Dana and Sean were captured by the Vietcong, who kept them for a few months before turning them over to the Khmer Rouge, who executed them.

In the evenings in Saigon, I liked to go to a restaurant near my apartment called the Aterbea, where they served delicious pepper steaks and fresh asparagus, artichokes, watercress, and strawberries from the old French mountain resort of Dalat. The French-style cook would plan his menus around whatever was the freshest veg-etable from Dalat trucked into Saigon that day.

I also enjoyed Caruso's, a wood-paneled bistro that served French-Italian dinners by candlelight with imported French wines and brandies. Caruso's was down a side street off Nguyen Hue, the wide boulevard of flower shops. Often you would have to sidestep mounds of uncollected garbage to get in the restaurant's front door. One night a dead white dog lay outside the restaurant. Nobody both-ered to haul away the bloated animal. Dinner patrons sidestepped it all night as they made their way down a few streets to Jo Marcel's, a discotheque where wealthy Vietnamese lycée-educated girls danced the frug in the shortest of Parisian miniskirts and sipped Coca-Colas costing 400 piastres (about $3.40).

One morning, after a very late night of drinking and nightclub-bing with my friends, I was jolted awake by an early phone call; my landlord, Nguyen Oanh, rang the shrill bell from the store below, a system he had devised to signal the telephone call was for me. Dehydrated, my head pounding, I rolled over to pick up the receiver: "Hello, Denby, this is Ann Landers. I am here in Saigon." I mumbled into the telephone, "Stop joking," and then I hung up. A minute later the phone rang again: "I really am Ann Landers." Eppie Lederer, the syndicated newspaper columnist known as Ann Landers, invited me to meet her at the Caravelle Hotel and spend the day with her in the city, visiting wounded soldiers at the 3rd Field Hospital. Eppie Lederer was an old friend of my *Honolulu Advertiser* editor, George Chaplin, who insisted she call me when she got to Saigon. The U.S. Army sponsored her on a ten-day trip to cheer up soldiers in hospitals. She told me she wanted to come to Vietnam because lots of soldiers and their families read her column and wrote to her; some asked her if she thought the Vietnam War was right, a question she would never answer then. "I think it is something that people should make up their own minds about," she said. She also wanted to come to Vietnam because she felt she was skilled at comforting injured people. As a young married woman, she had been a successful hospital volunteer at La Garde General Hospital in New Orleans, soothing injured World War II soldiers evacuated home from Europe and the Pacific.

At the 3rd Field Hospital, the official assigned to escort Ann Landers and the photographer documenting her visit mistakenly led us into a soundless and dark room lined with rows of metal beds holding motionless young men, most in their twenties, all grievously injured, many soon to be dead. The kinds of patients some field hospital doctors categorized in triage as "expectants"—people expected to die yet watched carefully for any signs of hope. Celebrity visitors were rarely taken to the rooms of the dying; instead they were shown recovering soldiers, young men who looked good, patients who would not depress or trouble the celebrity.

In earlier wars, many of these gravely injured would have died alone and in pain at the battlefront. But the extensive helicopter evacuation system used in Vietnam allowed medics to stabilize the wounded in the field and speed them to hospitals faster than in any previous war.

Medical facilities in Vietnam were crowded with serious casualties. The modern medical techniques at field hospitals saved many lives that would have been lost in previous wars. But the terrible irony was that the quick access to sophisticated treatment that kept wounded soldiers alive also led many of them to suffer prolonged deaths or to endure years of gruesome recovery only to be burdened for the rest of their lives with major handicaps.

No matter what sadness or shock she felt in the room of the gravely injured, Ann Landers, an intelligent and self-assured woman, collected herself and acted as though everything were normal. She walked calmly through the ward of the dying, speaking softly to each young man, asking which state he was from, offering words of encouragement, smiling gently. One soldier with a scratched face and no arms or legs seemed surprised to see me walking with her. He came out of his stupor and lighted up. "Why are you here? Where did you come from?" he asked, probably amazed to see a young American woman his own age in a minidress in the quiet, gloomy room, so far from his home. Unlike Ann Landers, I was not composed. I forced a smile and asked how he got so banged up. He told me he had stepped on a mine. The next day, when I called the hospital, I found out he had died shortly after we saw him. As we were talking to him, a hospital official rushed in and grabbed Ann Landers by the elbow and quickly escorted us down a dark hall and into the ward we were supposed to visit in the first place, a cheerfully lighted room with flowers, army nurses, and smiling, chatty, recovering men, all soon to be sent home to their families.

Later Ann invited me to dinner at the Caravelle Hotel's rooftop restaurant, where we ate frogs' legs and rice and had chocolate éclairs and espresso. She did not drink, but she urged me to order a glass of Chablis. I asked her what she thought about the war. She said: "As you can gather from what I've said, I am more of a dove than a hawk, but let's not go into it. I did not come here to expound on my political views. There is something wrong here when you see a twenty-year-old boy with both legs blown off." She seemed shaken by our walk through the room of the dying.

When I returned to my apartment to write my report about Ann Landers for the *Advertiser,* I was so upset by what we had seen in the hospital that I wasn't able to write about the horror of the dying soldiers, only about the "happy" patients we were rerouted to visit in the recovery ward.

To this day I am uncomfortable remembering Ann Landers's visit. I hate to admit how selfish I was then and probably still am today. When Ann was led into the room of the gravely wounded, I wanted to leave. Even though I covered combat, I tried not to think about the painful deaths of soldiers in lonely hospital wards or of the permanent mutilation so many suffered. I had already learned how to tune out the dead to keep functioning as a reporter in the field; the quick disposal of the bodies helped, the corpses dehumanized as they were zipped into black plastic body bags, to be ferried out by the helicopters coming in with food, ammunition, and more soldiers. Food arriving. Dead leaving. The terrible routine of war.

The badly wounded also disappeared quickly, swept out of sight and memory by medical evacuation helicopters. But in the 3rd Field Hospital with Ann Landers, there was nothing between us and the injured. I was shaken, too.

The longer I stayed in Vietnam, the more cynical I became. When I arrived during the huge 1966 buildup of American troops, everything seemed possible. Enthusiasm was high about the notion of protecting the South Vietnamese from the Communist North. But the more I saw in Vietnam, the sadder I got, finally concluding we had no business there—that each death, American or Vietnamese, was senseless and that we were hurting the Vietnamese more than we were helping them.

Small cruelties made me hate the war, such as the day I watched a GI threaten a Vietnamese peasant woman who was begging to stay with her husband, whom the GIs were taking away from the village as a Vietcong suspect. The woman rightly feared she would never see him again. A soldier kept pushing her back as she pleaded, the woman crying, then finally screaming. The GI yelled at her, "Shut up, *ba* [Vietnamese for woman]. Shut the fuck up." Then he yanked the woman to his side and jammed his .45 automatic to her forehead, saying, "Shut the fuck up, or I will crocodile you"—GI slang for *cat cai dau*, "cut off your head." The woman, unflinching, stared defiantly at the GI. Her husband was then taken away, the husband and wife calling to each other until he disappeared in a bamboo thicket and was no longer heard.

On another patrol, we came across a Vietnamese village just strafed by American helicopters. Nobody was there. I looked into the darkness of one of the huts to see a dead woman in the corner, curled in a fetal position, her white blouse spattered with blood. Outside in the sun, her pigs grunted in their pen. When the soldiers weren't looking, I quietly moved the pen's wooden bars to release the pigs.

Since the woman could no longer feed the pigs, I figured at least they could survive by foraging. There was so little you could do to help.

Much of the cruelty of the war was senseless. The subtle brutality of boredom. The result of infantry soldiers spending sweat-filled, tedious days on platoon patrols looking for the enemy in villages. Vietcong . . . like ghosts . . . appearing out of nowhere as deadly snipers, but usually invisible, blending seamlessly into village populations. Days when nothing happened, but you could never relax because there was always the possibility of getting shot to death or stepping on a mine. Hot days when soldiers were bored yet at the same time relieved not to find the elusive "Charlie."

In November 1967, I spent days on such patrols with Captain Davison's C Company, 5th Battalion/7th Cavalry, 1st Cavalry Division, in the Que Son valley. By then more of the soldiers were draftees. They wore helmets stenciled with the words *Pot, LSD,* and *Nobody Loves Me* and draped peace symbols from their necks. Their main goal was to finish their one year of duty and get out of Vietnam alive.

When Davison took over the company, the soldiers told him their previous commander always stayed back at the base camp. On their daily patrols, the troops tricked that commander by finding a place in which to hunker down all day, relaxing and having fun as they ate their C rations and called in false locations.

Soon enough, Davison's Charlie Company would go into deadly battle against a Vietcong regiment as they pushed deeper in the Que Son valley, twenty-five miles south of Da Nang. Months later, they fought against North Vietnamese regulars during the Tet offensive in Hue. Many of Charlie Company's draftees died in Hue in La Chu Hamlet, a place survivors remember better as TT Woods. TT was short for "tough titty" because it was a tough place to penetrate; it was the heavily fortified North Vietnamese logistical base for the NVA operation in Hue. TT Woods, a bloody, sad battle. On the first day alone, nine soldiers in the battalion were killed and thirty-five were wounded.

But when I was with Charlie Company prior to TT Woods, the company spent day after day on grueling, mean-spirited village sweeps. On a platoon patrol led by Lt. Winfield Beck, soldiers torched the villagers' hay supplies and rounded up teenagers, some as young as twelve years old, as enemy suspects. The haystacks were burned because the soldiers said they were good hiding places for enemy weapons. The purpose of the mission was to kill or capture Vietcong believed to be helping soldiers from the North Vietnamese 2nd Division operating in the valley.

As the radio operator, Chuck Spencer, a red-haired draftee from Nashville, kept herding up village children as suspects, Lieutenant Beck, uncertain, repeatedly asked the interpreter, Vo Bay, "Are you sure they are the Vietcong?"

Vo Bay spoke a cloudy English, a mixture of GI slang, bar girl chatter, and schoolbook English. "I think big one, yes, he VC. *Baby-san*, no. He no VC."

Sam Harris, another enlisted man, protested. Harris, a twenty-one-year-old art student draftee from Sacramento, California, whom the men called "Hippie" and "the Peace Freak," said, "They are only farmers."

"A farmer can still pull out a rifle and shoot at you," Spencer snapped back.

"What are we supposed to do? Kill all the farmers?" Harris asked.

"No, but we can take them all in," Spencer said.

The two Vietnamese boys they were questioning said they were just farmers. No, they were not Vietcong. No, the boys told the interpreter, they had never seen any Vietcong in the village. Yes, they hated the Vietcong.

Spencer grabbed a village woman and ran his finger across her throat. He ordered the interpreter: "Tell her if she shows me where her husband is, we won't kill him. But if she doesn't, we are going to crocodile him."

The woman just glared at Spencer. When the village women were asked where their husbands were, the women's answers were always the same. With a defiant or frightened look, each woman would say her husband had "died from a bomb the other day" or that he was "hiding because he hated the Vietcong."

What could you expect, considering that the Vietcong were fellow Vietnamese the villagers may have known and helped forever, and the Americans trying to capture and kill the Vietcong were foreigners, big and redheaded like Spencer, with a nasty way of talking.

"Are you sure they are Vietcong?" Beck kept asking. Beck was a lonely soldier whose wife never wrote to him. Three months later, he would be dead, fatally shot in the neck by the North Vietnamese at the infamous TT "Tough Titty" Woods, cradled in the arms of Captain Davison as he died.

But on this day, Beck could not stop worrying. More village haystacks were set afire by Zippo lighters. The hay burning in the background, Private First Class Joe Mead went in to search another house.

"I hate this," said Mead. "Before, we didn't do this. We just stayed in the mountains, and anything we saw was fair game. But yesterday we got fired on and a whole bunch of people came running across the field. We wounded a woman, killed an old man, and got one VC."

Someone set another pile of straw ablaze. Then the platoon began to march back to the rocky hill a mile away, where they would spend the night.

I came to hate the war, because I felt helpless watching the so-called pacification operations in which Vietnamese were forced to move out of their ancestral villages into stark refugee settlements a South Vietnamese commander I interviewed called "peace hamlets."

The last military operation I covered was in November 1967, with the marines in a complex of villages in Dai Loc district fifteen miles southwest of Da Nang. Operation Foster, led by Lt. Col. Roger H. Barnard of the 3rd Battalion, 7th Marines, was a search-and-destroy effort to wipe out the Vietcong, who were mounting mortar attacks on the American air base at Da Nang. By the time the operation was finished, more than 11,500 Vietnamese villagers had been forcefully evacuated from their homes into a refugee camp at Duc Duc district headquarters.

Such forced evacuations were happening in many areas of Vietnam. Villagers in Vietcong-controlled areas were herded out of their houses, and the houses were burned. Their ancestral villages were leveled and bulldozed and turned into free fire zones, where any living thing could be shot or shelled. It was a drastic and final solution to separate the people from the Vietcong.

The most famous operation of this kind was at Cam Ne village near Da Nang on August 3, 1965, when the crew of CBS News correspondent Morley Safer photographed marines burning down village huts with Zippo lighters. American war critics came to associate such Vietnamese village demolitions with the ironic phrase "We had to destroy the village to save it," a justification offered years later by an American major in Ben Tre during the Tet offensive.

It takes a great deal to make a Vietnamese forsake his land and the graves of his ancestors. Women and children wept during Operation Foster. Others were either sullen or terrified.

When I asked a high-ranking marine officer whether he thought the people would sneak back to their homes, he thought about it and later said, "After the taste of freedom the people have been given, I don't think they will want to return to the slavery they escaped."

Lt. John MacNamee, one of Barnard's platoon leaders, was more realistic. "I imagine many of them do not want to move, but they are not going to resist when we have the guns."

A Vietnamese journalist watched as the peasants were herded out of helicopters to the dusty relocation spot. "They move the people into areas where there is no work for them. They are peasants used to working ten and twelve hours. Their human dignity is taken away from them. They are forced to become beggars."

I left Vietnam in December 1967, exhausted and sick. I had the often deadly strain of malaria called falciparum. I didn't know I was sick then; I thought the war had made me crazy. Anything slightly sad would make me cry. In malarial dreams, ghosts hovered in the ceiling fan above my bed, eager to sweep down and steal my body. I had fevers and the chills. My weariness I attributed to personal depression over the hopelessness of Vietnam. I would slap my face to try to keep awake as I struggled to write stories, working a little and then slumping over my typewriter. Worried, Oanh and his wife, Tai, summoned their traditional healer to help; the glass suction cups she slapped on my back gave only temporary relief.

I flew home to Honolulu, certain I was suffering a nervous breakdown. My mother drove me directly to the suburban office of our family doctor. After about a week of blood tests and consultations with army doctors at Honolulu's Tripler Army Medical Center, our doctor, Felix Lafferty, diagnosed my illness first as hepatitis, then as malaria.

Malaria was a scourge in Vietnam, especially in the highland forests, where I had spent much time. Epidemiologist Robert Bwire, in his book *Bugs in Armor: A Tale of Malaria and Soldiering*, says more than 50,000 U.S. Army soldiers were afflicted with malaria in the Vietnam War, and 80 died from it. The U.S. Navy and Marines counted 24,606 malaria cases and 40 malaria deaths during Vietnam.

The Honolulu Advertiser

Tripler said I could be treated at the hospital for no charge; the doctors there were eager to study falciparum malaria, which was proving to be increasingly drug resistant in Vietnam. But the army hospital with its huge rooms full of war-wounded was a depressing place. I opted to stay at our beach house, with Dr. Lafferty making home visits. I recovered slowly over a period of two months in my oceanside bedroom . . . watching televised soap operas and taking quinine pills and other malaria medications Dr. Lafferty got from Tripler.

I returned to Vietnam briefly in 1969 and again in 1972 with Bob Jones, the former *Honolulu Advertiser* reporter, who gave me the incentive to go to the war in the first place. Bob now was my husband, and he had been hired to cover Vietnam as an NBC correspondent.

The next year, in the midst of the Saigon rains, a French doctor delivered our daughter, Brett Jones, at the Grall Hospital, the old French colonial facility in the center of Saigon. Each night of my hospital stay, the nurse poured me a glassful of red wine. My hospital bed, an old French army cot, was cooled by a ceiling fan; the fan's creaking rotations kept time to the music of crickets in the lush tropical gardens in the courtyard below. Outside my room, in the shadowy hallways, Vietnamese cooked food for their hospitalized relatives. They heated soups and stir-fried vegetables on small charcoal braziers; their simple meals were supplemented by lemon-pepper crabs and rice noodles purchased from dozens of food carts outside the hospital gates. The Grall was where Vietnamese babies and an occasional American child were born while people were dying in the rice fields so close to the city.

I never talked about my life in Vietnam until now, thirty-six years later. And even today, when I think about those days so long ago, I feel as though I am gazing down a long tunnel, at another person, a well-intentioned young woman in a dark dream. The many boring days we spent sitting in Vietnam waiting for the war to happen are long forgotten; all I can see down the tunnel now are the moments of terror and passion, an intensity of experience I have never felt since.

When I am asked about the war, the most difficult question is: "In what ways did Vietnam change your life?" I have difficulty answering, because Vietnam is my life. If you pinch my skin, Vietnam is there. If I rub my eyes, Vietnam is underneath. The rice fields of the Mekong Delta are where I became an adult. The French villas of Saigon are the settings of my most passionate love affairs.

My deepest friendships were forged in the heat of battle: some of my dearest friends lost forever.

Vietnam is where I walked through a field of dead soldiers always looking ahead. Vietnam is where I saw butterflies dance in the sun while soldiers tried to kill one another.

In the fear of death, I felt most alive. Vietnam is everything brave about me and everything that still makes me uncertain. Vietnam is where I lost my sense that everything was going to be all right. I pray to leave Vietnam, but I never can.

Ann Bryan Mariano

Vietnam Is Where I Found My Family

Alzheimer's disease blows through my memory like wind through a Buddhist sand painting. Vietnam is still the most beautiful country I have ever seen. But images once so fixed in my mind are now dancing ghosts. Just as I grab one, it's gone.

What no disease can ever erase is that Vietnam is where I found my family. In the anguish of war, I found lasting love. Shortly before my fortieth birthday, I adopted my daughter, Jane Catherine, a six-week-old Vietnamese orphan, when I was the bureau chief for the *Overseas Weekly* in Saigon.

The following year, I married Frank Mariano, a striking army captain whom I'd met several years earlier. He was a public information officer and helicopter pilot. We met when he offered me a ride on his chopper. He had a hearty laugh and an unquenchable zest for life—but he was so handsome that I was sure he was up to no good. At first, I turned him down every time he asked me out. But he was persistent, and his love and determination eventually capsized my doubts.

We were married in 1972. A bonus for me was Frank's son, Tony, a vibrant teenager who became an integral member of our family, often joining us in Vietnam for extended visits. After our marriage, Frank and I adopted a second child, a daughter we named Anna

ANN BRYAN MARIANO retired from *The Washington Post* as a reporter in 1996. A devoted grandmother, she and her husband, Bob McKay, live in Boston.

Francesca Hoa Mariano. She became our miracle child. When I first saw her at Nhi Dong hospital, where she'd been rushed from the orphanage, she was sick, malnourished, and completely listless. Dark circles were carved under her eyes. My heart sank. She was six months old and too weak even to lift her head. Doctors did not think she would survive. One of her problems was a severe iron deficiency, but the hospital was out of liquid iron. I asked a friend to mail me some from the States, and after taking it for a week, Anna was able to hold up her head. After a month in the hospital, she was strong enough to leave.

She, at least, survives. My husband died in 1976 following complications from cardiac surgery for pericarditis. He was forty-five. Katie died seven years later in the recovery room after surgery for a malignant brain tumor she'd been battling for two years. She was thirteen years old.

I fell into despair and depression. I had left Vietnam blessed with love but could not outrun its harrowing legacy of loss. I was grief-stricken and made despondent by my inability to save my daughter's life and to protect her sister from another shattering loss. Anna was eleven when Katie died. Within several years she had lost her father, her sister, and the grandfather whom she'd adored. Her biological family had been unable to keep her, and her country was gone. Would my love be enough to help her survive?

I found a family in war and lost nearly all of it in peace. Frank and Katie now live only in my memory. I hope Alzheimer's will not insist they die twice.

I can no longer write. But I am still able to talk and tell. My words in newspaper stories from years ago give voice to fleeting memories. Friends and colleagues have written about what they remember of me, my work, and my family and in doing so are giving me my life back.

Texas wasn't big enough for me. I knew that early on. I wanted to get out and see the world. I always knew I wanted to work on newspapers. Always.

I was an only child, born in 1932 in Bollinger, a West Texas town that was green and lush. But the color was all that was extravagant. My father was an IRS agent, and my mother taught second grade.

Dad and I were always reading, and Mother kept complaining that we forever had our noses in a book. Books for me were a way to escape into a world more exciting than my own.

My mother was harsh, domineering, and a devout member of the fundamentalist Church of Christ. We drew closer later in life, but when I was young she never understood why her way of life wasn't good enough for me and made it almost impossible for me to break away. I didn't push hard enough when I should have, and when I did, it was even more difficult. I'm not sure I could ever have made my mother happy, but staying in Texas and marrying a hometown boy would have certainly been a step in the right direction.

Rural Texas was as traditional as it was conservative. I remember sneaking around to read *Gone with the Wind,* a book my mother considered too risqué. I wrote for the high school newspaper and continued writing when I went to Texas Tech, where I majored in journalism and English. I graduated in 1954 and was hired by the *San Angelo Standard Times,* where I worked as a reporter and then as the women's editor until 1957.

I was destined to write for newspapers. I never wanted to do anything else, and that was one of the few things in my life that never changed. Mother kept expecting me to come back and replicate the life she'd made at 113 Glenmore Drive. But I knew there was no chance of that and just kept heading east.

In New York, I tried to get a job at *The New York Times* in 1958, but I was unsuccessful. I was disappointed but decided that even if I couldn't work for the *Times,* I could still keep having adventures. I applied to be an airline stewardess.

The U.S. government had contracted with independent airlines to fly troops back and forth to Europe. I got a job flying on military flights between the United States, Ireland, and Germany. I spent a lot of time in Shannon. The hard-drinking Irish were rowdy, funny, and unpredictable. I probably drank and partied too much, but I didn't care. This was the exciting life I'd always dreamed of finding.

But I knew I would find a way to return to writing and reporting, and on a trip to Germany, I met Marion von Rospach; she had founded the *Overseas Weekly* after she'd become disenchanted reporting for the *Stars & Stripes,* the army's newspaper, which always reflected the view of the military establishment. The tabloid's mission was to advocate for soldiers by reporting their version of events and saying what the brass would not want to hear. Marion hired me to work in Frankfurt in 1959.

The *Weekly*, at that time, had the largest circulation in Europe of any privately owned newspaper. It was distributed on military news-stands and reached thousands of American soldiers in Europe. As an investigative tabloid, the *Weekly* prided itself on being the "cham-pion of the GI" and consistently covered issues relevant to soldiers. The military justice system was a good example of the kind of regu-lar coverage the *Weekly* did that most other media ignored. But a se-rious story often shared the front page with a model in a bıkını (or less) to quicken the pulse of the paper's tabloid heart.

By 1965, the war in Vietnam had escalated, and we received nu-merous letters from U.S. servicemen and officers asking for the paper to be sold in Japan, Vietnam, Thailand, Korea, the Philippines, and other places where they were stationed. But when I contacted U.S. military authorities for permission to distribute the paper through-out the Far East, I was bounced around like a billiard ball before reaching the Pentagon, which said no.

But that did not stop us. I was assigned to Vietnam in late 1965 to open a bureau for the *Overseas Weekly* and plan for the paper's Pacific edition. While that was under way, I began covering the war for the *Weekly* in early 1966. I was introduced to readers in this way: "With this issue, the *Overseas Weekly* begins regular coverage of the Viet-nam War.

"Outfitted in jungle fatigues and combat boots, our girl on the scene Ann Bryan moved out to the field this week to file reports from Bong Son with the 1st Air Cav Div's 3d Brig. Her dispatches will be published as they arrive. . . ."

The column went on to describe the *Weekly*'s determination to follow the troops and voice their concerns. It talked about the paper's popularity in Europe and the intense interest U.S. soldiers stationed around the world had in following news from Vietnam, since many knew they might soon be on their way there.

The column continued, "Besides, as Vietnam information chief Col. Ben Legare told Ann when she first arrived, officials are sick and tired of reading dispatches written by newsmen who cover the war from the safety of a briefing room.

"The sight of a round-eyed gal reporter admittedly shook up the troops momentarily when Ann first appeared in the midst of the action at Bong Son. But she is not the kind of woman to stay behind in headquarters.

"That, briefly, is why Ann Bryan and the *Overseas Weekly* are in Vietnam today. Please stop by and say hello next time you're in Saigon. The address is 86 Nguyen Van Thinh." I was off and running.

My first apartment in Saigon was only a slight improvement over life in the field. It was across a bridge on the other side of the Saigon River. It had no hot water, no air-conditioning, and no kitchen—but that was not a problem since I lived over a French restaurant, Guillaume Tell. A stocky blond Alsatian woman named Madeline was the owner. It was not the best restaurant in Saigon by a long shot. But it was a cozy place. Madeline was very kind, and she served a delicious chicken in cream sauce. I ate there almost every night.

On the waterfront across the street, American soldiers and sailors unloaded trucks, tanks, jeeps, and tons of construction materials for the bases they built throughout South Vietnam. I lived near Trinh Minh The Street, the "black" bar area. Some of the bar girls on Trinh Minh The were the daughters of Senegalese soldiers from the First Indochina War. It was a hangout area for black noncombat soldiers assigned to the Saigon area, a "self-segregated Soulsville," as a friend of mine once described it. The bars were as busy as those across the river on Tu Do Street, where young Vietnamese women served American soldiers beer, whiskey, marijuana, and themselves. Soldiers would call their forays into Saigon "L&L" leave, for liquor and ladies. Marijuana cigarettes loosely disguised as cartons of U.S. brands sold for not much more than the real things cost on American military posts.

My apartment was furnished with plastic furniture, and it was cheap, $250 a month for two rooms. But since it was on the second floor, the constant din of street noise made sleeping difficult. Even so, I could not have been happier. Finally, I was living full throttle, doing work that I loved in a country where my heart found its true home.

Working in Vietnam was far more difficult than working in Europe. It could take half a day to make a crucial telephone call to Da Nang to clear up an essential fact in a story. Traveling by military aircraft to get to a story might take an entire day. During my first year and a half in Vietnam, I spent at least half my time in the field with U.S. troops.

"Gal from Texas Meets 270,000 GIs" was the headline on the *Weekly*'s article marking my first six months in-country. "I'm no Angie Dickinson, but like every unattached woman in Vietnam, I get an abundance of invitations for lunch and dinner—and a few of another kind." But those invitations were always from the officers who felt women were both a distraction in the field and a potential danger. They'd say that soldiers would be forced to protect us at the expense of protecting themselves or their units. I never experienced that at all. The grunts were always respectful and welcoming.

Sometimes an officer would say, "What the hell is a woman doing here?" and I'd shrug nonchalantly. "My editor sent me to cover the fighting." There were struggles with the military over where I could and couldn't go, what I could and couldn't do. I tried never to back down, and usually my dogged persistence prevailed.

I was out in the boondocks, where soldiers hadn't seen a Western woman for many months. Even in baggy fatigues and combat boots, I was always well treated. Even when there were several hundred accredited journalists, there were only about a dozen women reporting regularly from the war in the mid to late sixties. A sergeant once asked me to take off my sunglasses so he could look at my eyes. Another made me sit down and talk with him so he could see if he remembered what an American girl sounded like.

Soldiers offered me pistols or knives, believing that I should have some kind of weapon. Even though I was from Texas, guns made me uncomfortable. I was given a snub-nosed .38 pistol as a farewell gift from an officer in the 1st Cavalry who was returning home to the States. He was sure I'd need to shoot my way out of a Vietcong ambush one day, but of course I never did. I was afraid if I had to shoot anything it would probably be my own foot.

Cynical male colleagues said they liked to stick close to me because I always got rides on choppers and the best food. One of my more embarrassing moments occurred when I got the only empty seat in a colonel's chopper while ten annoyed men waited to get off a mountain. In those awkward moments, I did what felt right at the time. It helped that I was older and had been a reporter for nearly ten years. I paid my dues and earned my place in the field, but even so, as women, we still had to assert our right to cover the war in Southeast Asia.

Back in Saigon, I typed my stories on an old office typewriter and mailed them back to the *Overseas Weekly*'s main office in Germany, a procedure that seems so antiquated in this era of instant communications. I wasn't trying to do breaking news stories. I couldn't compete with the wire services, nor did I want to try. I wanted to write about the impact of the fighting on the soldiers. There was no live coverage in Vietnam. Television pieces were shot on film, which had to be shipped to Hong Kong or Tokyo to be developed and processed in a lab and then transmitted by satellite back to the United States, where it was edited. The war that people watched in their living rooms was always at least a day old.

I was opposed to the war when I arrived in Vietnam and left as a true pacifist, more convinced than ever that humanity had to find peaceful ways of resolving conflict. Being in the field proved to me that while there are many cases of individual courage and heroism among soldiers, there is nothing about war itself that is heroic. The suffering and deaths of soldiers and casualties among the Vietnamese civilian population were staggering. I had no doubt that America's involvement was tragic and doomed to fail. There was nothing to prepare me for the death and devastation I saw.

At times it was dangerous and frightening, and the adrenaline raced through me. At times, fear was a hurdle to clear. But I think my determination to continue doing what I was doing was always greater than anything else. I was also in my mid-thirties when I arrived in Saigon and ten to fifteen years older than most of the GIs I saw bloodied and dying. My fear always paled beside the suffering they endured.

The day-to-day frustration during my first six months in Vietnam was that I was writing for a newspaper that couldn't be sold on newsstands in Saigon or in military PXs. We fought the ban by trying to have it printed in Vietnam and sold on the streets. But I found out that no American publication could be printed or sold in Vietnam without permission from the U.S. government, and that was repeatedly denied. Even if we had successfully obtained permission from the Americans, the South Vietnamese government would have been legally allowed to censor it. Our only recourse was a lawsuit.

On July 25, 1966, in Washington, D.C., lawyers representing the *Overseas Weekly*, Warren Woods and Betty Southard Murphy, filed a lawsuit against Secretary of Defense Robert S. McNamara in U.S. district court. Our brief alleged that McNamara was violating the

First Amendment by banning the *Overseas Weekly* from distribution in the Pacific. We also sought a preliminary injunction to stop him from blacklisting the newspaper, arguing that this violated the due process clause of the Constitution. Word was that McNamara hated the *Overseas Weekly* and found it personally offensive. He was the engine driving the Pentagon's opposition to its sale on newsstands in PXs in Asia, whose excuse was that there wasn't any room.

I did the investigating for the lawsuit in Saigon and found that thirty new U.S. publications were added to the PX newsstands after the *Weekly* was banned. I also took photographs to show that there was still plenty of space on PX newsstands for our newspaper. There were, at the time, about 30,000 GIs stationed in and around Saigon, but only 750 women with PX privileges. Yet the three main PXs in the Saigon area that allegedly had no room for the *Weekly* had plenty of shelf space for *Better Homes and Gardens, Woman's Day, Hair-Do, Lady's Circle, Teen* magazine, *Romantic Confessions,* and even *McCall's Patterns and Fashions.*

On October 23, 1966, we published the Pacific edition of the *Overseas Weekly* for the first time despite the ban. The headline read "Hell with Red Tape—*OW* Hits the Pacific." In an editorial, the paper staked out why it thought the government was trying to keep it off newsstands. "It certainly isn't for the reason given—'there's no space on the newsstands.' (Have you looked at your newsstand lately?) It's because *OW* prints hard facts, and not even our worst enemy has questioned the paper's accuracy. It steps on toes. It never has been and never will be bought by pressure groups. It fights. It backs the little guy against the impersonal machine. A newspaper is a living entity with responsibilities and rights. The only people who should judge it are the readers—not timid officials. How can one defend fighting for democratic ideals as we are the world over while denying them to our own citizens?"

Since we couldn't print the paper in Saigon, we rented facilities in Hong Kong to publish the Pacific edition. Then we had the paper flown back to Vietnam, and I hired a few dozen Vietnamese paperboys to hustle it on the streets and outside military barracks.

But before long, the South Vietnamese began meeting the planes, removing the newspapers, and censoring them. Any stories that indicated problems of morale, corruption, or failure in the war effort would be cut out of the papers. One example was the reporting we did when soldiers stationed near Long Binh, just outside Saigon, complained that they did not have enough rifles and ammunition to go around.

Time magazine wrote about the lawsuit, making note of my gender: "Pacific Editor Ann Bryan, 35, is praised even by officers in Viet Nam. Without sacrificing femininity, the comely redhead has repeatedly gone out into the field under fire and written knowledgeably about combat troops."

Although we lost in the district court, we ultimately won at the appellate level on October 3, 1967. In a unanimous decision, the court ruled, "It is impossible to say at this time that the necessities of military operations justified the ban of the *Overseas Weekly.*" Our scrappy little tabloid had taken on the Pentagon and won. It was a fine moment for the First Amendment. We were soon on military newsstands in Vietnam and throughout the Pacific.

Over the years, I pushed the *Weekly*'s coverage in a more substantive direction than the pinup on the front page suggested. Our reporting could range from stories about racial prejudice in the army to the peculiar pacifism of the Daoist "Coconut Monk," who lived mostly on top of a coconut tree on an island in the middle of the Mekong River. We ran stories on war profiteers, officers involved in black marketeering, pot smoking among soldiers, profiles of Green Berets, and a look at life in a Montagnard village and the civilian doctors and relief workers who came to Vietnam to work with orphans and refugees. One of our freelancers (it might have been John Steinbeck, Jr.) got a scoop and managed to get on a plane carrying U.S. soldiers across the border into Cambodia, something our government insisted it wasn't doing at the time.

It was also important to me that we cover the military justice system and report on GIs who were court-martialed for drug abuse, attacks on Vietnamese civilians, or fraggings, the attacks on their commanding officers that often resulted in murder. The brutality of the war spread out in concentric circles from the places where battles were fought and bombs dropped.

As it became clear that the troops could trust us, soldiers began calling our office directly with tips and information, bypassing official channels, which undoubtedly would have thwarted the information. We began getting stories that ran counter to the rah-rah military point of view, which, of course, kept us often at odds with the Pentagon.

The army once tried to get me to kill a story about a crazy colonel who commanded a helicopter unit. In order to impress whomever he was trying to impress at the time, he'd order his chopper pilots to do dangerous maneuvers that were supposed to be used only to bring a chopper under control after it had been hit by enemy fire. The army said exposing the officer would be bad for the army's image. I thought putting pilots' lives at risk unnecessarily was outrageous. Once I had a story confirmed, no one was going to talk me out of running it.

I depended on freelancers, or stringers, to help staff the bureau. I couldn't pay very much, but that didn't keep people from showing up on our doorstep. Kate Webb, Don Hirst, and Cynthia Copple were some of the best people I hired; they'd simply walked in the door looking for work. They were young and intrepid and brought a passion to their reporting that was exciting.

I explained to those I hired the *Weekly*'s determination to ferret out the truth of events by interviewing the grunts and enlisted men who were actually there on the spot. I described the *Weekly*'s style as that of telling the story from the point of view of the main person in it, with a beginning, middle, and end, which is much more common today than it was in the late sixties. I reminded them that job description of the information officers said that journalists should get access only to people, places, and information that would support the official version of events.

Richard Boyle was one of those who just showed up one day, fresh from the battle at Ben Het, a Special Forces outpost at the Laotian border, not far from the DMZ. Ben Het, which was eventually overrun, had been attacked by regular North Vietnamese troops using Russian-made tanks for the first time in the war.

Boyle was still in his filthy fatigues, a stinking mess of mud. I had been trying, unsuccessfully, to get someone into the area for days. I put Richard in front of a typewriter and told him to write a first-person account of what he'd seen. He had shot some film, and after I developed his photographs, I offered him a job. Boyle had that renegade spirit that made him both dangerous and successful. He would take risks that were insane but often came back with stories no one else could get.

Boyle was working for the *Weekly* when Seymour Hersh, writing for Dispatch News Service, broke the story of the My Lai massacre.

On March 16, 1968, American soldiers led by 2nd Lt. William Calley, opened fire on the villagers in My Lai. In all, 347 men, women, children, and babies were killed in the slaughter; ninety more unarmed villagers were killed in a nearby hamlet by soldiers from another company of the 23rd Infantry Division. Both the government and military officials denied the first reports of the massacre.

Boyle was eager to go to My Lai and see what he could learn firsthand. I sent him with Jacqueline Desdame, a French Vietnamese interpreter. An old woman who had survived the rampage showed them where to dig for bodies. They were spotted by the South Vietnamese secret police, who shoved a submachine gun into Jacqueline's side to get her to stop translating. But she and Boyle held their ground and managed to get back with further confirmation of the massacre.

Reporting like that helped make the paper distinctive. In late 1969, fraggings were becoming increasingly common, as soldiers sometimes turned against their commanding officers. One day we were tipped off to an incident in which a black medic had allegedly killed his racist sergeant. Boyle managed to sneak onto the firebase, get the story, and get out. The commanding officer was shocked when Boyle confronted him with the story, seeking confirmation.

You never knew in Vietnam when a routine assignment could

turn deadly. I was going out to Bien Hoa in late 1968 or early 1969 with Don Hirst, a photographer I hired for $100 a week after he got out of the army, and Frank, who was going to do a radio piece for ABC on the one thousandth American helicopter that had been shot down.

We were riding along a road in the Bien Hoa air base, just outside Saigon, when shooting began. Several of the rounds hit near our vehicle, which I think was a jeep. We could see the puffs as the bullets hit the dirt nearby. We all bailed out of the vehicle, looking for cover. A few moments later, a white medic began giving mouth-to-mouth resuscitation to a black GI. Don was taking pictures, and someone started to call him a ghoul and I kept saying, "We're press, we're press." The victim died and we all felt awful. At first we thought a soldier had gone berserk and started shooting, but as it turned out, I learned a few days later that the man who died was a military prisoner who was trying to escape. All of that on the way to do the chopper story. But that was Vietnam. The deck was stacked with wild cards.

Frank Mariano and I were becoming closer. He was separated from his wife and was back for his second tour of duty in Vietnam as a helicopter pilot and public information officer. As a career army man, he was gung ho about the war and always believed it was winnable, even up until the bitter end. I knew it was not, and this was often a point of serious disagreement between the two of us.

What drew me to him was his exuberance for life and his passionate attachment to whatever he held dear. I have always been quiet, if not shy, and I loved being in the presence of Frank's boisterous personality and marvelous sense of humor. Once when we were in the field together in Cambodia, Frank was doing a radio report and some incoming rounds landed nearby. Without thinking he yelled, "Honey, get down!" When friends heard the broadcast, they fervently hoped I was the "honey" in question.

By the late sixties, I was living in a rooftop apartment in Saigon, which looked out toward the cathedral, that friends called Flowering Heights. It was the scene of many happy and boisterous parties. Frank had a way of drawing people in. He was the sun in a circle of friends that orbited around him. His capacity for friendship was magical and his empathy almost boundless. When you were weak, he was strong; and if you were down, he lifted you up. Frank had a generosity of spirit that eclipsed how hard he worked and sometimes struggled in his own life. Frank was an undereducated overachiever who always used to say, "If you flounder, you can't swim." He had a steely determination to persevere and did, but when he kicked back, it was with great gusto. Frank loved to cook and would make Italian feasts for our friends with recipes he swore had been passed down in his family for generations.

One night in July 1969 when friends were over, we watched the first American walk on the moon. Someone arrived late and asked what was happening. "We landed on the moon." She had been away from America for a year and was incredulous. An Australian journalist who'd had a lot to drink said, "Yes! Bloody Americans are on the moon even as they're killing people here in Vietnam."

The children of Vietnam captivated me from the time I first arrived. I was mesmerized by their beauty and soulfulness. The Vietnamese, with some exceptions, cherished children. But mixed-race children were looked down upon, especially those fathered by black GIs. They were called derisively *bui doi,* which meant "dust of life." Vietnamese who could afford to adopt children—and there were plenty in the South who could—usually didn't because of their traditional beliefs. The Vietnamese revere their ancestors, which helped create strong familial ties. But it made many wary of bringing "bad blood" into their own family lines.

Through my friend Anne Allen, whose husband, George, was in Saigon with ABC News, I had become friends with a Vietnamese nun, Sister Robert Tron, who ran an orphanage in Saigon. I never expected to become as involved as I eventually did in helping her arrange adoptions, but she had an irrepressible spirit and became almost a surrogate mother to me. Her mission was simple: Get as many children out of Vietnam as possible. We helped dozens of American families adopt Vietnamese children. The best estimate at the time was that there were about twenty thousand mixed-race orphans in South Vietnam. Those who survived the ravages of infancy in the understaffed and underfinanced orphanages were destined to grow up there. In 1970, for example, only twelve hundred children were adopted from South Vietnam.

I had a terrific network of friends that I often reached out to for help. I remember once calling my close friend Betty Southard Murphy, the attorney who had been instrumental in winning our lawsuit against the Pentagon, and telling her she had to help find a family for two beautiful African-American-Vietnamese sisters who were languishing in an orphanage. She did. The sisters were soon on their way to Michigan.

At best, it was tedious and frustrating to get exit papers for the children we were trying to help. Most often, it felt impossible. The Vietnamese government was in turmoil and labored under a byzantine bureaucratic structure that was a legacy of the French colonial rule. There were miles of red tape to cut through in Saigon, and it was equally difficult at the American end. I trekked from one office to another, returning as many times as necessary until I got departure approval. Getting U.S. visas for the children who were being privately adopted was exceedingly difficult. Betty, back in Washington, D.C., worked what I called her "immigration magic." Then we had to try to arrange free airfare and find escorts to accompany the children to the United States.

Once, when my sixteen-year-old stepson, Tony, was returning home to high school after visiting during the summer in 1973, I asked him if he'd be willing to take a six-month-old baby to her adoptive parents, who were waiting in Ohio. As spontaneous as his father, he agreed without a second's thought. In the cab on the way to the airport, I asked him if he'd ever changed a diaper. He hadn't. I gave him a crash course in the cab, and he and baby Pamela endured the twenty-two-hour flight together. How hard could it be to fly with a baby? Plenty, as Tony found out and never let me forget over the years.

But the rewards always outweighed the frustrations. Working with children filled me with hope, and that helped keep the staggering futility of the Vietnam War from overwhelming me.

I remained in Vietnam for five years, until 1971, when Frank, Katie, and I moved to San Francisco for a year. We always knew we would return to Vietnam, so leaving wasn't as difficult as it would have been otherwise. Frank and I were married on September 5, 1972, five hours after Frank's divorce was final. Tony was his father's best man, and our daughter Katie was a bridesmaid. Four hours later, we were on a plane to Vietnam. Frank had become a correspondent for ABC News, and we returned for two more years. I freelanced for the Associated Press and London's *Daily Express*, covering South Vietnam and Cambodia.

When we finally left Saigon, we moved to Hong Kong. By early

April 1975, eight months after we left Vietnam, it was clear that the country was on the verge of collapse; the war was about to end in a Communist victory. Frank, who had been covering the fall of Phnom Penh for ABC News, was in Bangkok after leaving Cambodia and was pressuring ABC to send him back into Vietnam and let him stay until the end. But the network refused. He was told that if he went back on his own, he'd be fired. ABC knew how much of Frank's life was invested in Vietnam and, I suspect, doubted that he could remain objective. He certainly would have spent a considerable amount of time and energy trying to help our friends escape.

With Frank sidelined in Bangkok, that task fell to me. I was determined that I would do whatever was necessary to get Do Van Kien, who had worked with me at the *Overseas Weekly*, and his wife, Vuong, out of Saigon. Kien had more energy than anyone I've ever met and was a devoted colleague who became a beloved friend. His family was entwined with mine because Vuong's mother helped care for our daughter Anna after she was strong enough to leave the hospital but still a weak and sickly baby. For five months, Kien's mother and sister loved Anna back into life. When Kien and his wife didn't have money to have an extravagant wedding—a huge occasion in Vietnam—Frank and I suggested they hold their wedding party in our villa, and we happily moved into a hotel for a few days.

But time was running out. By late April, Tan Son Nhut, Saigon's only commercial airport, was already closed. Since the beginning of the month, Kien and his wife had been on the U.S. embassy evacuation list because of his affiliation with the American media. Kien and his wife were told never to be away from home for more than two hours. If a bus came by and missed them on the first try, it would be back within two hours. But the bus never came.

I couldn't do anything for Kien and Vuong unless I got back into Vietnam, so the first thing I needed was a plane. I chartered one. Then I needed a cover so I could get a visa. The Associated Press was happy to endorse me as a freelancer. I left as soon as I could. I knew I was going into a dangerous situation, and it was hard to leave my two small daughters in Hong Kong. But I also knew that their father was safe in Bangkok and that we couldn't live with ourselves if we didn't try to evacuate Kien and his wife.

The pilot had only enough fuel to fly to Saigon. At first when we radioed the tower at Tan Son Nhut on April 26, we were denied permission to land. The pilot said in an urgent tone of voice that we were rapidly running out of fuel. The air traffic controllers were forced to let us down, and we landed safely. I got into a cab and headed straight for Kien's house.

By the time I rang the doorbell, my eyes were filled with tears. Kien and I embraced, desperate and scared, but happy to be reunited. I ran through the names of our friends and acquaintances to see who was around to help or pull strings. Everyone had left. I didn't know what I was going to do, but I was determined to do something. One thing I learned after seven years in Vietnam was never to take no for an answer. But this was hard. Kien didn't say so, but I knew he'd almost given up hope. He was sure his future, if not his safety, would be in jeopardy under a Communist regime because of his long association with Americans.

Midmorning two days later, I went to Kien and Vuong with good news: The embassy had a special pickup point for Vietnamese who'd worked for foreign media. But they had only five minutes to pack. Vuong spoke no English, but she understood what was happening and began to sob. Kien told her to get their papers and their wedding album, which had all the pictures of their families. He ran next door to their neighbors to telephone their parents and say good-bye.

Moments later, we were in a cab. Vuong was inconsolable. Kien had traveled outside Vietnam and had American friends, but Vuong, who had never been more than fifteen miles from where she was born, was being severed from everything she'd ever known. I had $300 and gave them $280, along with the phone numbers of friends in the United States who could help them once they arrived. We hugged one another quickly at the pickup point, and I watched as several armed Americans escorted them to a bus, which headed to a waiting C-130 transport plane. Within hours, they were gone.

Words can't capture the intensity of the feelings, sadness, relief, and the overwhelming sense of loss. I was able to help Kien and Vuong, but what about the thousands of others? It wasn't a good time to be asking why. Later that day, I went over to the AP office and found the cryptic message we agreed Kien would telex me when he and Vuong were finally safe: "Two packages for Kien have arrived safely in Guam." Kien and his wife now live in Los Angeles, where he works as a computer analyst for the *Los Angeles Times*.

I went to see my beloved friend Sister Robert Tron at the Viet Hoa orphanage. I asked her to go with me in the American evacuation, but she refused to leave her children behind. "I cannot go. My obligation is to stay here. I will die in Vietnam." By then Sister Robert was in her early sixties and still wearing a white habit and veil.

She knew the end was imminent and was making plans to destroy documents and records at the orphanage because she feared reprisals if the Communist leaders found that the nuns had permitted American, French, and other foreign parents to adopt Vietnamese babies. She gave me photos of dozens of adopted babies sent to her by their new families to show how the children were thriving in their new surroundings. She treasured the photographs but feared that they might endanger the children remaining with her.

As I was about to leave, she asked only one favor. "Please pray for me that I will have courage when the Vietcong come for me," she said. But courage was one quality that the frail, gentle nun had in greater measure than most of us. We never spoke again. I never wrote to her after that for fear of incriminating her. I still yearn for her, though, and mourn the years with her that I missed; she was a mother and a friend to me, one of the dearest I have ever known.

The next day, April 29, was my last in Vietnam, a country that had been more of a home to me than any I'd ever known. I left in a helicopter and was flown to the USS *Mobile*, a small navy ship not far off the coast. The vessel had a landing pad with room for one helicopter. The ship remained off the coast of Vung Tau for several days, picking up refugees. On May 2, the American task force steamed away from South Vietnam, heading toward the Philippines. The ships carried eighteen thousand refugees and Americans, like me, who were there at the end of the war.

Just as the USS *Mobile* was getting under way, the last of the Vietnamese refugees arrived, pulling near our mammoth ship in two small fishing boats, crewmen waving frantically from the bow. An American sailor waved them off in the direction of the ships that were not yet under way, and they were picked up.

The *Mobile* started moving just before dusk. A brief rainstorm brought behind it a half rainbow. Flying fish jumped in the distance.

I began a letter to my daughters.

To Catherine and Anna—

There has been an end and a beginning in Vietnam within the last seven days. It is far too soon to know what the new order that is beginning in South Vietnam will be like. But I can tell you something of how the old order ended.

Your lives began in Vietnam and by birth you are Vietnamese. By nationality and upbringing you are Americans. But I hope you will grow up to think of yourselves first as citizens of the world, involved with and connected to the human race more than to any national boundary. Ties much stronger than blood and birth bind you to your father and me. They are ties of love, concern, caring and need. We chose each of you for our children, because we met you when you were babies, loved you and wanted you. I hope you will grow up to feel yourselves bound to humanity by ties of love and concern.

The Vietnamese people have suffered terribly in recent decades. The fighting and dying have ended now. As the war neared its end with the encirclement of Saigon by the Communist forces, many of the Vietnamese I have known, loved and admired for years were very frightened. They feared reprisal for what they believed the new regime would regard as anti-Communist activities and connections; some feared they could not live as they wished, in their accustomed ways, under a Communist government. Many fled Vietnam. Many stayed because they felt their ties to Vietnam were stronger than their fears of the unknown of the new ideology, which would soon govern the country. The large majority of the Vietnamese, I believe, were not afraid of the new order and did not expect it to change their lives greatly.

This has been a time of sadness for me because I knew I would be separated from people and places I loved. . . .

My friend Cynthia Copple once said that Vietnam was like a poem because it could only be experienced emotionally and could not be understood through logic or reason. For me, that has been true.

Twenty-one years later, in 1996, shortly before I retired from *The Washington Post,* where I had worked as a foreign editor and as a reporter, I returned to Vietnam and walked along the sandy beaches of Vung Tau with my daughter, Anna, who now prefers to be called Mai. The fourteen-hour flight to Vietnam was returning Mai to a homeland she did not know, and me to the foreign country that had become synonymous with home to me.

Mai inherited memories of Vietnam. She has seen the photographs, heard the stories, and known our friends from those years. But my vivid memories, of the rich green rice paddies and slate blue mountains, are barely more than adjectives in her heart. My hope— really my dream—was that Mai would come away with memories of her own that would nourish and sustain her as mine have strengthened me.

My daughter has endured terrible losses in her life. I want her to find peace and be proud of the ancient culture and tradition from which she is descended. Those were the simple reasons. But no mother-daughter trip is ever simple, ever neat.

"It's no fun being an outsider," she wrote in the diary she kept during our trip and allowed me to read afterward. "I am ashamed of growing up in America. I am ashamed of the privileges that I have been given and taken for granted. And worst of all, I don't know how to relate to Vietnamese my own age who grew up in Vietnam, experienced hunger and poverty that doesn't allow them to develop fully.

"I share no common history with these people, no common experiences and no common hardships. I have lived a privileged life and so many millions have not."

As we walked along the beach where her chubby toddler legs once churned through the sand, I realized how much everything has changed. Vung Tau is almost unrecognizable from what it once was. Hotels and restaurants line the long beaches, curling around the little peninsula that makes up part of the city's coastline. Swimmers crowd the water, a few of them women still wearing their street clothes.

Mai and I stopped to watch a volleyball game. One by one, the young men dropped out of the game and made their way over to Mai. Each tried to begin a conversation with her in Vietnamese. Who could blame them? Mai is Vietnamese; her glossy black hair hangs straight down her back and below her hips in a style that has always been popular with young Vietnamese women.

The young men looked bewildered as Mai explained in English: "I can't speak Vietnamese." It is a phrase she was forced to repeat over and over during our trip. "I can't speak Vietnamese."

Back in Saigon, I looked for two of the houses where our family had lived during our years in the city. I found only one. It was located across from the South Vietnamese Presidential Palace and has been converted into offices. I looked for our favorite house, a villa with balconies and a front courtyard where the girls liked to play, but I couldn't find it. Too much in the city had changed. Anna had no interest in seeing the houses where she once lived. She wouldn't say why.

I went alone to the orphanage to find out the fate of Sister Robert Tron. Several of the nuns I'd known twenty-three years earlier were still there. The Communists had forced them to close the orphanage, and instead the nuns now baby-sit during the day for children of working mothers.

I was told that Sister Robert had died a few years before. She'd retired from the orphanage several years after the Communist takeover and moved to Dalat, a delightful city perched beside a lake and surrounded by water where her order had a home. I missed her and yearned for her goodness and friendship. It was hard to be back in Saigon and know I would never see her again. Even though I knew her age precluded it, part of me hoped that somehow I might find her full of years somewhere. Another link in my chain of memories snapped.

Mai had decided not to visit the orphanage where she arrived when she was only a few days old. Shortly after she was born, her birth mother had taken her to a hospital in Binh Duong province. She pleaded with the hospital to take her tiny daughter because the family had so little food that she feared Mai—the youngest of nine children—would die from malnutrition. Hospital workers brought her to Sister Robert Tron at the orphanage, which is where Frank and I first saw her. Mai knows this story and knows she was not an abandoned or unwanted child. I have always stressed to her how much her birth mother loved her and how deeply she wanted to protect her. Mai listened impassively to details of my afternoon visit to the orphanage but asked no questions.

It puzzles and troubles me that my daughter does not want to talk to me about her sister's and father's deaths and the pain those losses have caused her over the years. Mai was open and talkative until Katie died. Then she stopped talking, which made me feel more alone.

Personal collection

When we were planning our trip back home in Washington, D.C., we talked about trying to find her birth family and Mai seemed genuinely interested. I thought it was important to try, although we had such scant information that I was not very optimistic about our chances for success.

We hired a good interpreter and drove from Saigon to Song Be province, which was known as Binh Duong before the Communist takeover. The provincial hospital where she was first taken by her parents no longer exists. We began our search at two Catholic churches, not because we knew her parents' religion, but because most churches had schools attached to them and, we hoped, had kept good records. Since we knew Mai's family name was Huyen, we thought there was a chance of finding a sibling. As we drove through the neighborhoods near the first church, I found myself scanning the twenty- and thirty-somethings, wondering if any could be Mai's brothers or sisters.

At the first church we talked to a priest, explaining our reason for coming. He agreed to look through their records, but he wasn't encouraging. After a few minutes, Mai walked away from the group and stood alone under the rich foliage of trees and of vines climbing over the church buildings. She smoked and watched, saying nothing and frequently looking away from us. When I asked her whether she wanted to ask questions, she shook her head and seemed somewhat angry.

At the second church, we did the same thing. The priests said they'd look in the files and sent us over to the school, where they thought the teaching nuns might have some information.

Mai would not sit down to talk with the two nuns. I stood, not wanting to speak for her. When the sisters asked the name of the orphanage where we had adopted Mai, I couldn't immediately remember it, astounded by my memory lapse. I thought it was nerves. Now I know better.

The nuns gave us the names of some other schools and churches to try, but they were not optimistic because so many records had been destroyed as the Communists were taking over. My memory lapse seemed to frustrate Mai, and she did not want to continue the discussion of how we might find members of her birth family. The next day she called off the search entirely. "I don't think there is anything to find."

I think there may be in Mai a deeper, cultural anger that made her want to push me away physically and mentally. But she disagrees. As she wrote in her journal, "Mom thinks I'm afraid of something. She wants there to be some deeper meaning to my not caring about this search but there isn't. I just figure that any documents that might have existed were probably burned in 1975 when the Communists established control over the country. That is about all I have to say on the subject."

But we had happy interludes. Water buffalo and oxen working the rice paddies mesmerized Mai, who grew up in cities. She was, like most newcomers to Vietnam, dumbfounded by the sheer number of Vietnamese who can be compressed onto a motorbike or bicycle. Four adults seemed to be the limit, but a few children might still be added on, balancing like trapeze artists. A charming young man named Mike Nguyen, who had moved from Hawaii back to Vietnam, took Mai out for a fish-and-shrimp dinner at a small beachfront restaurant. Mike also taught her how to say "I don't speak Vietnamese" in Vietnamese.

The exquisite scenery melted some of the tension between us. We drove through plantations of rubber trees that stood as tall and straight as soldiers on parade. The treetops formed a canopy that provided shade for miles at a time. We drove up into the Hai Van pass through intense jade green mountains eclipsed by clouds. At an elevation of 3,500 feet, the breathtaking views are soaring and spectacular, as the mountains seem to stretch endlessly into the sky and, at the same time, drop dangerously down to the sea. I had flown over these jungled green mountains in helicopters during the war but had never seen them from this perspective.

Farther north, in Qui Nhon, we had a room in a hotel on the beach just outside the city. In later afternoon, the hills stretched away from me, ethereally beautiful. At one end of the bay, a fishing fleet anchored for the night. Mai seemed enchanted with the beauty of the fields, water, and the endless stretches of rice and other crops. As she wrote in her journal, "The countryside is spectacular here. What stands out most are the rice paddies. They are everywhere. I have never seen anything so beautiful. They are vibrant and green . . . no shade quite like the next."

Our birthdays are three days apart in August, and we celebrated them in Hanoi. By this point we had been in Vietnam for almost two weeks, and Mai had just recovered from being sick. Weariness was settling in, more on Mai than on me. We were increasingly edgy around each other.

We went to visit the Ho Chi Minh mausoleum and the park and gardens surrounding it. Ho's body is displayed inside a glass case and guarded by four soldiers twenty-four hours a day. The chill in the room seems to match the macabre site of the revolutionary leader condemned to spend eternity under scrutiny. His maxims are displayed throughout the building. Outside in the gardens, vendors sell souvenirs and booksellers display works about Vietnam's history and struggle for independence. Mai and I shopped independently, but she made a point of showing me one of her purchases, *The Ugly American.*

One of our hardest encounters was at Hanoi's Army Museum. It was high on the list of places Mai wanted to see. We saw some of it separately but were together at the harrowing display of the infamous "tiger cages," holes dug into the ground where prisoners were entombed with grates over their heads. Guards would walk across the grates and look down on them. Prisoners were kept in them for weeks and months at a time. The cages were so small that some captives' legs would be permanently atrophied.

While Mai and I were looking at the tiger cages, I remarked that at least the U.S. forces did not use them for the prisoners they captured. Mai became furious with me and turned away in anger. Beyond the immediate losses of her father, sister, and grandfather, she has also lost a country and her racial background. I became a target for her fury. We didn't talk much more for the rest of the day.

We flew back to Saigon for five days before returning home. Mai asked me to go with her to the Museum of War Crimes, which according to one of our guidebooks is one of the most popular stops for Western tourists in Vietnam, although it's now called the War Remnants Museum.

The museum has many of the deadly weapons that were used to wound, maim, and kill thousands of soldiers and civilians during the long war. More disturbing are the photographs of atrocities. One of the most stunning is a photograph of a small child born without arms or legs. The child's deformities, according to the museum, are a result of the chemical defoliation used by the American forces and their allies in Vietnam.

Scores of other photographs show badly wounded and maimed women and children in rural villages decimated by bombing and fighting. Mai made sure I saw them, but she said little. I think she wanted me to feel the anguish and anger she felt at seeing her fellow Vietnamese tortured and killed.

I wish now that I had told her while we were in the museum that I did feel some of that pain when I worked as a reporter in South Vietnam. I saw frightened, injured people in the refugee camps after they fled when the combat erupted, and I saw them running from the fighting that broke out around their homes. It was terrifying, and I was watching out only for myself.

Disturbing photographs of Vietnamese families killed by American troops in the infamous My Lai massacre were printed in a large book of war photographs on sale in the museums; I bought a copy. Only one officer was punished, Lt. William Calley, and he spent only a few days in jail. As a nation, we have never owned up to our actions for this terrible massacre. I believe it is a factor in Mai's alienation. She is of a different racial background and knows that her fellow American citizens murdered hundreds of Vietnamese civilians at My Lai because, in part, they looked the same as she does.

By the time I had been through the war crimes museums in the north and the south of Vietnam with my daughter, I realized that at some level she saw me as a war criminal, allied with the Americans who had shattered her birth country with bombs and bullets.

The anger and scorn she has directed at me have caused me pain, and I have cried. My husband and I took her away from her country and her culture. As American adoptive parents, we may try to rationalize what we have done and try to make up for the alienation our children feel, but sometimes it is not enough and sometimes we fail. Mai still calls me Mom, asks for help when she needs it, and, I believe, still feels I'm her mother. I will always feel that she is my child. But on some hidden level, I believe she feels I am complicit with U.S. soldiers for the massacre at My Lai, for the napalm attacks on Vietnamese soldiers and civilians, for the chemical defoliation of thousands of acres of forests, and for pursuing a war that turned hundreds of thousands of Mai's countrymen into refugees.

One of her final journal entries that she wrote during our trip read, "I don't know how to end this. I just know that I have a lot of questions about my life and who I am. Not who my natural parents were or which village I was born in. I guess going back to Vietnam didn't answer any questions but presented even more.

"Vietnam is just as foreign to me now after my trip as before it," she added. "Except now, I don't feel like I belong in either place: Vietnam or America."

But five years later, as the birth of her first child drew near, Mai seemed closer to finding the sense of belonging that has been so elusive throughout her life. I tried to give it to her but always seemed to fall short. I would have given my life to spare Mai the cruel losses she's endured. But all I could do was give her my love.

After traversing a landscape of loss for years, my daughter and I have finally found common ground in happily anticipating the birth of her child. Whether it's a boy or a girl, Mai plans to call her baby Tam, the Vietnamese word for "heart." My daughter and, now, my grandchild will always be my treasures from Vietnam, my joy, and my heart.

I want my story to be remembered as one of hope, so it seems fitting that the last words here should be my daughter's. From the moment I first saw her as a desperately sick baby, all I could do was hope. Because of Mai, I have learned just how much hope the human heart can hold. Hope is the pulse of love.

Mai was asked if she wanted to contribute thoughts for this chapter, and she did. When I read what she wrote, I began to cry:

I used to have so much resentment for my mother growing up, which got even worse as I got older. My mother and I were never really close, but over the last ten years we grew even further apart. Our phone calls diminished to about twice a year and visits home about every two or three years, but seven months ago, most of that resentment disappeared.

Eight months ago, when I found myself pregnant and alone, I was apprehensive about telling my mother. I was afraid she would be disappointed with me. But I was facing being a single parent, hundreds of miles away from any family, and absolutely terrified of what the future held for my baby and me. And I realized that after ten years of distancing myself from her, I really needed her in my life now. It was the first time since I was a child that I admitted to myself that I needed my mommy.

Although it took me about two weeks to finally get up the nerve to tell her—and it took a few more days after that for the news to sink in for her—I was so relieved when she finally called back with her support. And with this gift of unconditional love of my mother for her child, I found that most of my resentments and anger towards her were gone, replaced by a new admiration and awe of what an amazing woman my mother is.

She gave me life, not in the traditional sense, but by making sure I received the proper medical attention unknown to an orphan in the middle of a war; and by giving me the opportunity of a life I would never have had in Vietnam.

Although the last twenty-eight years haven't been easy—filled with more than our share of sorrow, pain, fights, and anger—there was also a great deal of love, caring, and support. I'm not saying my mother is perfect, for no one is, but she did the best that she could, given the tragedies that life dealt for us. And through it all, she managed to raise me to the best of her abilities. And I think, all in all, I turned out all right. No matter what our problems, I guess deep down, I always knew that she would be there for me, loving and supporting me as only a mother can.

As Tam's arrival into the world approaches, I am thankful my mom will be a part of Tam's life. And I can only hope that one day, Tam will know that my love for her (or him) will be as unconditional as my mother's love for me. And through that love, Tam will grow up knowing love, learn to be strong and independent, and will always be able to depend on Mommy like I have.

The fact that I am going to be a mother in a few short weeks has made me realize what a strong, independent woman my mother is; what an amazing life she has lived; and that I owe everything I have and everything I am to her.

Katheryn Tam Mariano was born on July 11, 2001, in Columbus, Ohio. She weighed six pounds, eight ounces.

UPI

Kate Webb

Highpockets

I left for Saigon in March 1967 at the age of twenty-three on a one-way ticket, giving up my job as foreign-wire copy taster in the News Limited newsroom in Sydney, Australia.

Afraid I'd be laughed out of court—as I had been by three wire service editors when I asked for an assignment there—or dissuaded, I said no good-byes but sent instead a resignation letter while on an overnight stop in Hong Kong. In it I stated matter-of-factly that since the period required for notice and my annual vacation were the same length—three weeks—I was resigning.

There was no political motivation. It was simply the biggest story going, it was affecting the lives (and the arguments in the pubs) of everyone around me, and I didn't understand it.

Nor did I understand why, when Australian and New Zealand soldiers were being drafted, News Limited and others were sending no one to cover the war.

With no job lined up and only an old Remington typewriter, the name of a UPI photographer, and a couple of hundred dollars in my pocket, I nearly lost my nerve in Hong Kong when I read of the death on Highway 1 of Bernard Fall, the French writer/reporter on Vietnam.

KATE WEBB worked for UPI for ten years. She has written for *The Economist* and *Business Week* and for the last thirteen years was a correspondent for Agence France-Presse based in Southeast Asia. She retired from journalism in 2001.

In antiwar protests in Australia and in my cubbyhole in News Limited back in Sydney, Fall had been my only dictionary to the stories of the war clattering in on the Teletypes.

I had, I realized only then, an impossible vision of sitting at Fall's feet, perhaps on the "Street Without Joy"—the coastal highway on which he died, which now runs from south to north but during the French and American wars was a symbol of futility—and learning to trace the historical faultlines leading to today's war.

But thanks to three U.S. Air Force pilots in the bar of the August Moon Hotel on the Kowloon side of Hong Kong, where I'd gone to toast my loss of nerve, I made the flights to Bangkok and on to Saigon.

It was simple. They asked where I was going, and I replied Saigon.

The war I flew into was in the "pile-on phase"—Secretary of Defense Robert S. McNamara had won approval for his appalling refinement of the concept of cannon fodder, and instant GIs with only a few weeks' training were being sent straight to the battlefront, with predictably appalling casualties.

Australians, New Zealanders, South Koreans, Filipinos, Thais—and, more covertly, the Nungs of Taiwan—were piling in, too, as were the riffraff that accompany any war: the black marketeers, construction workers, whores, entertainers, gamblers, and profiteers.

It all made for a surface hectic gaiety and a frenetic mix of military and civilian traffic in the Saigon that greeted me—tall, high-ceilinged, gray stone buildings flanking tree-lined boulevards, honeycombed at ground level with seedy bars.

I quickly realized that my few dollars wouldn't last in a place where "war correspondents" seemed to me then to spend at least as much time in expensive cocktail lounges as in foxholes, and after the first few weeks, I was hanging on by my teeth.

Piastre-per-column-inch articles for Vietnamese newspapers—courtesy of UPI's Paul Vogel, a fluent Vietnamese speaker—kept my head just above water. But the rebuffs from news agency editors who seemed to think I was sixteen were firm, and I was getting seriously hungry from eating at pavement food stalls and still no nearer to finding what I had come to find out—what the Vietnamese, from both North and South, wanted.

Ann Bryan (Mariano to be) was responsible for my first paperwork break—a stringing job with an alternate GI newspaper, which gave me my ticket to ride, accreditation with the Military Assistance Command in Vietnam (MACV)—the Great Classifier on the Ground—according to whose book I was now a journalist. I was granted and issued a visa extension and a laminated plastic MACV ID.

The MACV card also got me into the daily briefings (known as "the five o'clock follies"), rides in helicopters, and the "right" to go into battle.

But I was still Saigon-bound, and my most dangerous assignments to date had been to interview a gentleman by the name of Joe de Marco, who lived in a high-walled old French villa protected by five Doberman pinscher dogs, on PX scams, and two veteran Air America (AA) pilots who decided I was about to get the law on to them.

The AA pilots, who had been drinking beer in their skivvies and ten-gallon hats in their driveway when I found them at home late one morning, left me locked in a room in their villa. It took me about six hours to bash-squirm my way out of a high barred window, leaving them a note on a page torn out of my notebook saying some birds didn't like cages.

The reason they had freaked out was that I was following up a hometown story request, and one of them, whom I shall call Tex, decided that the request was a disguised way of getting him for some offense back home, the nature of which I shall never know.

Tex later saw me in a bar, threw his arms around me, roared with laughter, and yelled, "The bird!" At least twice, stranded at isolated airstrips in impossible places in the boonies, I heard the Texan yell, "Hey, Katie-bird!" and I was airborne, learning to handle a light plane and hearing stories of what to me then were the largely undocumented "missing years" of U.S. involvement, mostly air support, from the end of World War II when the French war started in earnest through their collapse at Dien Bien Phu in 1954—and the so-called U.S. advisers stage before the pile-on.

Plodding those unevenly paved, tree-lined streets of Saigon, I tended to find my friends among the Vietnamese—from MPs, journalists, priests, and students to soldiers, bar girls, and street kids, made easier by my being a French speaker, and the likes of "Tex."

My stories then were small—hometowners thrown reluctantly my way by then–UPI bureau chief Bryce ("What the hell would I want a girl for?") Miller—but they got me a stringing job with UPI, enough money to rent a cold-water room above a shoe shop owned by refugees from the North, who mercifully let me use their iron.

But it came together.

More than a year later, the hungry shoestring phase was over. Tet had come and gone and won me bylines and even a front-page photo of kids in the rubble in *The New York Times,* as well as *Newsweek* and *Time,* and recognition as the first wire service reporter at the U.S. embassy on the morning of Tet.

I had seen friends die. My French language had gotten me a UPI assignment to Cambodia, and again largely because of the language I was on the political staff of UPI, gofering for Dan Southerland, with a bunk in the second-floor dormitory of the UPI office on Ngo Duc Ke Street near the Saigon port.

I had also broken the story of a high-profile and poignant defection, that of a Korean war orphan who had followed his adoptive American army major father into the U.S. Army. He slipped out of Cam Ranh Bay by ship and remained holed up in the Cuban embassy in Tokyo for the rest of the war.

Apart from the 1968 Tet and May offensives—the two big North Vietnamese pushes on the capital—I did not cover the other big-name battles of those years, such as Khe Sanh or Hamburger Hill.

But kitted out with the obligatory military uniform, boots, and helmet from the black market, I found myself as often as not in the field as in parliament (yes, there was a parliament) and passed the test of finding out whether I could function and write amid the knife-edge fear of battle.

The political fear was different. My political articles were being censored in the South Vietnamese press. Truong Dinh Dzu, the peace-ticket presidential candidate who ran against Nguyen Van Thieu on a New Dai Viet Party ticket, was convicted, to my horror, and sentenced to years of hard labor on the basis of an interview conducted by myself and the BBC.

When Mrs. Dzu, days later, called me to say her husband was being tortured and starved in Saigon's Chi Hoa prison, I knew I had to get in to see him.

From several Vietnamese friends familiar with the inside of Chi Hoa I learned the layout, and with the help of UPI colleagues I wrote an application for an interview using the longest, most official words

I could think of, stamped it with Singapore coins rubbed in an ink pad, wet it in the gutter outside the office, folded and refolded it, and ironed it dry until it looked well used.

Then, on crutches with a broken foot, I hobbled off to Chi Hoa at siesta time—those three somnolent hours from midday when the population of the city succumbs to the heat and hides in the shade.

The letter got me past the sleepy main gate guard and the political block guard. But once inside, a young Vietnamese major sat with it in his office, read it carefully, then looked up and grinned at me.

"Nice try," he said in French.

In the welcome cool of his office, I explained the urgency of the story and told him of the calls from Mrs. Dzu.

"Do you think," he asked me, "that we would do that to a man who could be our next president if the political situation changes?"

"But I have to have proof."

"Wait, I have an idea," he said, starting to play the game. "I can't let you into the cells, but Mrs. Dzu will be here shortly. She comes every day with his food, sometimes twice."

I waited maybe an hour, during which I talked to some of the imprisoned Buddhist monks from the Quang Tri uprising, who assured me Dzu had an air-conditioned cell with all the mod cons.

Sure enough, Mrs. Dzu marched into the major's office, resplendent in full *ao dai*, war paint, and jewelry, a bag crammed with a thermos of coffee, fruit, hot food, and toiletries, and began giving instructions to the major, who managed to keep his face deadpan and angle the conversation in a way that assured me that Mrs. Dzu had no doubt her husband was getting the full VIP treatment.

The abrupt change from the glaring sun in the prison yard and the dark of the major's office meant that she hadn't seen me at the back when she first came in. When she did, I was a little concerned that my eyes would not survive her long red fingernails.

I also had my crutches. "You!" she said in the same voice that had hissed at me in the courtroom and when I had walked into her house to find some mysterious Americans there the night after the trial.

Politics and the war inevitably intertwined, with so many questions hanging to this day.

In the May 1968 offensive in Saigon, I had been trapped overnight in Cholon with the Vietnamese police. The following evening, just before sunset, the battle finally seemed to be turning against the North Vietnamese. I was sitting on the steps of a high school with the top Vietnamese brass, including the police, who had given me shelter overnight. There was U.S. helicopter support, and on the radio crackling beside me on the steps, I heard them asking us to mark our position with purple smoke.

The purple smoke grenade went off—marking the school steps as a friendly no-strike zone—and the next thing we knew, the last thing most of the thirteen officers there knew, was a barrage of rockets that exploded in our midst.

I screamed for the medic, but he too was dead. The young colonel who had joked the night before about his long lifeline was dead, as was the chief of the Saigon police and the chief of the Cholon police.

Someone riding past on a motorbike yelled through the haze of plaster smoke in English: "Get out of there now!"

I did, and I ran for miles through the dark to the office. I babbled out my story, but they all just stared at me. I was covered with white plaster and bits of people's brains and bone.

It was during the 1968 offensives that I learned from a press-escort noncom in the Hawaii-based 25th Division, Sgt. Bill Jackson, that I had a nickname. I was covering the battle for Saigon's Y-bridge—the beginning when the "friendlies" were driven back—and I too was moving in a "discretion is the better part of valor" mode. I stopped Bill and yelled into his ear in my notoriously too soft voice, trying to get him to hear over the shelling and the staccato of the M-16s. "There's someone left behind, they say someone's missing."

"Who?" he said.

"Someone called Hapockets, they keep saying Hapockets hasn't been seen."

Bill doubled up, not shot, but laughing. "That's you. Highpockets."

In the middle of a battle, I blushed.

Jackson had a narrow escape. Caught by the North Vietnamese, the man I had thought a gentle PR, whose aim in life was to run a photo studio devoted largely to high school yearbooks, had been captured overnight and held in a Saigon graveyard. They disarmed him but forgot to take his knife. He got away. His eyes when I first saw him after that looked as though someone had shot the daylight out of them at point-blank range.

It was coming back from the field, I think, that made those tree-lined streets of Saigon special—returning there became a symbol of survival. When an out-of-town assignment turned "sad," you always wondered if you would ever see them again.

Lots of assignments turned sad. Small kids stepped on land mines. Units called in artillery even though they knew a deserter from their own side might be there. A GI next to you got hit, and you didn't. A kid who the night before had been whispering over a Dear John letter from his girl in Puerto Rico was a cold, gray weight in a slimy poncho hung on two poles.

U.S. troops operated mostly in the full heat of the day, through jungles, along roads, in the southern Mekong Delta, along rivers, plodding, sweating with fully laden packs.

The attacks by the other side, apart from the mines, came almost invariably at night.

On one of these nights, crammed breathless in the bottom of a foxhole in a rubber plantation after the first mortar barrage had landed, I listened to two GIs, one from Detroit, discussing in whispers in the dark the price of cars.

"Wonder what happened to that lady reporter," said one.

"Probably flew out on the chow chopper," replied the other shadow above me.

"I'm down here," I piped up, scrambling up from under the boots that had been standing on me.

On that same operation, a young kid from New York died of heat exhaustion—one of McNamara's ten thousand. He died because he hadn't taken his salt tablets.

On a peninsula in I Corps, the part of South Vietnam just below the demilitarized zone that split the South from the North, the medevac helicopters clattered back and forth to a Seventh Fleet hospital ship. Most of the wounded on the choppers had their feet blown off by peanut-butter mines. Gray-faced, in shock, in morphine-blocked pain, they would yell for us to find their feet before they boarded—clinging to the grisly, severed boots and the hope that the surgeons could sew their feet back on again.

I wrote a story: "This is a place where marines wear dogtags on their boots."

On the hospital ship, after filing one of my stories, I was waiting in the ready room for the medevac to return. The ready room movie had a sloppy, happy ending, and tears were streaming down my face.

One of the pilots told me later it was one of the darnedest things he had ever seen. There was this chick, he said, who they all thought was hard as nails, going back and forward day after day to the peninsula with the body bags and the wounded, blubbering over a sad movie.

On the same peninsula, about a week later, a press chopper touched down not far from where I was sitting with a group of marines, and out poured about ten reporters, cameramen, and TV crewmen—all nice and clean and showered, uniforms crisp, led by a press escort officer by the name of Major Martin.

"Hey, lookitty," said the marine next to me with a grin, leaning back on his pack as I was on mine (the usual way of trying to relax when sitting).

"Yeah," I replied with the same grin, as we watched Martin confidently leading his men toward the minefield we had stopped to clear.

I choked back my laughter, though, and spoiled the fun by racing over and grabbing Martin, yelling, "Minefield!" He mistook the roar of laughter from the rest of the unit as a joke and angrily threw me off so forcefully that the weight of the pack sent me flying into the minefield.

For about thirty minutes—which felt like a year—I lay watching ants near my face, as sweat trickled and itched all over me, with disembodied voices of the men whose stories I had been writing telling me repeatedly, "Don't move."

I think it would have been the end of the war for me if the marines who risked their lives to get me out had been blown up.

Out in the field you were all in the same predicament, with nothing between you and the piece of metal with your name on it except the whim of the Great Classifier in the Sky.

But back in Saigon it was different. You got back more often than not stinking, sweat caked, mosquito bitten, and badly in need of a shower, the images of the last week or ten days—the loss, the nerves, the bitterness, the adrenaline, the fear—to lights, booze, laughter, and martinis on the terrace of the Caravelle or the Continental.

I would find myself mesmerized by the little pats of butter, the fresh French bread, the clink of ice, the feel of silk underclothes, and the whiteness of the tablecloths. I reveled in it, and I felt guilty and a sham. The people I had been with were still out there.

It was weird. It was Alice through the looking glass.

Often only hours before you took that first sip of Ricard or your martini, the ice cold on your tongue, you had been watching a medic give up on a kid of eighteen or nineteen and flip a cold poncho over his face. Often you could hear the artillery of a battle across the Saigon River.

Some things I couldn't hack.

I couldn't face boiled eggs. They reminded me of how thin people's skulls were. Cars backfiring made me jump. On my first R&R (rest and recreation, a GI term that the journalists adopted), I found I couldn't run over grass for fear of mines. I also found that survivor's guilt is a fact of life.

But it had become my story, and I would no more have thought of leaving than I would have handed in a half-finished story to an editor.

Then there were the ARVN (the Army of the Republic of Vietnam), troops for whom the dragging war usually spelled dishonor, death, injury, or imprisonment. (I'm speaking not of a number of *very* rich generals, but the line troops.) They were, unlike the GIs, in for the duration, not for one year.

In I Corps, that treacherous area south of the DMZ, 4th Company, 1st Battalion, 1st Division—many of them from jails in Hue—became my adopted unit.

They operated at night, without helicopter support. The North Vietnamese artillery walked toward us. We carried our wounded out on foot. I helped scrounge a pallet of beer for *Dai Uy* (Captain) Truong when he became *Thieu Ta* (major)—the same man I had watched shoot a man in the foot when he pleaded that his other foot was in too bad shape to go on patrol.

"That way," *Dai Uy* Truong told the troops, "he won't be able to patrol for the other side, either."

I saw *Dai Uy* Truong wounded, I helped carry his young number two on a stretcher back to Quang Tri, where his arm was amputated. And when they threw the ARVN 1st Division, in my mind the country's best, into "the Tiger's Mouth" in Laos and lost them all, I was angry. I will always wonder if it was deliberate, to hasten the end.

If my thoughts return to Vietnam, it is often to *Dai Uy* Truong and his men, the pitch-black night patrols with only the tiny phosphorous mark on the pack of the man in front of me to follow. The sliver of tart green mango with salt to slake your thirst, our conversations about the war, usually at dawn with the first cups of hot tea or coffee.

Often I went out with his men on my own time; the U.S. papers at that stage, when the political clamor over the war was at its height, were not much interested in the ARVN.

Another friend, President Thieu's bodyguard—whom I met by accident when he gave me a lift in his jeep when I was on crutches—became another point of sanity and source of news. He would pick me up to accompany him to opium dens at night. He was a Hoa Hao—a strange sect with no political affiliation, which gave him relative immunity from the approaches of Thieu's political enemies.

He introduced me to the Hoa Hao and their unique world; they were one of the few groups that both the North and the South tolerated as neutral. No such immunity existed for other minorities—that cost was high.

Then the inevitable happened. I fell for a soldier, a Special Forces officer (yes, we talked about Fall and Lateguy and what the war was all about for whom; about Wilf Burchette, and the China-Taiwan factors, the Korean War and Cambodia and Laos; and about the corruption, the deception, and the lies), got to know the secret war on the ground—and I got egg all over my face.*

My falling for the officer, who of course had a wife and family back home, landed me alone, miserable, and jobless in the States, until UPI's Jack Fallon found me a slot in the Pittsburgh bureau at the time of Kent State and Cambodia's entry into the American war.

When I heard there was a possibility of going to Phnom Penh, I grabbed it.

A now fly-specked black-and-white photo, falling in flakes from my album, shows me arriving back in Saigon in an Yves Saint Laurent mini, high-heeled sandals, and long hair, arm in arm with the staffer I considered my greatest UPI buddy and one of the best rewrite men in the business, Bert Okuley. Within a day my hair was back to GI short.

Cambodia was a different war.

No helicopters, no MACV, no special passes for U.S. or any other transport, no U.S. military hospitals—just a beautiful old French colonial city on the Mekong River dotted with graceful pagodas, en-

---

* Bernard Fall and Jean Lateguy, two French authors on the Vietnam War. Wilf Burchette, an Australian who wrote publications about the South Vietnam Liberation Front, as perhaps the only Westerner allowed to accompany their troops.

gulfed in chaos, and on the bum end of a war the United States was pulling out of with a final, wrenching kick.

French rubber plantation owners—in dark glasses, open-necked white shirts, and gold watches—who had lost their plantations to the North Vietnamese army and hoped the Americans or someone would get them back, sat daily in the shade of the sidewalk Hotel de La Post café, sipping endless glasses of *pastisse* and *bebés* (babies, or single whiskies).

Whole battalions of ill-armed and unarmed students charged into the front lines and never came back. Small farm kids ran squealing in delight toward the "pretty" napalm.

Here, in a way, the Alice in Wonderland feeling—the jarring contrast between khaki fatigues and silk dinner dresses, death in the mud and haute cuisine—was even madder.

The foreign press, most of them "old Saigon hands" now in bungalows and rooms in the old colonial Hotel Royale set among flowering trees, drove out daily in civilian clothes in rented Mercedeses in the morning. In the evening, the first back would pull up a chair by the swimming pool and wait for the others to return.

The casualties and the list of missing got so bad so fast that François Sully of *Newsweek* went around the hotel swimming pool in the evenings, snapping everyone's photographs, joking that he'd make money out of the obits. When Sully, who had survived the French war, was killed in the worst way, *Newsweek* used the famous and fatalistic "Today your turn, tomorrow mine."

The day came when my two colleagues from UPI, Frank Frosch and Kyoichi Sawada, did not come back. It rained all that day and was still raining the next morning when my Cambodian colleague Khauv Bun Kheang found their bodies facedown in a paddy field off Highway 2.

Those weren't the days of hand phones, satellite phones, or, in Cambodia, even working phones. The quarter-speed telex ticker in the post office seemed to take forever to get out the words: "R-e-g-r-e-t t-o i-n-f-o-r-m y-o-u . . ."

I remember trying to smash the camera of a TV team who tried to film the bodies at Calamette hospital when they came in, that Ray Coffey of the *Chicago Daily News* quietly helped out, that it kept raining and raining, that in the middle of it all I thought it was hysterically funny that I had to keep getting ice from the Coca-Cola factory for the morgue, and that finally, when I was on my own, I just kept repeating one word: no.

I stepped into a dead man's shoes, Frank's, and was named UPI bureau chief in Cambodia. Khauv's only son was killed. Riding protection for the U.S. ambassador, he took the full force of a Plastique charge. Khauv wrote the story first, then told us. At the funeral, one of the son's colleagues was killed when he got a grenade tangled while relieving himself against the back wall of the pagoda. They cremated him, too.

I broke the story of Lon Nol being incapacitated by a stroke. Someone high up in Washington called UPI and tried to have the story stopped, and at my end embassy officials tried to persuade me I had it wrong. It was one of the most nerve-racking forty-eight-hour beats I have had in my life.

One of my permanent stringers, François Bailly—who always went to battle with his pet monkey on his shoulder—died in an insignificant battle, in an area to the northeast, beyond a line I had come to suspect was the cutoff point (unknown at first to the Cambodian high command) of U.S. air support. A Cambodian photo stringer's spine was severed by a sliver of shrapnel.

I tried to take the risky assignments myself and was tough on those I thought were taking needless risks.

But it was only months later, in April 1971, that I was captured by North Vietnamese troops along with five others, four Cambodians— Tea Kim Heang (Moonface), Chhim Sarath, Vorn, Charoon—and Toshiishi Suzuki of Japan's Nihon Denpa News, during a battle on Highway 4—the road that runs through the Kirirom mountains down to Sihanoukville on the south coast of Cambodia.

We had crawled together in the roadside scrub during an ambush in which the North Vietnamese turned a several-kilometer stretch of the highway into a shooting gallery that effectively wiped out the Cambodians. The last paratroopers who tried to fire back were riddled with AK bullets.

We had no helmets or flak jackets. Heang had two old bullet wounds, which had opened up in the scramble for safety. The killing of the last paratroopers showed us that trying to reach friendly lines by going forward down the road was impossible. Going back was the same.

In whispers, we decided we had to belly-crawl sideways out of

UPI

the scrubby roadside ditch we were huddled in before the North Vietnamese troops emerged from the trees behind us to count the dead.

For the rest of that day, the night, and the next morning, any bits of white color torn off our clothes, we crept through the trees and their lines, sometimes holding our breath as they walked within inches of us, chattering. Thirst plagued us, insects bit us as we hugged the earth, branches crisscrossed us with scratches. Then the friendly artillery started and the allied bombing, obviously called in by the Cambodians. The bombing was with fléchettes, those small, razor-sharp bomblets that shredded people. Zillions packed into one big bomb.

At eleven-thirty the next morning by the watch on the hand that went up next to my head, they got us. We simply ran into them, two skinny young soldiers as surprised as we were—probably more surprised seeing a Western woman, a middle-aged Japanese, and four Cambodians, all in civilian clothes and all looking as if we'd been mauled by tigers.

We kaleidoscoped into one another in the face of the two AKs, caught in a small clearing.

"Kasset"—press—we croaked in Khmer, then *"Nha bao"* in Vietnamese, the words pathetic in the face of the rifles, the memories as

fresh as echoes of the volleys of shots that had finished off the paratroopers.

They were standing higher than us, we realized, as we stood frozen, our arms high. On top of a large bunker. Unable to help ourselves, we started croaking for water: *"Nuoc."*

They gestured for us to squat and stripped us of our belongings—shoes, cameras, my bag, notebooks, and binoculars. Gestured us to empty our pockets. Then one ran off and returned not with water, but with baling wire, vines, and tape to tie us up and bundled us squashed into the dark of the bunker.

I thought that was it. I was sure they were simply going to toss a grenade in on top of us. But eventually they gestured us out back into the dappled light of the dry jungle floor and, ensuring that we stayed squatting, handed me a small tin pannikin of water. I passed it around, thinking we could all get a sip, but when it had gone the full circle, it returned to me empty.

That the others hadn't left me anything, and what it meant, shocked me more than the rifles. I said nothing, but there was a huge loneliness in my head that didn't leave me.

More soldiers in their floppy green fatigues and soft bush hats emerged silently from the foliage, ignoring our cries for more water. Tied in a chain with the baling wire, which bit deep into our arms, we set off single file—rifles ahead, alongside, and behind—into the dappled jungle.

It was the first of many long marches.

I tasted it—the feeling of being a prisoner—underneath the burning thirst, the new loneliness in me, and the compulsive documenting of every detail.

We were a mindless, cattlelike line, shuffling in our wires.

They hacked branches from the trees and stuck them upright into our bound hands as camouflage against the planes, then directed us into the open and onto a side road.

Once on that road, whose surface burned our feet, we ignored their yells and tumbled toward a pool of black, fetid water scummed with jungle debris and insects. Flopped on our bellies like turtles, we stuck our faces in it and sucked at it desperately.

It impressed the guards. Two of them went off and returned with a poncho, slung between two poles, full of water.

"This is my blood which I give for you. . . ." It was like a strange jungle communion, as we knelt one by one to drink from the poncho.

At one place, still tied in a chain, we had to cross a single log over a small ravine. A slip would have sent us all tumbling. I still dream about that.

Every detail and smell of those nights and days—the nights walking from dusk to dawn and the days often crammed stifling in bunkers—is etched in my memory, like the time when in the light of a small oil lamp I was showed crude propaganda drawings of GIs peering in the lighted windows of their homes at Christmas.

The night of the first day, the others were led off one by one, and I lay breathing the earth smell in the dark, heard spaced shots, and believed I was next.

The same with the first long interrogation—not just the endless repetition of name, age, rank ("*No rank*, not military"), nationality, and length of time in country—but also the shots.

After those, I was known as *co Anh*—the English girl.

The first long interrogation came as we were lying in the dirt, trying to dig body crabs out of our skin, after waking almost fizzy with life after surviving an overnight march that I at least had doubted we would finish.

They summoned us one by one, at intervals of about thirty or forty minutes. A single shot would ring out, and as our numbers slowly dwindled, we couldn't meet one another's eyes.

My turn came.

I was led into a clearing, at one end of which a thin, white-haired Vietnamese of about sixty, his face etched with fatigue and, I thought, illness, was sitting at the center of a flimsy table set up in the shade of a canopy of green camouflage silk, strung on low tree branches. He was flanked by what I supposed were junior officers.

My place was to sit in the sun on a log at the opposite end of the clearing as a North Vietnamese military photographer clicked away. I had managed to whisper to Moonface and Sarath (UPI photographer and driver, respectively) in the bunker on the first day not to mention any connection to me—the only one in our group clearly working for an American company, something that could easily be checked in Hanoi—but I had no way of knowing whether they had admitted, or been forced to admit, it.

An odd thing happened as question followed question, and the young interpreter struggled to translate from English. I found myself thinking of the senior officer interrogating me as a professional soldier.

The flip side of that was that I stopped feeling like a filthy, scared prisoner from the other side with U.S. (UPI) and MACV ID cards, and probably on my way to execution, and like a professional reporter instead. He was taking what the war dealt out to him, and I was taking what the war dealt out to me.

The questions droned on and on, and my head began to swim. I half joked in some of my replies.

"Who won the battle on Highway Four?"

"How can I tell who won? I am a prisoner."

"Why were you down on Highway Four?"

"To find out what was happening."

"Why would you risk your life to find out what was happening? You must be paid a great deal of money."

"Now I wish I hadn't, but I am a reporter."

At one point, when the interpreter translated two and a half years into twenty-two years, I decided to drop any pretense of knowing no Vietnamese at all (in fact I knew very little) and corrected him.

When it was over, I was told to stand. I tried, almost fainted, and succeeded on the second try. This is it, I thought for probably the tenth time since our capture.

But the interpreter led me not to my execution, but along another narrow jungle path to where Suzuki was sitting, not dead but alive.

"I think we will go to the north," the interpreter said brightly.

Silently Suzuki tore out the cotton lining of his trouser pockets and began trying to tie them on my feet, suppurating, cut, and oozing pus from the walks.

I knew I would never survive the walk north, to the Hanoi Hilton (the prison camp for U.S. POWs), and changed the subject, congratulating the interpreter on his English.

"Oh," he said. "I learned it from a New Zealand woman, a Mrs. Freda Cook."

(After our release, when I later described this, Freda Cook wrote to me and asked how "her boys" were doing. It turned out she had been to school with my mother, had answered the call of "the cause," and had gone to Hanoi as a teacher.)

Night marches followed night marches. We slipped like shadows through the villages and jungles, across paddy fields, and over mountains and small mountain streams, starting at dusk and stopping just before dawn.

Our feet mushed and remushed, until they finally had to untie Moonface, whose weight made walking hideous for him, from our chain and provide him with a staff to walk with—this after, to our horror, he just lay down.

In one village we passed through I held my head high, hoping that some gawking kid would spread the word that a *co Anh* was being held by the North Vietnamese. In another the soldiers flushed a young couple making love out of the undergrowth—in others the North Vietnamese were not welcome; and in one they fought.

The guards, whose names we never knew, changed. One Cambodian guide got us lost. When the bombs fell, we ignored their threats to shoot and fell in a heap, protecting one another's heads.

Our guards would shoot upward—both actions, theirs and ours, futile.

Strange to think you might have drunk a Budweiser with the pilot who killed you.

Just before dawn one morning in a large, unfenced paddock, we were led to an open-sided thatched shelter—equipped incongruously with a blue iron bedstead straight out of a Matisse painting—and learned that we would not march that night.

In the predawn light, shadowy figures came to look at us, then melted away. The "empty" paddock was obviously a military complex.

The second or third day there, a tall young soldier I nicknamed the Carpenter came and built, in two days, an additional small open shelter alongside the first, which they told us was for Suzuki and myself.

It was an order.

The interrogations resumed, and the "history lessons" started, separate lectures for Suzuki and myself, and for the Cambodians, telling us their version of the war. Very little mention was made of Cambodia—and we found they did not know what the Cambodian liberation flag was, or if there was one. They also told us of the terrible cost of the Tet offensive and that they had been so sure of victory that money had been printed. Westmoreland would have liked to hear that.

Our health was deteriorating fast. Both Sarath and I were shitting blood, trekking time and again to the latrine—a hole under a distant tree whose lower branches soon ran out of leaves. Moonface had shed kilos; though I managed to take the stitches out of his two old bullet wounds, he had lost too much blood. Suzuki, the oldest of us at forty-one, was helpless without his glasses and severely worn down. I had a fever and was shivering and throwing up.

Their medic, a skinny kid with a pathetic little tin of sulfur tablets, came often to lance our feet, the soles of which they had earlier "sewn" with strong black cotton so that we could pull the cotton back and forth and let out the pus.

With the lack of any news or reference point, any reality check, in the gray limbo of the "prisoner"—where you are not among the living or the dead of the war, but trapped in a gray twilight with no links to the living world—you reach a point inside yourself that you wouldn't reach otherwise.

I mark three points that braked my descent. One day, after I returned from a daylong interrogation, my head splitting with fever, Suzuki picked up a condensed milk can with a stick handle, sat me down under our tree, and took me through the steps of the Japanese tea ceremony.

Another time was when I stood on my head. It was like playing a violin on takeoff in a 747—there are no rules covering those kinds of things. It sounds Zen in retrospect, but it cheered me up enormously, as did the perplexed reactions of the guards and my fellow prisoners.

Then there was the morning I saw the dawn reflected upside down in a dewdrop hanging from a leaf—an exquisite miniature in rose, peach, and green.

We were by this stage all dressed in black pajamas, to our surprise tailored to measure. And sitting at night, blowing out the tiny oil lamps at the first call of *Mai bai de quoc My* (Imperialist American planes), we knew that even if one of us ran from the guards, the pilots of any low-flying, rocket-equipped spotters would see us as VC and open fire.

Under close twenty-four-hour guard, we never saw the complex, only heard it—men carousing at night, the Carpenter playing a haunting tune on his flute, the food being carried to a haystack and different clumps of trees.

But the camp dogs adopted us, and we them, nicknaming them Thieu, Johnson, and Nixon.

Because we thought this was just a staging point on our way north, when after a new tense round of interrogations they said we were to be released, we hardly reacted. Hope, we had fast learned, was as treacherous as an oasis mirage, and as cruel.

So it was with resignation rather than hope that we went through a Mad Hatter's tea party farewell in the interrogation hut, complete with candy and coffee loaded with condensed milk and our small speeches of thanks, ending with pleas for news of our missing colleagues. They returned our personal belongings to us—our watches, pens, and wallets—but we were told our cameras and notes had been "liberated"—a cruel blow for Suzuki, a film man.

The presence of newly arrived guards with the old belied to us the release "plans" and suggested we were on our way north.

But, twenty-three days after our capture, we were released, a strange moment—their whispered farewells dying as they melted silently into the jungle behind us and we stood alone in the dark on a roadside in no-man's-land.

I hoped that one day I'd be able to meet at least some of the guards again, over beers, with no rifles in our hands or theirs, prayed that the Cook, the Carpenter, the Medic, Dad, L'il Abner, and the others—some of them obvious shell-shocked cases, and all homesick—would not all die in the Cambodia they feared and hated and that they'd be able to return to their homes in the Red River Delta or Hanoi or Haiphong.

But like the South Vietnamese, they were in for the duration, and many nights we heard the groans as the bombing wounded and malaria cases were carried past us.

As strange as being a prisoner is, coming out, something I have not until now tried to write about, is traumatic.

Straight from the gray, almost silent limbo into, in my case, the glare of TV lights and a bizarre mixture of fan and hate mail, it was doubly bizarre for me, as I found that I had been reported killed, a body had been found and "identified," my family had held a memorial service for me, and I read my own obits.

For the first hour or so I was okay, just fighting back the tears. The incredulous relief that we had all come out alive.

Then I found I couldn't talk normally. I was measuring every word, as with the interrogators, as if all our lives depended on it.

Three people figured large in getting me back to the so-called real world—French planter Renee Maureau, U-2 pilot Frank (Gary) Powers, and British journalist Donald Wise.

Maureau, a man of very few words who had been born and raised in Cambodia, watched me besieged by fellow journalists on my return to Phnom Penh. He sent his Mercedes and driver with a message that they would take me to an empty apartment with a maid and a bath and that the driver should let him know if I needed a doctor. (I had lost ten kilos, and my feet were like sacks of jelly.)

I was able to get clean. Bath after bath, until the black, buggy water turned dark gray, light gray, then finally colorless. I tried the soft bed with clean sheets and the radio, then finally gave up and lay listening to the street noises under the stars on the hard balcony.

Frank, sitting with his arm lightly over my shoulders, looking down on the lights of Los Angeles, taught me how to deal with the deeply divided U.S. press and my own shakiness.

Wise, who had been a prisoner on the Burma Road, came quietly to my rescue when he saw me unable to walk into a room full of welcomers in Singapore.

What they said at the time, I don't really remember, but they knew.

It also helped that I sat down once I was out of the hospital (vivax and falciparum malaria) and wrote what I had learned behind the lines—Martial's "To tell the story is to live it a second time"—kept honest by the minuscule notes I had kept and managed to hide on a torn scrap of a cigarette packet.

Though we all came out, only three of us are alive today—Suzuki, Vorn, and myself. Chhimmy was recaptured (there were reports he was sighted later with the other side), Moonface was shot outside the French embassy in the last evacuation, and Charoon disappeared in the killing fields.

Against UPI's wishes, I returned to Cambodia but did not last too long. Chhimmy and two more stringers had gone missing, and I was spending more time looking for them than reporting. Part of that time I covered a major North Vietnamese offensive in the northern provinces of Vietnam. Then, despite my reluctance to leave the story and Khauv Bhun Kheang, my office manager and probably the finest colleague I have ever had, I left.

But though I was based in Hong Kong, and then in Jakarta and the Philippines, Vietnam and Cambodia were very much with me. The false hope that my survival roused in the wives of the missing was hard to live with, and the shooting of Cambodian colleagues and friends outside the French embassy in Phnom Penh, the whole killing fields, as they came to be known, became devastating.

The first day the Khmer Rouge entered the city—before Pol Pot's children started marching the whole population out of Phnom Penh—I was in Clark Air Base in the Philippines on hold as wire service pool correspondent for the Saigon evacuation (AP had the pix).

With the help of the air force, UPI Hong Kong/Manila patched me through to the Cambodian staff who had elected to stay behind, filing copy from the post office. I can't remember how many hours it was, but the second-to-last message joked about a pay raise, the last one said the KR were approaching the post office. Then there was no reply.

I went to a bar off base and drank martinis.

At about four A.M., the members of the four-man Filipino band carried me to my hotel room, telling me sympathetically not to worry—it often happened to wives of downed pilots.

I knew who Pol Pot's children were—the baby-faced but expressionless kids who came in from the countryside and stove people's heads in with hoes. They weren't a front for the Khmer Rouge. They were the Khmer Rouge.

One day in the Hotel Royale bungalow, a police officer we knew dropped by and asked a favor. He had, he said, orders to round up kids caught carrying plastic explosives taped to their bodies, after one had been caught taping an explosive to the corner of a ministry building.

The officer had found this small barefoot boy of about eight, Plastique taped inside his shirt and detonators in his shorts pockets, trying to take a ferry across the Mekong River to his village, where he had been snatched in a raid.

The kid had put his mission—blowing up government buildings—on hold and was trying to find his father. The cop, himself a father, said he felt there was some hope for the boy and couldn't bring himself to take him in.

Khauv, who is a Pied Piper with kids, and I agreed without hesitation, and the kid stayed in the office for a week.

He told us that in the raid, which was at night, the Khmer Rouge took all the young children, boys and girls below about eight, then burned the village. They then moved them north into the jungle, where they lived in a camp and learned about weapons and explosives.

Anyone who was good was loved by the "family," and anyone "naughty" disappeared.

Not once did the kid smile. He showed us expertly how to wire detonators, ate the food we gave him, slept in the office, and even went with Khauv to the village to see if his father was there.

Nothing was left of the village except burned huts. It was empty of people.

When we were out, we'd come back to find the kid still stony faced and still trying to make bombs. Khauv then took him home to stay with his own children, but he still never smiled, and still he kept fiddling with anything he could make bombs with.

We stored gasoline in the office and had batteries for tape recorders stashed there. We decided we had failed to undo the brain-washing, couldn't take the chance, and returned him to the cop. It was one of the most terrible decisions I have ever made.

Survival miracles did emerge from the nightmare of the killing fields. The books have started to come out now, Dith Pran's (*New York Times*) and others'. But at the time, when the first crept across the Thai border, the survivors didn't speak.

My only personal experience was when I got a message from the AP's Denis Gray, longtime bureau chief in Bangkok. Denis said there were two small kids who were approaching every journalist who came to Khao-I-Dang camp, asking in French: *"Où est Mademoiselle Kate?"*

Denis guessed rightly that they were related to my close friend Ly Eng, the editor of the Cambodian newspaper *Koh Santhapheap* (*Island of Peace*).

Then in Indonesia, and close to broke, I couldn't have done much without Denis and other go-betweens who relayed letters back and forth until I had established that they were the only survivors of Ly Eng's extended family.

All we had between us to try to convince the United Nations and other refugee agencies of a connection was an old group photograph of the family and me taken together at a party during the—by com-parison—halcyon days of pre–killing fields Phnom Penh.

I think I can be forgiven for thinking the worst of a UN official who met me in Jakarta and accused me of faking the connection be-cause I was a bleeding heart. The two kids, he pointed out, didn't look at all like the ones in the photograph. I restrained myself from throttling him (counterproductive), reminded myself that the UN was struggling with a huge burden, and signed form after form after form.

Did he really believe two primary-school kids would look the same after four years of terror and hard labor when they didn't even dare speak for fear their language would brand them as having been to school, or that a word of French might slip in?

The kids are adults now, the girl working as social worker in Orange County and the boy as a mechanic.

They told me in one letter all the details of when they had last seen Ly Eng, their mother, brothers, sisters, and the rest of the family—about twenty in all. All gone.

Then they never spoke or wrote about it again.

An old 1968 *Washington Post* newspaper clipping dug up for me by Beverly Deepe (*Christian Science Monitor*), written by J. W. Cohn (would you believe of *Women's Wear Daily*), focuses on five women who covered the war, including me, Bev, and Denby Fawcett of *The Honolulu Advertiser.*

In it, Cohn says that we "ask no favors and want none . . . cover the same assignments as men reporters . . . write and think, and even in the field dress like men."

He also says that back in Saigon, we were just as "feminine as any girl back home" and, although deeply concerned about the issues of the war, "refuse to be classified as hawks or doves."

Bravo, Cohn, on all the above points!

In the field, the troops mostly took us for granted. The only real incredulity among the younger American GIs, the draftees, was when they found out we didn't *have* to be there. The Koreans and Australians (with the noted exception of the Aussie advisers to the Vietnamese troops in I Corps) simply said no women.

Not that we didn't have our embarrassing times. As I marched out into leech-infested paddies one day, my turn came to pass a top sergeant handing out condoms. "Jesus, Katie, I don't have a cork!" he said.

And taking a pee in the field was a problem, until solved for me by another U.S. top sergeant, who equipped me with a lightweight poncho. Voilà! Small tent latrine. Not always easy, though, and when a serious and puzzled tropical medicine specialist asked me after my capture if I had "a habit of retaining your urine for long periods of time," I couldn't stop laughing.

The North Vietnamese troops had women troops among them—though except for some officers they were in separate all-women units—and in all their long interrogations I don't think it ever occurred to the North Vietnamese that it was unusual to find a woman in the field.

But the Great Classifier in the Sky doesn't trouble with the details, leaves those to us—and when tied in a chain of men for days and nights on end during the capture, I had some problems. I owe the men in the group for their decency. But it was pretty humiliating.

Back in Phnom Penh, at the first sort of debriefing, we are describing this heroic return—our crossing the lines from the North Vietnamese to the Cambodian side, the little column of stick-thin prisoners shuffling along a deserted road toward the oncoming troops, me in the lead, waving a white flag.

Okay, they say, where did the white flag come from?

Sarath looks at me sideways and says something vague about me finding it. My head was down, and I didn't say anything. It was, in fact, as Chhimmy and the others well knew, a piece of parachute silk that Suzuki with his near fluent Vietnamese had begged from the guards because I had the curse. I had washed it as best I could in a roadside puddle and tied it to a stick to use as a white flag. What the hell, it was all we had, and it worked.

But our biggest problems were the same as those of the men.

An ongoing fight during the war—waged in our consciences and among our editors—was whether we should take positions as hawks or doves or not.

I was unequivocally on the not side. Cohn was right on that, though I don't remember telling him so.

One of the most troubling times for me was when addressing the Washington Press Club. Though proud to be there, I did not acquit myself well at all—too nervous. And I was horrified to find that Washington's Finest to a man all seemed to feel that a field reporter was morally bound to take a hawk or dove stand.

In vain did I argue that that was their job, not a field reporter's, and that what newspapers wanted from me and my colleagues was what was happening and what people were saying, feeling, and doing on the ground, and without that hard, unbiased input they had nothing to opinionate, or stand, on.

I felt like swearing—but did not; it ain't what you do in Washington. What had all our people died for? As is obvious, I can still get worked up over that.

Then what do you do with classified stuff you stumble on? One time with Vietnamese troops in I Corps, we were policing the dead after a firefight, and I came across a lot of Chinese papers—railway tickets, ID cards. I mean a lot, not a few. When the Vietnamese intel officer handed them over after we got back to Quang Tri, plainclothes U.S. intel guys ferreted me out and argued with me long and hard that if UPI went with the story, it could widen the war.

I argued that this showed that the war had already widened, but eventually I caved in. I still wonder about that decision.

Then there was the perennial—journalists don't carry arms. Nearly all of us stuck to that. But there were always exceptions. That old Great Classifier again, He leaves it to you. One time in Cambodia, I was with a small unit and couldn't get out. We were surrounded, outnumbered, and when night fell these guys were having fun getting their mortars homed in on us.

The U.S. pilots in the planes out of Thailand were pretending to be Cambodian pilots, but their French wasn't good enough and it was one of those nights when Sam, the friendly Cambodian FAC (forward air controller), was not around. The Cambodian colonel in the group, knowing my ground rules, helped me out of my dilemma by holding a pistol to my head and I called in the strikes.

I am almost 100 percent sure he wouldn't have shot me. But I did call in those strikes. My jury's still out on that one.

After the war, a lot of us survivors had trouble with what I call the lack of bridges to cross or rafts to hang on to—this time to get us safely over to the post-Vietnam time.

After the first mad drunks, there were books, some just cathartic, some bad, and some good; some, like Jon Swain's and Tim Page's latest ones, showed, I think, that they had made it across—the books their rafts, their bridges.

But there were suicides and divorces, a lot of editors saying what do we do with these madmen, and quite a few of us madmen not knowing what to do with ourselves.

One time, despite a fair amount of official press/military hostility, an ex–U.S. Navy friend asked me to a ball for returned POWs in San Diego after I got out of the hospital. With some qualms I accepted, and rustled up some clothes that would do justice to their dress whites. They weren't quite up to snuff, so I bought shoes and a white stole. In fact they wore dress blues and it was fine after my nerves settled down. I thought, Hey—POW survivors dancing. Then I looked down and saw that I had left the price tag on my stole.

Now, all these years later, the Vietnam War is overlaid for me by the war in Afghanistan, and I see it, like Afghanistan, the Korean peninsula, the Indian subcontinent, and the Indonesian archipelago, tossed and battered in the churning wakes of the death of colonialism, the mad post–World War II divvying up of countries and peoples, and the cold war.

The Vietnamese singer Trinh Cong Son used to say that Vietnam was a football field for foreign powers, a description I thought beat the hell out of geopolitical faultline, and I guess what I call the "sandwich countries" like Afghanistan and Cambodia will always continue to fascinate me.

Trinh Cong Son was still in Saigon when I began to write this, a cynical but oddly gentle skeleton of a man, ground ruthlessly between two stones—both sides of the war, each one accusing him of being "on the other side."

When I first met him it was in Hue, one of Vietnam's most beautiful cities, in 1972. A group of us were sitting on the floor of an empty apartment, watching star flares falling slowly, lighting up the night and the Perfume River, and listening to the sounds of the bombing and the Bee Gees.

We all knew it was a matter of time. I asked Cong Son, whose haunting songs had earned him the American label of the Bob Dylan of Vietnam and several spells in jail under the Thieu regime, whether he would stay or go.

He would stay, he said. It was his country.

When in 1975 the refugee ships started arriving in Guam (I was there for UPI after covering the evacuation), I searched and searched, but he wasn't aboard any of them. One U.S. Marine, seeing me rush futilely from passenger to passenger on the docks when the last ship arrived, told me he had watched me for the past few days.

"Whoever your boyfriend is, ma'am," he said, "I'm sorry," and handed me a Styrofoam cup of purple Kool-Aid.

To this day, purple Kool-Aid, or any purple drink, takes me back to the stench of the refugee ships, the glaring heat of the docks, and the long lists of paper scraps flapping in the wind, all with names of missing relatives, people separated in the scramble out.

I hate Kool-Aid.

In Saigon in March 2000, I found Trinh Cong Son again. The Hanoi regime liked him as an individual no better than the Thieu regime had.

He had, he said, spent four years as a forced human minesweeper, and survived. Many of his fellow minesweepers had not. We sat in his upstairs studio in a villa at the end of a back alley and drank quietly—he as usual Scotch, me as usual beer—as the sun set.

Around him were his guitars and paintings. Tolerated, he told me. A fellow Vietnamese reviewer said of his postwar songs, "There is the feeling of something unsaid."

He had a sister in the States he couldn't visit, because her Vietnamese neighbors labeled him a Communist for staying behind.

On April 2, 2001, Trinh Cong Son died. At first the official press ignored him. From what I have been able to gather, only one friend, Buu Y, risked writing of him and what he stood for—in an article entitled "Crying for Trinh Cong Son."

In Jakarta, a young colleague saw the news on the wire from AFP's Hanoi office and said, "Hey, isn't this your buddy?"

Then, in a bitter irony two days later, the Party in Hanoi decided to adopt him posthumously, and thousands turned out for the funeral. No one could claim him while he was alive.

Journalism and women have changed.

When I first joined newspapers as an apprentice in Sydney, there was one woman editorial writer, a few on the desk, with most of the other women on the women's page. For years after Vietnam I had to get used to those wary "she must be a freak" looks from people, especially from women.

Then there was a group of women in the UPI New York headquarters who gave me a very warm welcome but the next day told me severely that my miniskirts were too short. That was my first brush with the women's libbers. The last was with a woman who called and asked if I would talk to a group on the lack of work for women professionals. I replied that I was sorry, I was too busy with work, and the irony of it made me laugh out loud on the phone. Not polite.

One day in Sri Lanka in the early 1980s, Barbara Crossette of *The New York Times* was waiting with me at a heliport. I was an admirer of her writing. And since discovering she raised a daughter pretty much on her own, as well as writing the good stuff she does, I am an admirer of her as a person as well.

But then she said to me, "You know, if it wasn't for you, I probably would never have got overseas." She explained that my being a bureau chief in Cambodia had been her most persuasive argument to her editors.

By the time of the Gulf War, which I did cover, and certainly by Bosnia, which I did not cover, people were more inclined to ask why you weren't there.

I did not stop after Cambodia. With UPI, later as a freelancer, and the last seventeen years with AFP, I moved on to cover India and sometimes Pakistan, Sri Lanka, Nepal, Bangladesh, Afghanistan, the Philippines, and East Timor and Indonesia.

Other Vietnam survivors didn't stop, either—like Derek Williams and Digger Williams in Asia, Jon Swain in Ethiopia, Al Webb in Beirut, Dan Southerland in China, and Joe Galloway in Moscow. Two I know of—the French writer François Bizot and the U.S. photographer Al Rockoff—went back into that dark place to explore the fountainhead of the horror of the killing fields. To them and to most of us, the U.S. support for the Khmer Rouge at that time for "geopolitical reasons" (Cong Son's football field again) will make a black mockery any attempts to convene a war crimes trial all these years later.

Personally, I think I've finally found my raft—my bridge. It has taken all these years, including trips back to Vietnam and Cambodia. I went through a rough patch following Afghanistan after a similar cycle of losing friends and watching another country destroyed— and finding that the old wounds reopened so easily, and there was no armor against new ones.

The Vietnam War didn't change me. I was quite truthful when I told a TV interviewer that the biggest difference was that I now appreciated such simple things as clean, white-tiled bathrooms. But all

Personal collection

that baggage was crushing me, the lost friends, the responsibility as bureau chief of sending people into the field who didn't come back.

I was given six months' leave by UPI one time after the war in Hong Kong when the boss reported a barman telling him I had been sitting laughing and talking to six guys I had kept buying drinks for who weren't there. I don't remember it, but I don't doubt it.

The baggage is still there, but it's a part of me, and because of that it's now weightless—and as Bao Ninh wrote, I can revisit that time now.

Anne Morrissy Merick

My Love Affair with Vietnam

My arrival in Saigon was a disaster.

There I was, at the top of the metal steps leading from the Air Vietnam plane that had flown me from Hong Kong to Saigon, looking down at the faces of my ABC bureau colleagues waiting on the tarmac. It was a beautiful hot day, but Saigon was always hot. And the wind was blowing. I waved. Suddenly my travel papers, ticket, passport, visa, landing documents, and immunization records were blown out of my hands and went cartwheeling down the runway of Tan Son Nhut airport, with my bureau chief, Elliot Bernstein, and his Vietnamese aides in frantic pursuit. I'll never forget the look on Elliot's face. Disbelief, despair, dismay? He must have been thinking, Is this a harbinger of worse things to come?

In 1967 I had been working for ABC News for seven years. Starting as a newswriter in radio, I had worked my way up the ranks until I was a producer for the Special Events Unit.

During those years, I was involved with many of the events that changed America, including the civil rights movement from its early beginnings in Selma, Alabama, to Martin Luther King's March on Washington, and the early space program, starting with the eight

ANNE MORRISSY MERICK worked in the Washington, D.C., area as a television producer of news and public affairs. She now divides her time between Naples, Florida, and the western North Carolina mountains, working on her golf and tennis games with her husband, Don Janicek, M.D.

Mercury missions and continuing through the Gemini flights. I specialized in political coverage: conventions, elections, and inaugurations, beginning with the Kennedy years. Sadly, I also covered that era's rash of assassinations.

It was a dream assignment, because I was there on the spot as history was being made.

It never occurred to me that I would be sent overseas for ABC. We had a foreign staff that was responsible for the stories happening outside the United States. But I guess the time was right. Elections were over and we were between space shots. I was an unassigned producer with the right credentials. I don't know if the fact that I was a woman was a help or a hindrance. I do know that I was overjoyed when my boss, Sid Darion, asked if I had any interest in going to Vietnam.

It was decided that I would leave in January and do a three-month tour assigned to the Saigon bureau. That three-month tour ended up lasting nine months and was the most exciting nine months of my life.

There still weren't a lot of women in television in those days. Each network had its token correspondent. But the women's movement had started to influence television executives, and the fear of class-action lawsuits, like those at *The New York Times*, forced them to add women to the payroll.

I was used to being a woman pioneer. During college at Cornell University in Ithaca, New York, when the Ivy League was still predominantly male, I had been elected to the position of sports editor of the college newspaper. As such, I broke a lot of professional barriers, from interviews in the locker rooms to sitting in the previously sacrosanct press box at Yale.

Famous sportswriter Red Smith chronicled the event when he wrote in his column: "This sportswriting doll breached the last bastion of masculinity left standing this side of the shower room." I got a lot of publicity that day, which helped me two years later to be hired as sports editor of the International Edition of the *New York Herald Tribune*, better known as the *Paris Herald*.

That really launched my career. I spent two and a half wonderful years in Paris. I wrote my own column, kept our American readers abreast of stateside sports by recapping line scores, and covered such European athletic contests as the Tour de France, the French Open Tennis Tournament at Roland Garros, World Cup soccer, and rugby. I even learned the finer points of cricket.

Feeling that my career needed a change, I took an assignment with the Israeli newspaper *Yedioth Ahronoth* and spent six months traveling in the Arab countries gathering material for a series on Arab life. This was not one of my smartest career moves.

Relations between the United States and Syria were strained at the time, and my interviews aroused the suspicions of the Syrian authorities, who suspected I might be a spy. So I was summarily arrested and escorted out of the country.

My arrest and deportation piqued the interest of the foreign press, and I was met at that Syrian-Lebanese border by a *Manchester Guardian* correspondent named Kim Philby. It was only a few months later that he fled Beirut for the Soviet Union, where his true identity as a Russian spy was finally revealed.

This was the first but not the last time that I put myself in a dicey situation.

To cover the Vietnam War, most of the networks sent in their headliners for brief stints in the field: Walter Cronkite of CBS, David Brinkley of NBC, and Howard K. Smith of ABC. They came for what we called "face time" in front of the camera. A few days in the field, a couple of on-camera stand-ups to show that they really were in-country, and then home.

A second tier of reporters were sent in for longer periods, staying three months to a year. Most of them were young, and their excellent reporting established them as first-class broadcasters: Ted Koppel, Bill Plante, Ed Bradley, and Morley Safer are good examples.

The Vietnam War also attracted a large number of freelance journalists who were not unlike mercenaries. They sold their services to any news organization that would pay. They were fearless and willing to go to any lengths to get a story that might ensure a broadcast career.

Only a handful of women were covering the war. Their arrival on the scene was to make many changes in the news coverage of the war.

SAIGON

I was not prepared for Saigon in that year of 1967. I guess I had envisioned something Graham Greene might have described in his book *The Quiet American*. Instead, it was like being in the middle of a maelstrom. The traffic was madness, the worst I had seen in Asia, including the clogged arteries of Tokyo and Bangkok.

It was a hodgepodge of civilian and military vehicles. U.S. Army two-ton trucks and jeeps competed for the roadway with the ubiquitous motorbikes and bicycles ridden by the Vietnamese.

Since cars were at a premium in Vietnam, most affluent Vietnamese owned either a Honda or a Lambretti for transportation. It was not surprising that Saigon was called Honda Heaven.

Motorized three-wheeled cyclos and blue-and-yellow mini Renault cabs added to the melee. The motorized cyclos belched great clouds of exhaust for instant and perhaps deadly air pollution. Their fuel was often stored in discarded military barrels that once had held the deadly defoliant Agent Orange.

You put your life in jeopardy if you jaywalked. One military doctor told me he got more patients from traffic accidents than from war casualties.

Fortunately, in downtown Saigon there were traffic lights that sometimes worked and traffic controllers who worked sometimes. The controllers were part of the Saigon police force and known as "white mice" because of their white uniforms, which resembled workmen's coveralls, and white gloves.

The drive in from Tan Son Nhut airport, which should have taken twenty minutes, took over an hour because of the traffic congestion and construction. Work crews were busy removing the standing trees along the route. It was assumed that this was to widen the highway, but in Vietnam one could never be sure.

The work crews were made up of six women all dressed in white Vietnamese blouses, loose-fitting black pants, and conical straw hats that were tied under their chins to protect them from the sun. They were usually accompanied by a man past military age. Presumably he was the foreman, because he could usually be seen sitting in any available shade along the side of the road.

My first impression of the city of Saigon was that it was dirty and seedy. There was little vestige of the days when it had been the southern capital of French Indochina.

(During my tour of duty I visited Phnom Penh, which in the mid-1960s had not yet been touched by the war. I am sure its beauty, with broad tree-lined boulevards, palatial villas, and well-groomed gardens, was reminiscent of prewar Saigon, once known as the Paris of the Orient.)

Now the city was like a gracious lady who had seen better days.

There had been little or no upkeep on the buildings. The paint had been allowed to fade, and only a faint reminder of the original yellow ocher color remained. It was very much a city dictated by war.

Barbed wire and cement-filled oil drums ringed government buildings guarded by American MPs or Vietnamese soldiers, depending on whose provenance they were.

Independence Palace, housing the president of Vietnam, was in direct contrast. The original building had been blown up in 1963, and its replacement was surrounded by a rolling green lawn. It stood at the end of Thong Nhut Street. Smartly dressed guards at the gates stood at attention in white uniforms adorned with red sashs and berets. It was the Vietnamese version of our White House.

There were three major civilian hotels in downtown Saigon. The Majestic, very French, was located on the Saigon River at the beginning of Tu Do Street. My favorite was the wonderful old Continental Hotel, which harkened back to French colonial days with its wide verandah begging people to sit and sip a *citron pressé* or a *33 bière* and watch the bustling pedestrian and motor traffic go by.

Across Lam Son Square and the Parliament Building stood the most modern and Westernized of Saigon hotels, the Caravelle, which was owned by the Catholic Church.

It was to the roof bar of the Caravelle that correspondents gathered to talk over the day's activities. And from this venue you could often watch as American fighter planes dropped flares out in the countryside.

The Caravelle had an elevator that worked most of the time. It had an excellent restaurant featuring French cuisine, spacious rooms, and a large staff of employees to fill our Western needs.

It was headquarters to a number of American news organizations. ABC and CBS had their Saigon bureaus in the big corner suites on the second and sixth floors. Several major publications, including *The Washington Post, Baltimore Sun*, and the *London Daily Telegraph* and the *Daily Express*, also had their offices there. It was my home for a good part of the seven years I lived in Vietnam.

ABC originally assigned me to a room on the third floor. It was small but adequate. Its size eliminated any need to share in this city of limited accommodations. Fellow ABC colleague Roger Grimsby, who gained fame as an anchorman in San Francisco and New York, had lived there when he did his tour of Vietnam. He told me that most of his time was spent on the commode—a problem that eventually affected all of us at one time or another.

On my first morning "in-country," I was awakened by the sound of squealing in the walls near the head of my bed. I had visions of being overrun by rodents. I later learned that my noisemakers were a covey of starlings that had found a home in the eves outside my window.

Rats were a frequent menace in Saigon. I had several invade my room while I lived there. Whenever I saw one, I would ring for the hall boy, stand in the middle of the bed, and wait until it was chased away. He never killed them, so I assumed they continued to multiply—not a pleasant thought.

My first days in-country were spent getting credentials and being outfitted for my military excursions. My five-foot-two-inch, 110-pound frame meant that army-issued uniforms were not going to fit. The only solution was to go to the black market and buy uniforms made for the ARVN. This shopping expedition was clandestine, since buying stolen goods in Vietnam was highly illegal (but done all the time).

We went to Cholon, Saigon's sister city and home to the large population of ethnic Chinese that lived in the capital. I was ushered into a small house on a side street. When the goods arrived through the back door, the doors and shutters were closed. Then I tried on the contraband. It took several trips by the purveyors before we found the right size of boots and camouflage fatigues. To this we added a blanket roll, poncho, web belt, and two canteens. It reminded me of being outfitted for Girl Scout camp.

This was the field uniform. While some more macho male correspondents wore their combat gear in town, most substituted the correspondent's suit, also known as the television suit. The mufti was a short- or long-sleeved multipocketed shirt, similar to the safari jacket. It was made of cotton, usually khaki in color. It was cool and very practical, with lots of places for pens, pencils, extra rolls of film, and the ubiquitous reporter's notebook.

Most of the correspondents' suits were made by Mr. Minh, the tailor, whose shop was located on Tu Do Street a few doors down from the Caravelle. He had a corner on the market, was an excellent tailor, and made a very nice living during the war years.

I was also introduced to the use of chopsticks during those early days. Two of our ABC cameramen, Tony Hirashiki, Japanese, and

Terry Khoo, Chinese from Singapore, took me to the Eskimo in Cholon. It was a small, one-room restaurant with tile floors and rickety tables and chairs from its former days as an ice-cream parlor serving Eskimo Pies.

One wall was adorned by a huge poster featuring a robust Occidental boy with a large grin, showing off enormous white teeth and an oversize jar of Ovaltine. I never figured out the significance of this unless it meant you could have a glass of Ovaltine with your Eskimo Pie and be blessed with white teeth.

The menu featured northern Chinese food (hot) and fiery kim chi, a Korean cabbage salad of extraordinary heat.

To partake of the meal, one had to use chopsticks or go hungry. There were no Western utensils. I was not even allowed to use my hands to help myself to the bowl of peanuts. Instead I had to pick up each morsel with the chopsticks. It was a tough lesson, but one I had to master or go hungry.

Terry Khoo worked for ABC News for seven years during the war as a staff cameraman and was one of the best-liked men in the Saigon press corps. In 1972, ABC assigned him to the coveted job of cameraman for the Bonn, Germany, bureau. It was on his last day in-country that he and his replacement, Sam Kai Faye, decided to take one last look at the fighting north of Hue.

They were caught in an ambush. Bullets from a single sniper killed them both on July 20. It was several days before the bodies were recovered.

HELICOPTERS

The helicopter was an integral part of the Vietnam War. Few battles were fought without the inclusion of helicopters. They were essential to move troops, supplies, and ammunition; to provide reconnaissance and fire support; and, most important, to furnish medical evacuation capabilities for the wounded. These medevac, or "dust-off," choppers were modified for their medical mission and carried specially trained medics with up to nine litters to care for the critically wounded. They stayed on alert and could be airborne to a battle site within minutes.

Several types of helicopters were used during the war, and according to Pentagon statistics, they flew over thirty-six million sorties. The most frequently utilized chopper was the Bell UH-1H Iroquois, better known as the Huey, which is still flying. Even today, the *whap, whap* of chopper blades brings back vivid memories of my years in Vietnam.

The Huey was the correspondent's best friend. It was our major means of transportation in-country. While we would fly long distances in C-123 or C-130 cargo planes, short hops were usually made by chopper.

My love affair with the chopper began a few days after I arrived in-country. We were going up to Lai Khe in the middle of Military Zone III, known as the "Iron Triangle." It was located about twenty miles northwest of Saigon.

We were going up to interview the owner of a French rubber plantation. We went out to the airport before first light. On the flight line, the choppers were lined up in their sandbag revetments, each about four feet high.

There were some advantages to being a woman correspondent. I usually got a good seat on air transport planes, behind the pilot on a chopper, or on the flight deck of most cargo planes. I thought the flight deck was the best spot on the plane, but later learned I was kept up front so the soldiers in the cargo area could use the relief tubes. So much for chivalry.

My colleagues thought it would be fun to introduce me to a little contour flying on my first chopper ride. This meant following the contour of the land, often below treetop level. It is not for the faint of heart or those who suffer from motion sickness. I loved it!

Actually, this is one of the safest ways to fly when there are enemy snipers on the ground. It is more difficult to get a bead on a low-flying object than a high-flying one.

One of the major concentrations of airmobile troops was the 1st Air Cavalry Division, located at An Khe in the Central Highlands. This was to be the subject of my story on helicopter warfare.

The 1st Air Cavalry was radically different from the usual division in that it contained 434 helicopters, which were divided into two battalions of assault helicopters, a battalion of attack helicopters, a battalion of assault support helicopters, and a battalion providing aerial rocket artillery.

To get to An Khe, my crew and I took a C-130 milk run from Saigon. Making stops at other military bases in the Central Highlands, the flight, which should have taken forty-five minutes as the crow flies, took over four hours.

To visit this area, we had to take special malaria pills against a

U.S. Air Force

third strain of the disease that was prevalent there. We were cautioned to roll down our sleeves at sundown despite the hot temperatures and never, never, never forget to tuck in the mosquito netting when going to bed.

Press accommodations there were fine for the men but nonexistent for women. I was fortunate to have the loan of a major's "hootch." A hootch is a place to live. It could be a tent, a wooden structure, or a covered bunker surrounded by sandbags. In this case, it was a wooden structure reminiscent of Girl Scout camp. It contained two cots and a couple of footlockers. An electric light on a long cord was suspended from the ceiling and went out when the generators were turned off.

I was presented with a sleeping bag and, because of my gender, two sheets and a blanket. Believe me, a sleeping bag, used as a mattress, can be just as comfortable as a Sealy Posturepedic when one is really tired.

The latrine was a six-holer down the path, with the shower facilities and running water next door. One took care of one's needs before lights out because of what might be met on the muddy path from hootch to the facilities.

There was little privacy. Washing, shaving, and toothbrushing were communal affairs. There was, however, a lock on the latrine door.

There are few places in Vietnam that aren't dusty and dirty, especially in the dry season. During the monsoon season the dust turns to mud, so you got both wet and filthy. This was exacerbated by the hot and humid climate. One soon got used to being dirty all the time. At least we correspondents could get back to Saigon from time to time for a bath and clean clothes. The GIs in the field were not so lucky.

From my experience, the GIs were usually delighted to see a correspondent in the field. It broke the monotony, and I think in most cases they were also pleased to see a woman after all the male contact. The young information officers were especially friendly.

They worked at putting out press releases and stories for hometown papers. They were all sure they were going to become this war's Ernie Pyle and loved to discuss "the writing business."

My first assignment was with the 15th Transportation Corps. They were the men who kept the helicopters flying. They presented me with a plaque made from the rear rotor blade of a Huey, adorned with the 1st Air Cavalry insignia, a map of Vietnam, and a drawing of a flying chopper.

It was hard going. My cameraman was Vietnamese and had only a minimal knowledge of English. I had to translate my directions into French, which was only somewhat better than his English and was often drowned out by the constant roar of the helicopter engines.

My objective was to get "the story behind the story, not only what these men did but how they felt about it." This was not an easy task when half the guys were camera shy and had a vocabulary heavily into "yeah," "yup," and "I don't know." But one sergeant summed it up so beautifully that it was worth the hours we had spent on the story.

"We feel our job carries a great responsibility. We are not only fixing the plane that carries eleven men, but it also carries their mothers, their wives, and their kids, and with that many lives in our keeping, you've got to fix it right," he said. I believe a lot of our boys felt the same way, especially in those earlier days of the war.

I got my first and only war wound in An Khe. I was bitten by a monkey that was a mascot for one of the groups. Luckily he had had his rabies shot, and it didn't break the skin through the sleeve of my fatigues. But it left one heck of a bruise.

The next day I was off to "Two Bits," one of the forward base camps. It's a godforsaken place on the top of the highest hill in the area. It was originally a Special Forces base, so it had its own barbed-wire perimeter protected with claymore mines. When the 1st Air Cavalry moved in, it built another perimeter encircling the first with more barbed wire. In between the two camps was a Vietnamese village whose location was about as safe as dynamite.

My story was about one of the reconnaissance missions of the division. The pilots flew tiny bubble choppers over an area. They'd look for the enemy and hope to draw fire to identify his location. One chopper flew at one hundred feet, the other at eight hundred. Between those heights was considered dead man's altitude. Down low, the VC can't get a bead on the chopper, and up high they can't reach it. These aircraft still got shot down with alarming frequency. Some of the pilots had been hit as many as eight times, but they lived to tell and laugh about it.

Flying in the bubble enabled you to see the broad vistas of the Kim Son valley. It was like riding a magic carpet. And once again I realized how beautiful the country is. In my mind, Vietnam has the loveliest scenery of any of the Southeast Asian nations.

It was rice harvesting time, and we could see the peasants with their conical hats bending over the plants. The pattern of the fields was like a painting of curved lines, dotted with stands of palm trees providing shelter for the thatched-roof huts of the hamlets.

One small hamlet was built on the side of a hill, with a Buddhist temple perched at its pinnacle. A broad river ran across the valley, and the heavy vegetation of the An Ho forest made it difficult to spot the enemy. The strategy was that once the enemy was spotted, a squad of infantrymen would be dropped in to make contact and hopefully destroy them.

They, however, had no problem spotting us. Our military encampments showed up as ugly red scars on the high ground, where the bulldozers had scraped the vegetation down to the red clay to make clearings for the tent villages.

We spent the rest of the day filming the action around the landing zone and beyond into the jungle. But, like so many sorties in Vietnam, the enemy stayed elusive. We found packs and war implements, but no contact was made. They had slipped away again.

CU CHI

Whenever I went to Cu Chi, the place came under mortar attack. I figured the enemy knew I was coming.

The camp was located twenty-five miles north of Saigon, near a prime enemy supply line from Cambodia. It was headquarters to the 25th Infantry Division, which had originated in Hawaii during World War II and was known as "Tropic Lightning."

The area was honeycombed with underground tunnels. They had been originally built by the Vietminh during the war with the French. By 1968, this labyrinth had grown to some 125 miles. Some descended four levels into the dense clay soil and consisted of headquarters, barracks, classrooms, hospitals, kitchens, armories, and ammunition dumps—everything that a guerrilla army could need in enemy territory.

They were marvels of military engineering and today are a major tourist attraction for visitors to Vietnam.

The tunnels were discovered in 1966, and the 25th was given the job of clearing them out—a job that frequently had to be done by hand by a band of GIs known as "tunnel rats." It took well over a year.

But the camp continued to be a favorite target for the enemy. Its shelling was incredibly accurate, not surprising since they had mapped the entire area early in the war. If they needed additional intelligence, they could always get it from the *mama-sans* and their children who did the laundry and cleaned the hootches of the soldiers on base. It was very hard to keep good security when the enemy, or friends of the enemy, had such easy access. It was a continual problem for us and our allies.

The first time I spent the night outside of Saigon was at Cu Chi, and it also was the first time I experienced a rocket attack. I was bunking in with the nurses and Red Cross girls, who had kindly provided a cot for the night. Not long after we turned in, we received heavy bombardment. One shell landed so close to our quarters that the concussion knocked me clear out of my cot and onto the floor.

We usually had enough time after an alert was sounded to scramble for the roofed bunkers, which were located strategically around the base. Early on I learned to carry a small pocket flashlight. Its beam could scare off the rats and other vermin that lived in these belowground foxholes. I would sling my combat boots over my shoulder, since there rarely was time to put on protective footwear when the alert sounded. You can't cover a battle in bare feet!

Cu Chi was also headquarters for a long-range reconnaissance patrol (LRRP, pronounced "lurp") unit. This was an innovative military tactic designed specifically for the Vietnam War, where U.S. tactics were hampered by the lack of front lines and the difficulties of locating the enemy in the rugged terrain. It was so successful that General Westmoreland had ordered every division and brigade to create their own LRRP units on a priority basis.

This order was never fully carried out because of the lack of trained personnel.

Each LRRP patrol unit consisted of five men. They dressed in camouflage gear, including face paint, so they could blend into the jungle. They were inserted into an area where enemy presence was suspected and spent up to three days in the field, gathering as much intelligence as possible.

This was one of the most dangerous missions in the military, but one of the most effective. If you can't find Charlie, you can't fight him! The information these troops gathered was vital to the overall battle strategy.

The men who volunteered for this assignment (and they were all volunteers) were young, adventuresome, and somewhat nuts. Most had been awarded Purple Hearts.

ABC News wanted a story on this new military tactic. My camera crew and I would go in with a LRRP team and stay with them as long as we could, until our presence might compromise their mission.

After taking off from Cu Chi, we flew to an area where Vietcong had been spotted a few days before. We secured the landing zone (LZ) and went in. The insertion choppers didn't land but hovered a few feet off the ground. We had to jump. It was almost like jumping into a swimming hole, and I briefly thought about holding my nose. Over I went, and—surprise!—I immediately sank waist deep into the mud of the rice paddy. It felt kind of nice. The little holes on the side of the boot that let the water drain out . . . well, they also let the water drain in, and on a hot day the cool paddy water felt good as it soaked into my heavy woolen socks. Walking was something else. Paddy mud has similar qualities to quicksand and makes walking a slow and tedious affair. Despite my short legs, I made it to the jungle perimeter ahead of the crew.

My speed could also be attributed to my desire to avoid picking up any of the gruesome leeches that inhabited the paddies and quickly attached themselves to any exposed skin and had to be burned off. This was the reason soliders wore their fatigues tucked into their jungle boots: so the slimy creatures couldn't reach their legs and ankles.

For the next three days, these men would live in the mud and dense underbrush of the jungle, totally alone, searching for an elusive enemy while trying to keep themselves undetected. As you can imagine, the jungle is a dangerous place and totally inhospitable. It was heavily booby-trapped, and some areas were mined.

It is home to a wide variety of other dangerous animals, snakes, and insects. A thoroughly nasty place, as I soon found out. Leaning against a tree, I came too close to a nest of fire ants and was attacked. Fortunately, I was liberally covered with insect repellent so I suffered only a few of their terribly painful bites. They were quite enough. I also got a strong reprimand not to go any farther into the undergrowth because of booby traps.

Afraid of stepping on a land mine, I closely followed the squad leader, placing my size sixes in the indentations made by his size twelves. After a few minutes of this Indian file walking, he turned and asked, "What are you doing?" I explained my attempt to avoid injury. He broke out laughing, then explained that because I was following so closely, I was bound to blow up right along with him if he encountered a mine. I backed off quickly.

We got our jungle footage, and when we were told we couldn't go any farther without endangering the men, we called in an extraction ship. I felt bad about leaving this brave band of soldiers behind.

Again, as I had found throughout Vietnam when I interviewed these young men, I was impressed with their sincerity and dedication. They talked openly about their faith in God and how they believed it would protect them. They were an impressive group of men.

They had chosen this job, and they were going to do it right. You couldn't help but believe them.

In the later days of the war, the soldiers I met were not as forthright and outstanding. I believe they had been influenced by the growing attitudes against the war and the men who fought it. They questioned the inequities of the draft, which allowed the more affluent draft-age men to hide behind their education. Also, having seen our military strategy firsthand, they had begun to doubt its logic. Was this a war that could be won, and was it worth it?

THE WESTMORELAND EDICT

No one would have suspected it would be Denby Fawcett who came close to scuttling the women journalists' coverage of the war. We wouldn't have been surprised if it had been Cathy Leroy, the acerbic

French photographer whose bawdy language allegedly had gotten her banned from the marine base in I Corps. But not sweet, gentle young Denby from *The Honolulu Advertiser,* who had come to Vietnam straight from covering women's-page stories in Hawaii.

It seemed that Denby was with an American battalion in the Central Highlands near the Cambodian border when Gen. William Westmoreland paid an impromptu visit. The American unit had encountered a reinforced North Vietnamese battalion and lost 64 men, while killing 113 NVA. Westmoreland was there to cheer up his soldiers and congratulate them. Denby had known the general in Hawaii, where her family and the Westmorelands had been neighbors.

The general was horrified to find a young woman, and one that he knew, in the field with his troops, especially in such a dangerous area. When he got back to his Saigon headquarters, he issued an order banning women reporters from accompanying troops to the front lines. But in Vietnam it was impossible to determine just where the front lines were. The war was everywhere.

An edict like Westmoreland's would prohibit women from covering the war. It was a knockout blow to our careers. We had to fight!

Ann Bryan (later Mariano) spearheaded our attack. Researching the involvement of women journalists in covering wars, she came upon some incredible examples of women reporting on conflicts from the Civil War to the Korean War. She sent her statistics to the Pentagon. They were ignored.

We learned that Secretary of Defense Robert S. McNamara was planning a trip to Saigon. We asked for a meeting, and he agreed.

As the only woman TV correspondent in Saigon, I was asked to be the spokeswoman for the group. Accompanied by Ann and a few other women who would be adversely affected by the ruling, we drove out to Barry Zorthian's villa on the outskirts of the city. Zorthian was head of JUSPAO (Joint U.S. Public Affairs Office) and chief spokesman for the U.S. Mission.

Secretary McNamara didn't show but instead sent his deputy assistant secretary of defense, Phil Goulding. A former newspaperman from Cleveland, Goulding listened patiently to our position but failed to give us an answer one way or the other. Instead he suggested we all should check out the bar scene on Tu Do Street. So off we went with the car and driver I had borrowed for the night from *U.S. News & World Report.*

On the drive into town, my colleagues turned "chicken" and asked to be dropped off at their respective residences, blaming the approaching curfew. So when we reached downtown there was just Goulding and me.

The bar signs on Tu Do Street were dark, and the only available booze was in my suite at the Caravelle Hotel. There was nothing to do but invite him up for a drink. What lengths one had to go to for a cause—damned if you do and damned if you don't!

For the next two hours, I poured martinis for Goulding and listened to his take on the war, the problems they were having with women entertainers in-country, and stories of his six children. When he said good night, he added that Westmoreland's edict would be lifted and we could go back out in the field. I'm sure that decision had been made long before our meeting.

And, if you are wondering if I slept with him, the answer is no!

MARRIAGE

We can all say that Vietnam touched our lives and changed them in many ways. For me it was a milestone in my personal life. I fell in love in Vietnam, I got married in Saigon, and my only child, Katherine-Anne, was born there. It was my home for seven years.

It was inevitable that I would meet Wendell "Bud" Merick of *U.S. News & World Report*. He lived on the sixth floor of the Caravelle Hotel, next door to the ABC bureau. He always left his door open and could be seen sitting at his desk pecking away at his small portable typewriter or watching Armed Forces TV on his miniature Sony television set.

One Sunday afternoon, he came into the news bureau. I had the duty that day, and not much was happening. He asked if I wanted to come in and watch a Bogart-Bacall movie. I took him up on his invitation, left a note on the office door, and switched the phones over to his room. For the life of me, I can't remember the name of the movie.

Bud was a veteran Asian correspondent. He had originally come to the Far East in the 1950s to cover the Korean War. He had been a cub sports reporter in Detroit and was sent to Seoul by the United Press. After the war, he was transferred to Hong Kong and served as UP bureau chief there.

In 1965, he came to Saigon and joined *U.S. News & World Report* to cover the Vietnam War. He held this post until the fall of Saigon ten years later and was evacuated on one of the last helicopters to leave from the embassy in the early hours of April 30, 1975.

We were married in March 1969 in Saigon. We chose Vietnam because it was where most of our mutual friends were. I lived in New York, my parents were located in San Francisco, and Bud's family was in Vancouver, so Saigon seemed the most logical place for our wedding.

We found that it is no easy task to get married in Vietnam, a country that had been ruled by French bureaucracy for almost one hundred years. A lot of time and money was spent planning a wedding over transpacific phone lines.

My wedding dress was selected from I. Magnin in San Francisco. It had a lace bodice with a short skirt, in keeping with the 1960s, and was cool enough for the tropical climate.

The red tape and paperwork was endless. We needed seventeen separate documents, which meant lots of waiting in lines at government agencies and lots of translations. Fortunately, we had the help of the *U.S. News & World Report* Vietnamese translator.

One major stumbling block was getting the mandatory ten-day waiting period waived in time for the wedding. This was accomplished by Bud, who convinced the appropriate factotum that I was in the "family way." I had wondered about the solicitousness I had received at every office. Would I like to sit down, did I want a glass of water, some tea? It never occurred again during my time in Vietnam.

The day finally arrived. The actual ceremony was to take place at the First Arrondissement on the banks of the Saigon River. By Vietnamese law, any marriage had to be by civil ceremony, even if a religious ceremony was to follow. This again was a throwback to the French colonial days.

The First Arrondissement was in an old, deteriorating building that also housed the government functions for the district, including the police department. I could honestly say that I got married in a police station.

The room looked like a small classroom, with a table covered by mildewing green baize cloth. The magistrate stood behind the table, and the bridal party sat in a row of rickety plywood-and-metal chairs. He had asked if I wanted to brighten the room with flowers, but I declined because I really didn't think it would help.

The ceremony was well documented. An ABC camera crew covered the action as if it were a real news event, and the Associated Press sent one of its photographers. This probably was because our best man, George McArthur, was the AP bureau chief.

We also needed a translator for the ceremony, and his interpretation of the vows caused large guffaws when he asked Bud to promise to "practice conjugal love." Bud's reply: "Practice? I intend to indulge!"

The reception was planned for the top-floor dining room of the Caravelle Hotel. The hotel staff was ecstatic. They hadn't had a major reception in a decade. Our ideas of decor were somewhat divergent, and I still shudder when I think of the pink satin and tulle material they had originally selected to drape the buffet tables. It might well have been appropriate for a streetwalker's lingerie. We quickly changed it to white damask.

But the Caravelle chefs produced an excellent menu, complete with a three-tiered wedding cake topped with a Caucasian bride and groom they had managed to find somewhere in Saigon. It is hard to believe that the food bill came to only $2,000 at the black market rate.

Some 150 American and Vietnamese guests helped us celebrate the occasion. More people would have come had President Eisenhower not died the same day. Embassy personnel were told to observe a period of mourning and stay home for five days in deference to Ike's death, but a good number ignored the directive.

Bud had purchased the PX liquor rations from many of his correspondent buddies and champagne from his diplomatic friends. It was a great party! Ann Bryan caught my bouquet and was the next one married when she tied the knot with Frank Mariano.

We left the next morning for our honeymoon at the Oriental Hotel in Bangkok, followed by a week at the Mandarin Hotel in Hong Kong.

Our trip was cut short when Bud's Hong Kong doctor discovered he had an extremely elevated hematocrit and we were medevacked stateside on Pan Am. When I called my mother to report that I was returning home, she exclaimed, "You can't do that. You have to give your marriage more time!" I suppose she had good reason to jump to that conclusion, since I had broken three previous engagements before taking the plunge.

In Washington, we checked in to the National Institutes of Health, where Bud went through an extensive series of tests. He was diagnosed with the blood disorder polycythemia vera. Once diagnosed and determined that it was not life-threatening, we returned to Saigon two months later, where I set up housekeeping in a small suite at the Caravelle Hotel.

Bud's illness was the first indication of the precarious state of his health, which prematurely claimed his life in 1988 at age sixty.

BABY'S BIRTH

The doctor called me an "advanced primip," which means that I was an expectant mother of advanced years. I was in my thirties. I got a little confused and immediately told Bud I was an advanced primate. I sure was!

I sought out a gynecologist when I thought I was pregnant. The only one in-country was a member of the Central Intelligence Agency attached to the U.S. embassy. One of Bud's "spook" friends arranged for my appointment. His first question was "Do you want to be?" It seemed that many of his patients would not have been as happy as I to be in this condition.

They were still doing the rabbit test in those days, so I left a urine specimen and went home with the instructions to call his office the next day when the little bunny died.

The telephone system in Saigon was a disaster. The regular PTT system worked sporadically, so most of the American government and military offices were linked by a system called Tiger. To go from one system to another was nearly impossible. So at the appointed time, I walked over to the Joint U.S. Public Affairs Office (JUSPAO), which housed the U.S. Mission and the military press centers, to place my calls. They had plenty of Tiger phones.

Bud was up-country on a story, so I was on my own. I placed the call at the appointed hour and looked up to see a room full of military personnel all listening attentively to my conversation. Poor Bud, he was one of the last to learn that he was about to become a father.

My timing was fortunate. During my pregnancy, the head of Saigon's 3rd Field Hospital was the senior OB/GYN in the army. Career physicians took tours of duty just as field officers did, and it was considered an important career move to serve in overseas military hospitals, especially in a war zone.

Col. Warren Patou was one of the finest obstetricians in the army and came with a great reputation for delivering mothers of advanced age. Several years earlier, he had attended Gen. Creighton Abrams's wife when she was in her forties. He was wonderful, and I adored him.

The only thing that was different about my approach to motherhood was that I was in a war zone. I got plenty of TLC from everyone from war correspondents to embassy personnel and even the occasional military officer. They all made me feel that an expectant mother is really beautiful, a rumor I am convinced was originally started by a pregnant woman.

In my condition, I no longer roamed the country in helicopters, but I continued to report from Vietnam. When the labor pains started, I was working on a story about interracial births. I knew that first babies don't deliver quickly, so I just kept working while the dad-to-be kept pacing.

Good thing I did finish my work, because when I got to the hospital my labor pains stopped. Hooked up to an IV on a movable stand, I was directed to walk around the hospital grounds until things started again. I must have been a weird sight, an American woman with an immense belly, walking among the wounded soldiers.

The staff of the 3rd Field Hospital did very little civilian work, especially obstetrical. They delivered the babies of Vietnamese women who were married to American soldiers. But it was rare to deliver a "round-eyed" baby. Mine was one of the first born in that hospital.

Katherine Anne Merick put in her appearance at 2:44 A.M., November 23. She weighed in at 4.4 pounds but was healthy. She was a month premature, arriving for Thanksgiving instead of Christmas. Unfortunately, her birth coincided with the arrival of wounded soldiers who demanded attention. She was unceremoniously placed on a baby scale and given over to Bud's care.

There was no neonatal nursing facility. The only incubator available didn't work, so she was swaddled in blankets and kept warm under a gooseneck lamp. Because she was premature, we had not yet received the baby clothes I had ordered from Sears, Roebuck. We improvised by tracing the outline of her tiny body on a Chux. We sent this pattern along with a stack of Bud's underwear shirts to my dressmaker, who quickly ran up a complete layette in telltale gray cotton jersey.

Although her childhood was out of the ordinary, growing up in a war zone, Katherine Anne spent the next four years in Saigon, healthy, happy, and speaking Vietnamese until we were transferred to Sydney, Australia, shortly before the end of the war.

Today she works as a physical therapist at Massachussets General Hospital in Boston.

FEAR

The question I am most frequently asked about my time in Saigon is, was I frightened while I was there? I can honestly say that until my daughter was born in 1970, I was never fearful for my life.

You have to remember that my assignments were mostly feature stuff and did not involve combat. While I saw my share of action, I did not go out specifically looking for a firefight. We had a number of male correspondents, especially freelancers, who loved nothing better than to be where the guns were blazing. One reason, despite their being a little bit crazy, was that it guaranteed them a spot on the evening news.

Television producers were always delighted when they got a piece of action footage for the nightly newscast; the noisier the better. It showed that "war is hell" and fueled the growing antiwar segment of the population. But Vietnam wasn't all combat; there was lots of downtime. There were many other stories to be covered, and I was responsible for ferreting them out.

Also, I was fairly young, and like most people of an early age, I thought I was invincible. It just goes with the territory. Today, I would be terrified.

The press corps represented several media groups. There were the network and other broadcast teams. We had to get pictures and sound for our audiences. To do this, we couldn't just go to briefings or conduct interviews with the military brass who were masterminding the action. We had to go out in the field at whatever cost. Ours was also a team effort.

A camera crew consisted of at least two men. (To my knowledge, no women were working on camera crews in Vietnam at that time. That would not be the case today. Women frequently work at any and all technical positions.) The cameraman had the toughest and most physical job. He carried the heaviest gear: the camera, extra battery packs, the film. He often put himself in the most vulnerable position when covering the action.

I am not sure that network headquarters stateside were aware of the dangers some of their employees faced in the field. One angry telegraphed "rocket" from a hotshot producer at ABC News complained that our guys never got the right perspective on the action. "I want to see the enemy and what they are shooting at," he cabled. I wonder if he realized that this would have put us within enemy lines. Guess you had to be there!

The number two man was responsible for the sound. He carried the mikes and any lighting equipment that might be needed, such as a portable spot or reflector to fill in for shadows. Then, of course, came the correspondent and, if the piece or the reporter was really important, a field producer. Depending on the story and whether we were going to overnight in the field, we also carried whatever gear might be required. We always carried canteens of water. One memory I will forever carry about Vietnam is of being thirsty.

We were a team, and it gave me, at least, a feeling of security knowing I was not alone.

Some of the freelancers were what I called a "one-man band." They did everything: shot the film, monitored the sound, and read their pieces into a camera operated by remote control. They were exceedingly hardworking, but a lonely group.

All television coverage those days was shot on 16-millimeter film. When a story was shot, the film was rushed back to Saigon, where it was shipped stateside to be developed. Videotape recording didn't begin until many years later. Stories could then be edited in-country and sent to Hong Kong to be broadcast via satellite. With today's technology, it is possible to cover a war "live," as was done during the Gulf War.

The larger newspapers and magazines had manned bureaus in Saigon and often twenty to thirty staff members, including local translators and other support personnel. Smaller papers with more limited budgets often had a correspondent and a telephone.

I spent a lot of time in the field, but there were only a few times when I felt faint of heart or got sweaty palms. I still considered it an adventure.

However, when Katherine Anne was born, all that changed.

In 1970, we had moved to a small apartment in downtown Saigon on Hai Ba Trung Street, named after the two Trung sisters, who fought off Chinese invaders in the first century. It was a great loca-

ABC News

tion, located on the Saigon River across from the *33 bière* brewery. But it was not far from the South Vietnamese navy headquarters, which was the target of Vietcong rockets one night. We had taped our windows to avoid shattering glass, and while we didn't get a direct hit, the attack made a terrifying noise. Katherine Anne was six months old at the time, and she made her displeasure known by screaming bloody murder.

We kept a flak jacket and helmet under our bed. I wrapped her tiny body in the jacket and put the helmet on my head. Then we pushed apart the two box springs, and holding the baby, I crawled into the existing space, which was well protected overhead by the mattress. It was safe as a bomb shelter, and only a direct hit could have caused any real damage while we waited out the barrage.

Another night, the concussion from one of the mortar attacks did shatter the window glass in her room, and despite all the tape protection a shard the size of a dagger penetrated the crib's mosquito netting and landed in her bedding, missing her by inches.

Then there were the scares that were not war related, like the time I found a bat hanging from the balcony railing directly over her crib. Bats in Vietnam were usually rabid.

Because of the lack of American pediatricians in Saigon, Dr. Spock's original child care book became my bible. Years later, I met the renowned pediatrician when he did one of my television shows and told him that while I didn't agree with his views on the war, his child care advice carried me through motherhood in Southeast Asia.

Incredibly high fevers brought about by infections, diarrhea, and severe dehydration were constant worries. It was not unusual to have fevers spike over 105. When this happened, I would place Katherine-Anne on bath towels on the floor and bathe her with tepid water until the fevers subsided.

The Vietnamese thought I was crazy. Influenced by French and Chinese medicine, they believed high fevers called for bundling up the patient to keep him or her warm. Fry the brain, was more likely.

Then there was the time she drank the rabies vaccine we had imported for our dog and had to be rushed to the emergency room. No one there knew an antidote. Seems you don't need one.

She laughed at the rats that invaded our kitchen and were a continual challenge to the exterminators. She survived not having any baby food and thrived on pureed French and Vietnamese cuisine. She even liked Korean kim chi, which was so hot and spicy that it brought tears to my eyes. And she never got diaper rash, because, like Vietnamese babies, she didn't wear any diapers.

THE COUNTRY

Vietnam is one of the most beautiful countries I have ever encountered. It is hot and humid most of the time and dusty and dirty, especially in the cities. But there is nothing quite like its magnificent coastline, its forested mountains, and its fertile valleys. It is also one of the most interesting countries in Southeast Asia, and that adds a lot to its charm and mystique.

I loved Vietnam with a passion, not with the patriotic fervor that I feel toward America, but with an ardor that is as strong today as it was when I last saw Saigon twenty-seven years ago. I miss the sounds, even the squeal of the motorbikes. I long for the smells, sometimes perfumed, sometimes foul, but always exotic. Vietnam has burrowed into my very being, and I yearn to return.

Because my assignments for ABC News were not limited to the battlefield, I had the luxury of traveling throughout this fascinating country. Stories on pacification took me to the Mekong Delta. The *Chieu Hoi* ("Open Arms") program was a long-standing amnesty plan originated in 1963 by then-president Ngo Dinh Diem. It offered financial rewards to enemy soldiers who turned themselves in, gave up their arms, or revealed intelligence information about the Vietcong. Like most of the many programs created by American and Vietnamese bureaucrats to win over the "hearts and minds of the people," it met with only sporadic success.

Chieu Hoi was just one of the programs that came under the umbrella organization known as CORDS, or Civilian Operations and Revolutionary Development Support.

I learned early that most government programs, both military and civilian, could be translated into acronyms. New programs were being created daily, reminding me of heavy helpings of alphabet soup.

The Mekong Delta produced most of the rice in Vietnam for domestic use and export. Its scenery was a monotonous panorama of lush green rice paddies stretching as far as the eye could see. It was crisscrossed with canals, many having been built by the French during their occupation. The main means of transportation was by sampan or other watercraft. It was another example of the difficulties presented to the military in attempting to fight a nonconventional war.

Another CORDS program was Revolutionary Development (RD), which had its national training center in Vung Tau. Dressed in uniforms of black pajamas to resemble the Vietcong, these RD teams were assigned to villages throughout the country to provide security and promote economic development.

Vung Tau was a popular seaside resort, boasting lovely whitesand beaches. It was located only eighty miles south of Saigon. On weekends its population mushroomed with Saigon families surfing or sunbathing and dining with little apparent concern that their country was at war.

The mountain resort of Dalat was located in the middle of Vietnam in the Central Highlands. It was home to the Vietnamese Military Academy, which trained the elite officers corps, and was the site of the country's only nuclear reactor, an antiquated installation. It was also famous for prewar tiger hunts and its cultivation of fruits and vegetables.

I was to do a story on the last remaining railroad in South Vietnam, which ran from Dalat down to the coast at Phan Rang. The route went through some VC territory, and my Vietnamese two-man sound crew decided it was too dangerous to continue. So they quit. ABC's cameraman Tony Hirashiki, who was also my chopsticks instructor, continued the journey with me without incident. It was my favorite TV piece and certainly the most picturesque.

From Phan Rang we hitchhiked back to Saigon aboard a C-130. The bureau was happy to see us since we had been out of communication for three days. There was a stack of messages from Bud Merick on my desk. I was thrilled. This was the first time he had shown any interest in my whereabouts.

I was a sight: sweat-stained clothes, tangled hair, and skin caked with red mud. First I had to "freshen up." The bath-water was rust-colored when I finally bathed. I then called Bud.

"Where have you been?" he demanded. I explained my assignment, happy that he cared. "I can't get my tape deck to play," Bud wailed. "Come and fix it." So much for his concern.

The hill tribes known as Montagnards, or "mountain people," were the focus of a story in Ban Me Thuot. There I was inducted into the tribe by drinking their potent and very sour rice wine and then presented with a beautifully carved crossbow, their traditional weapon.

Not only did we all have prodigious hangovers the next day, so did the Montagnard animals who had eaten the fermented rice dregs. They spent the night staggering around their pens. I think we all did a little staggering.

Covering the marines in I Corps was probably the most challenging and dangerous of my assignments, because it was close to the DMZ and in the way of infiltrating North Vietnamese forces. The marines suffered some of the highest death tolls and casualty rates during the war.

The major press center was located in a former Vietnamese motel that had been requisitioned by the marines. Most of the major news organizations kept permanent quarters there, and we all took weekly turns living in Da Nang to cover the action. I remember the first time I stayed there early on during my tour and thinking after I crawled into the damp interior of my sleeping bag, What am I doing here? I hated summer camp.

One of my stories that I liked the best was the one I did about the ancient capital of Hue, with its picturesque Perfume River and its beautiful citadel. Located halfway between Da Nang and the DMZ, it was Vietnam's third largest city. It was one of my biggest challenges to try to explain the significance of this ancient place and its impact on the Vietnamese people.

Covering the war in Vietnam was exciting.

First there was the story itself. It was the major news story of the decade. It drew the most famous names of the journalistic community, and I was part of this illustrious group. While there weren't a lot of women correspondents in-country, we were treated as equals by the establishment and most of our peers. We asked no special favors and worked just as hard and under the same circumstances as our male colleagues.

Perhaps the only difference we experienced was the loneliness many of us felt being such a minority. It was probably the first time that I really missed the company of women. Maybe that's why we refer to ourselves as part of a sisterhood. I remember how surprised I was to admit this to myself and how grateful I was to my friend Ann Bryan when she revealed that she felt the same way. There is just something special about the closeness women have toward each other, and it isn't just "girl talk." We really do think differently.

Covering the war wasn't all work, either. The social life in Saigon was very active. Besides the military, there was a large diplomatic corps and a huge American community of people connected to the U.S. Mission. The major form of entertainment revolved around cocktail parties and dinners. It was a welcome break from being in the field, and we all got gussied up and partied.

We all had seamstresses and tailors who could create a dressy outfit from the elegant silks and cottons that were available from our R&R shopping trips to Hong Kong and Bangkok.

If you were a famous-name journalist or the bureau chief of a TV network or a major publication, you usually were on the "A list" and included in prestige dinners at Ambassador Ellsworth Bunker's residence, where dinners were always preceded by a pony of imported Russian vodka and concluded when the men repaired to the salon for brandy and cigars while the women were left by themselves with coffee.

Someone was always giving a party. American embassy workers had access to first-run films, and that was always an excuse to have a dinner and movie party. The military BOQs like the Brinks or Rex often had dances for the officers and female personnel. They also showed first-run movies.

Many of the correspondents had a houseboy or a woman who cooked for them. I was fortunate enough to have a French-trained cook and therefore entertained frequently. One time my guest list of twenty-four included three ambassadors.

Weekends often meant a trip to the seashore at Vung Tau. If you were up-country and lucky enough to get a chopper ride, you might sample the fabulous lobsters at the beach resort of Nha Trang. Both areas have become popular tourist attractions in today's Vietnam.

Sports were popular during our leisure time. The military had active handball and raquetball courts at their new complex, dubbed "Pentagon East." Saigon-based athletes could choose a lazy afternoon at the Cercle Sportif, a pool and tennis complex in downtown where our male counterparts especially enjoyed the lithe figures of the young Vietnamese ladies in their brief bikinis.

For the adventuresome, there was the Golf Club of Saigon, located near Tan Son Nhut airport. It was eighteen holes over a flat terrain, not difficult by American standards. The caddies were sturdy Vietnamese women not much bigger than the bags they carried. The real challenge came from the course layout, which was interrupted from time to time by an ARVN outpost, well fortified by barbed wire, land mines, and heavily armed guards. Should you be unlucky enough to hit your ball into its confines, you simply declared a "lost ball."

We even went waterskiing on the Saigon River. I was never sure whether I was more worried by the polluted water or the rifle-toting ARVN soldiers who could easily have taken potshots from their guard posts on the river bridges.

It's hard to believe that Saigon was considered a hardship post. The lively press corps changed all that. But you know the adage "All work and no play . . ."

FINAL CHAPTER

I lived in Saigon for seven years, and I did many jobs. I was a professional journalist. I was a wife and mother. I worked for the U.S. government editing translations of interviews with captured North Vietnamese prisoners of war. Like many of the other women journalists, I did a lot of volunteer work. I taught English to the Vietnamese officers of the national police force. As president of the Saigon Women's Association, I organized relief activities to help refugees from the war. I also edited and published a Vietnamese-American cookbook entitled *You and Your Cook,* which featured translations of old American favorites.

I lived through the American buildup during the early days of the war when the number of U.S. troops escalated in increments of

100,000 soldiers annually, from 385,000 at the end of 1966 to a peak of 543,400 in April 1969.

In 1970, influenced by the growing antiwar sentiment, U.S. policy called for the Vietnamese to fight their own war. Known as Vietnamization, it was an integral part of Richard Nixon's strategy to bring the war to a close. By December 1973, our military presence was down to fifty.

With this drastic reduction in the American presence, most news organizations decided to cut back on their personnel covering the war. *U.S. News & World Report* decided to close their full-time bureau and send in correspondents as events warranted.

It was with great sadness that we packed up our household belongings and moved with our daughter, Katherine Anne, then age four, to Sydney, Australia. Our Vietnam adventure was over.

But it wasn't over for my husband, Bud. Watching the tide of the battle turn toward the North Vietnamese, he returned to Saigon in April 1975 and was there when the final battle was lost. He was among the last Americans evacuated from the embassy compound, along with our child's godmother, Eva Kim, who served as Ambassador Graham Martin's secretary, and George McArthur, best man at our wedding.

I always thought that it didn't have to end the way it did. The Vietnamese could have saved their own country. Their soldiers weren't cowards, but their leadership was riddled with corruption and the price was the loss of their country.

The United States didn't have to be embarrassed by its first military loss in history. Simple military decisions made early enough might have stopped aggression from the North. Our participation in the Paris peace talks sold our allies down the river by allowing the North Vietnamese to remain below the demilitarized zone in the name of "peace with honor."

The war polarized the United States as no other military action has done since the Civil War, and its repercussions will be debated for years to come.

Jurate Kazickas

These Hills Called Khe Sanh

We are the intruder, we are the trespasser, we don't belong,
not in these hills, these hills called Khe Sanh. . . .

"Home from the Woods,"
by William Stross, 2/3 Marines

When I think of Vietnam, I think of the soldiers' faces. Unguarded, innocent, smiling. They were all so young, unprepared for the filth and degradation of war. No one wanted to be in that distant, strange land, but they did not complain. Some felt it was their duty to come to Vietnam. Some never stopped questioning why they were there. But they fought; they died.

I wanted to write about these men. I wanted to know who they were, where they came from, and how they coped with the madness of it all. Looking for them, I went far from Saigon, to the north near the DMZ, the imaginary line that separated the two Vietnams, into the dense jungle with its dark secrets. There was always a story in Khe Sanh. It was an important place in Vietnam. For me, it was where two significant events of my experience as a journalist during that conflict took place, bringing the war into my life in ways I never dared imagine.

The marine helicopter hovered a few feet over the freshly cut landing zone on that hot morning in late June 1967. Balancing a heavy rucksack and clutching a Nikon camera in my hands, I jumped to the ground, dashed beneath the swirling blades, and ran to a nearby tree line.

JURATE KAZICKAS, a former newspaper reporter in New York and Washington, has co-authored several books on women's history, and is now a writer living in New York with her husband and three children.

In a small clearing, marines from the two-hundred-man Lima Company of the 3rd Battalion, 26th Regiment, based in South Vietnam's I Corps, were busy packing their gear for a five-day patrol deep inside enemy territory. Some looked up in surprise at the sight of a woman reporter suddenly appearing in their midst. I nodded hello and headed straight for the company commander.

Capt. Franklin Delano Bynum shook hands briefly when I introduced myself. He was pleasant but seemed too busy to concern himself with a female reporter about to accompany his men on their patrol. He turned away abruptly and began ordering the troops in his low southern drawl to move.

Six feet four inches tall, powerfully built, handsome, and tough as the polished oak shillelagh he carried along with his .45 pistol, Captain Bynum was typical of the best United States Marine officers that were sent to fight in Vietnam. At age thirty-three, he was much older than most of his men, but he was aggressive, loyal, and brave, often rushing to the front of the line during firefights. He had already received two Purple Hearts. A white ascot stripped from a piece of parachute was wrapped around his neck, and the green forage cap he wore, rather than the standard steel helmet, completed the picture of a colorful but professional marine whom the men could trust to bring them home safely after a successful mission.

From their base at Khe Sanh, the company was planning a secret foray to the Laotian border, where they hoped to engage the enemy and intercept a suspected North Vietnamese supply route. As a properly accredited journalist, I was entitled to cover any military mission in Vietnam. However, securing permission to join this long-range patrol had not been easy. While male correspondents sometimes went out into the field unaccompanied, there was no way the marines were going to let a woman move around on her own, as I had been used to doing with army units. The military brass insisted that I have an official escort.

I tried to object, but eventually there was no choice. To my chagrin, the man assigned to watch over me, Staff Sgt. Les Johnson, an overweight, out-of-shape desk clerk, looked woefully inept. He seemed nervous at the prospect of going out on a patrol as we flew by helicopter from Dong Ha to a small landing zone hacked out in the wooded staging area by Captain Bynum's men.

By midmorning, the troops were ready and we began moving

through the dense triple-canopy jungle. Immediately, the difficulties of the terrain became apparent. The thick brush caught at our clothing and stuck sharp pins into our arms and legs. The stifling air made breathing difficult. For me, however, the satisfaction of being on a critical combat mission easily made up for the physical discomforts. This was why I had come to Vietnam, after all. I was, in a sense, a child of war.

Born in Lithuania, I was just a year and a half old in June 1944, during World War II, when Russian tanks rolled into Vilnius. My father, active in the anti-Communist underground, was a marked man, destined for death or deportation. We fled our homes in the night and joined a ragged band of refugees, trudging through the countryside with a cart for our paltry possessions and a cow to provide milk for the children. My lullabies were the sad songs of a lost homeland set to the distant thunder of bombs as we pushed our way west toward the unknown. Every day was uncertain and terrifying. Even the Allies strafed us innocent civilians when we decamped in Germany.

Then, in February 1945, in the Breslau (now Wroclaw) train station, surrounded by panicked crowds desperate to flee, my parents tried frantically to push their way onto a train carrying wounded German infantrymen from the front. Suddenly, a window opened and a soldier leaned out, reaching for my mother and me. "Give me the girl," he shouted.

In one of those maternal instincts for survival, without thinking, my mother thrust me into his outstretched arms. Then the young soldier pulled her into the wagon as well, just as the train chugged out of the station, and unbeknownst to us, my father leaped on somewhere in the rear.

The Germans hid me and my mother under a pile of bloody bandages and torn army blankets when the commanders came through looking for unauthorized passengers. I was quiet "like a little mouse," my mother often said when she recounted the story of our escape years later. The train stopped in Dresden, but luck was with us once again. We fled the city on the night of February 13, just hours before its awesome destruction. As wave after wave of British planes attacked, off in the distance my parents could see the raging fires that filled the sky.

I have no memory of the bombing, but World War II, its horrors, and our trials while fleeing to freedom was my family history, my heritage. I grew up in New York hearing the stories of our life in the displaced persons' camp in Germany. The GIs nicknamed me Shirley Temple because of my full head of curls and plied me with chewing gum and Hershey bars. When at last we received permission to emigrate in 1947, the ship that carried us across the turbulent Atlantic to America was the USS *Ernie Pyle*, named after the famed World War II reporter who wrote so movingly about the rigors of warfare as experienced by the soldiers in foxholes. It seemed preordained, I like to think, that one day I would seek out a war of my own.

When I told my parents almost a quarter century later that I was going to Vietnam, my mother wept. "Everything we have done in life was to keep you from ever having to live through a war again." She was not alone in her concern. Few of my friends could understand what would motivate a woman to go voluntarily to Vietnam. Perhaps I wasn't even sure myself.

What *was* I doing here? I couldn't help thinking in my agony after five grueling hours of tramping through the thick underbrush. Finally, Captain Bynum called the patrol to a halt. The men sprawled on the grass, gulped water from their canteens, and broke out the C rations they had stuffed in socks strapped to their packs. My escort, Sergeant Johnson, seemed too exhausted to eat. He was breathing heavily as he mopped his wet face with a bandanna.

A young corporal named Tom, with a crew cut and narrow, tanned face, was sitting next to me. After opening a can of franks and beans, he asked my name.

"Oh, man, that's too hard to remember. Mind if I call you Sam?" he said.

Sam? I didn't like the idea of a man's nickname. Standing six feet tall in my clunky canvas jungle boots and dressed in regulation olive drab fatigues, I had to work extra hard to maintain some semblance of femininity. Even out in the field, I always wore a bold slash of Maybelline coral on my lips, gold studs in my ears, and sometimes a camouflage ribbon in my long brown hair.

"Okay, you can call me Sam," I said, shrugging.

Tom eyed me with curiosity. "So, what's a woman like you doing out here?" he asked.

"I'm a reporter, and this is the biggest story of our times," I answered. "I want to experience what's going on here so my reports will be accurate and truthful."

He shook his head. "Yeah, but this is dangerous. You might get killed here."

"That can also happen to a male reporter," I countered. "I just think it's important to let people know what this war is really like."

"Who do you work for?" asked another marine, named Scott, who had been listening to our conversation.

I explained I was freelance, writing for a variety of publications and whatever magazines I could interest in a feature story about the war.

"You mean you came over here on your own just to get shot at? Wow! Sam, you're nuts!" Scott said, laughing and shaking his head.

Serious again, he asked, "What do you think about all this? You one of those peaceniks that tell everybody we should get the hell out of this place?"

With a confidence that would soon change, I said I believed we were right to help the South Vietnamese fight the aggression of the North. "My country was taken away from me by the Communists. I know what it is like to be denied freedom."

Before the conversation became too political, we were called to form up and clear out. Once again, we began moving in a westwardly direction, away from the relative safety of the military firebase the troops had left that morning.

Tom, the young marine who had been so curious about me as a woman war reporter, was just ahead of me during the afternoon march. As we trudged on in single file in the blistering sun, I wondered how I could ever explain the complicated path that brought me to these hills of Khe Sanh.

Certainly, Vietnam was not on the original itinerary for my trip around the world. I was heading home in 1965 from Africa, where I had been working as a volunteer teacher since my graduation from college. I knew practically nothing about the crisis in Southeast Asia. I had tuned out civilization and the rest of the world while I lived in Kenya, where elephants trampled my garden and the stately Masai and their cattle roamed the land.

By then, the Vietnam War was moving into high gear. Bombing missions had intensified over North Vietnam. More than 120,000 ground troops had arrived in-country. In the States, the antiwar movement was gathering momentum.

While backpacking through Asia, I stopped in Bangkok, where I met dozens of GIs on "R&R"—rest and recreation—from Vietnam. In the honky-tonk bars of the Patpong district, they talked of war and an unseen enemy everywhere—in the lush jungles, rice paddies, and villages. It was a crazy, terrifying world that they had left behind, if only for a few days. My curiosity was piqued. I wanted to see this war for myself.

I hastily rearranged my travel schedule for a twenty-four-hour layover in Saigon. The American presence in November 1965 throughout the city shocked me. The trappings of war were everywhere sandbagged offices, armed guards, tanks, men in combat fatigues, rifles at the ready. And nowhere, it seemed, any Western women. I felt as I did in Kenya's Chalbi desert among the Gabra tribe—a lone woman from a different land, an eyewitness to an exotic culture. My senses were overwhelmed by the bizarre scene.

Something was planted in my soul during that day and night as I careened through the bustling streets in a cyclo, taking in the myriad sights. Skinny old Vietnamese men squatted on the sidewalks cooking noodles, porcelain-faced women in fluttering *ao dais* glided by. Baby-faced GIs lurched out of bars with their bought girlfriends, while jeeploads of their buddies headed off to nearby bases. In the distance I thought I heard the rumble of bombs exploding. I think even then in those few hours, I knew that I would return one day. A new and mysterious world was beckoning.

Back in New York, in February 1966, I took a job as a library researcher for $67 a week at *Look* magazine, gathering facts and writing memos for the senior writers. I began compulsively reading every story written about Vietnam and plotting my return to the war zone. The *Life* magazine pictures of soldiers in combat mesmerized me, the reporters' eyewitness stories were riveting. When Don Moser, *Life*'s bureau chief, was quoted as saying, "Send us some women," that was all the encouragement I needed.

But in May, Sam Castan, *Look*'s correspondent in Vietnam, was killed in a firefight, a devastating shock for everyone on the magazine staff, even those of us who had never met him. I don't know what possessed me to broach the possibility that I, an unpublished researcher and a woman, go in his place, but I did. The editors were appalled at my proposal and tried to discourage me by arguing that such a move would be disastrous for my journalism career.

Undaunted, I made the rounds of other magazines, hoping to get an assignment. Richard Clurman, head of correspondents for *Time* magazine, blustered at the résumé I pitched. "You mean to tell me that just because you've climbed mountains, jumped out of a plane, shot a leopard, hitchhiked in Afghanistan—I should send you to represent us in Vietnam?"

I thought at least my youthful ambition and sense of adventure counted for something. But in the end, no editors agreed. The only way I could work in Vietnam was to go on my own.

I found out that the U.S. Military Assistance Command in Vietnam (MACV) and the Joint U.S. Public Affairs Office (JUSPAO) in Saigon had strict rules for granting press credentials to freelancers. I had to have letters from at least three news organizations vouching that I would be writing for them. I lined up the North American Newspaper Alliance (NANA), a news and feature syndicate; the *Insider's Newsletter; Maryknoll* magazine (for a story about Catholics in Vietnam); and *Darbininkas* (*Worker*), a Lithuanian-language weekly newspaper.

These organizations were willing to help me with press credentials but I had to pay my own way overseas. My parents, genuinely upset at the thought of my going to war, did not offer to help with my finances. On a lark, I auditioned for a television quiz show called *Password*. I won the contest and, with my $500 prize money, bought a one-way ticket to Saigon and headed off to war.

And now, barely three months later, I was on a long-range patrol in the hills of Vietnam, where almost every foot of ground was controlled by the North Vietnamese army. When we finally came to a halt that evening, we stopped near a deserted Montagnard village, just three hollow huts on stilts. Here, Captain Bynum decided we would spend the night. The men put out some claymore mines and stationed machine guns around our perimeter. No fires were permitted, and radio contact with battalion headquarters was limited. The enemy was not supposed to know we were within striking distance. A few of the men warmed up their cans of C rations with small blue heat tabs. Most, however, were too tired to do more than slurp down some cold chow.

I too was aching and exhausted but kept my pains to myself. Sergeant Johnson, however, couldn't hide the strain from the first day's march, and I worried how he would be able to go the full five days.

That night, I slept on the ground wrapped in a poncho. A cool breeze swept through the camp, bringing a welcome relief to all of us as we drifted off to sleep. As I lay in my makeshift sleeping bag, looking up at a full moon so bright that it hurt my eyes, I remember thinking how extraordinary it was to be here with these men and experience all they were going through. The circumstances, to say the least, were unusual—I the lone woman with two hundred men in a remote corner of Vietnam. I tried to keep a professional distance, but I could not help being attracted to many of these men, and on nearly every patrol, there would be a soldier with whom I would connect in a special way. Perhaps we traded C rations or dug a foxhole together or simply marched near each other through the jungle, exchanging occasional glances in the spooky shadows.

Sometimes in the dark we would lie on the hard ground under our ponchos and watch the distant flashes of artillery, red-and-orange streaks playing havoc with the stars. We'd sneak some cigarettes and sip smuggled Scotch as we whispered stories of our lives through the long night. The sexual tension was intense, delicious, heartbreaking. Yet I was so careful of my reputation, I did not dare allow even our fingers to touch.

The men were very kind to me, and I was grateful for their acceptance. Watching them kidding around with one another, sharing letters from home, proudly showing off pictures of their sweethearts, I was always struck by how young and vulnerable they were. The thought that some of them might never come home from Vietnam was too terrible to contemplate. But I knew it was true. And so did they.

We woke early, and before the sun had risen far into the sky that morning, Captain Bynum had his patrol on the move. Once again, he set a hard pace, insisting we hike for hours without a break in the oppressive heat, which was reaching 110 scorching degrees. Several men complained of dehydration. But they pushed on, hacking their way with machetes through clumps of bamboo and ten-foot-high elephant grass. Sometimes the only way the lead men could get through was by hurling themselves forward and falling against the stalks of grass. The sharp edges slashed at our skin like a million paper cuts as we stumbled up the steep hills. Coming down the treacherous slopes, encumbered by packs weighing as much as one hundred pounds and filled with weaponry such as mortar rounds,

Personal collection

grenades, and machine guns, the men slid and fell, shredding their fatigues on the sharp rocks. I got an eyeful of hairy bare bottoms that day.

My escort was beginning to fade. Panting for breath and barely capable of putting one foot in front of the other, Johnson was clearly suffering. Soaked with sweat, he lagged far behind and slumped in an exhausted heap every chance he got.

"Are you all right, Les?" I asked.

"No problem," he said, waving me away.

My eyes scanned the landscape around me. Again and again, the inescapable beauty of Vietnam seized my heart and transported me to another world. The sky was a radiant blue, with dazzling chalk-white cumulus clouds. The hills around Khe Sanh were a patchwork of lush greens, so many different shades like emerald and jade that shifted in brightness as the sun dropped in the sky. It was all so peaceful, reminding me of the African highlands. But then, on some of the hilltops, one could see the intrusion of war. Ash brown tree stumps had been stripped by the napalm American jets dropped just two months earlier to support the marines in the fierce battles for Hills 861 and 881, named for their height in meters.

"If you see anything moving out there, once you ascertain that it is not one of our own men, open fire at will," Bynum announced.

But we saw nothing, heard nothing except the slashing of knives against gnarled vines and bamboo and the groans of exhausted men.

Despite the difficulties of marching through the dense under-brush and up the steep hills, we often had moments of sheer silliness and fun. When the men camouflaged their helmets with branches and leaves, I found some yellow flower blossoms to twist in my hair. Even Captain Bynum began to loosen up. He made his troops laugh when he gave his point man a bunch of *Chieu Hoi* passes, which of-fered amnesty to enemy soldiers who wanted to quit fighting and sur-render. "Hey, you can just hand these to any NVA you meet on the trail," he joked.

Once when I wasn't looking, some of the men strapped an extra mortar round on my pack as a prank. Though my shoulders were painfully blistered and I was so tired that I thought my legs would buckle, I pretended I didn't feel the extra seven-and-a-half-pound weight as I hoisted the pack and began to slog up the hill. "Hard-core!" the men hooted.

By midday we came to a waist-deep stream. After the first pla-toon had crossed, the slopes became muddy, and soon everyone was slipping and falling. Captain Bynum himself, shillelagh held high, was doused when he lost his balance and tumbled into the stream.

As I splashed through the cool water, holding my camera above my head, my legs suddenly began to itch. At our next stop, I slipped behind a clump of bushes and pulled down my fatigues. I was ap-palled to see my thighs all bloody and covered with disgusting leeches. I lit a cigarette and burned them off until the last one had fallen away.

As we slogged on, I concentrated on staying focused and keeping up without complaining. But I could not stop worrying about my lag-ging escort. Then, late in the afternoon, after more grueling hours of scaling impassable ridges, Johnson pulled a muscle in his groin and collapsed. Writhing in pain, he said he could no longer walk. A burly marine offered to carry him up the hill. Johnson looked miserable.

Clearly exasperated, Captain Bynum checked on the crippled sergeant. "We'll have to call a chopper to get him out of here," he said. Then he added that I too would have to leave the patrol.

"But it's not fair to make me go. There's nothing wrong with me," I protested.

The company commander shook his head.

"I was promised a five-day patrol," I argued.

Bynum, however, was insistent. "No escort, no reporter."

I reminded the captain that he had said there would be no helicopter relief flights during the mission so as not to alert the NVA to our activity.

Bynum glanced at Johnson, who was lying crumpled on the jungle grass. "We don't have a choice," he said with a finality I knew could not be changed.

Still, it was a dangerous move. Calling a chopper to get us out would reveal our position to the enemy in this hostile territory. It was also apparent to me that even though Johnson was the culprit, I, the woman, might be blamed for the compromise of Lima Company's security. Every suppressed anxiety I had about being an unwanted female in a war suddenly surfaced. After all, if I hadn't been there with my albatross, Johnson, Bynum wouldn't be forced to break radio silence to summon the highly visible chopper.

Perhaps sensing my concerns, Bynum seemed to go out of his way to assure me that his men could use some more water and that he would take advantage of the arriving helicopter to secure extra supplies.

It was twilight when the chopper appeared, clattering above the giant stalks of bamboo. Surrounded as we were by walls of thick brush, there was no place it could land. The men had to raze an area about ten feet square, just big enough for the Huey to hover over us.

The crewmen lowered us a cable. Then, belted into a harness, I was hoisted upward past the trees and the high grass. While twisting slowly higher in the fading light, I suddenly realized that I was the perfect target for any NVA snipers watching the maneuver. However, I soon swung through the open doors, where I clambered into the safety of the chopper. Johnson lumbered in after me. The engines roared as we moved up and away from the treacherous jungle floor.

The last image I had of the men of Lima Company that evening was of several marines turning their heads away from the dusty downdraft of the chopper. Captain Bynum, however, stood erect, a strong, lone figure in the wildly swaying grass, and saluted me goodbye. As the helicopter rose toward the heavens, I wondered if I would ever see him again.

Watching the darkening hills of Khe Sanh recede in the distance, I became so angry that I could hardly look at Johnson. I resented having to leave that patrol. I was sure that a firefight would erupt before the mission was finished. Intelligence reports had indicated that several battalions of NVA were massing in Laos to assault the area near the demilitarized zone.

Now I would miss the action that I might have photographed and reported with an exclusive byline that could have been flashed around the world. Instead, I was heading back to Da Nang with nothing but sore muscles and bloodsucker bruises, all because of my hapless escort.

Johnson begged me not to tell anyone what had happened. He looked so pitiful, I started to feel sorry for him. "Don't worry, I won't say anything," I promised.

A few days later, back at the press center, I was studying a map to figure out where to go next, when a fellow reporter called out to me.

"Weren't you out on a patrol near Khe Sanh?" he asked. "Lima got hit. Company commander was killed."

"What?" I was stunned. "I can't believe it."

As soon as I confirmed it was Captain Bynum, I was overcome with anxiety. I wondered if the company had been discovered by the NVA because the resupply chopper had appeared to extract me and my ailing escort.

I had typed up my notes from the operation, but I couldn't complete the story. Fear and grief prevented me from further checking out the details of the marine officer's demise. It was a story I didn't want to write. Nor did I want to open a Pandora's box of my own mixed emotions concerning the events of that hot June day in the jungle near the border of Laos.

I put aside the incident and tried to forget about it, a task that would prove impossible during the coming months and even years.

I headed back to Saigon for a few days of rest. The capital city was always a welcome relief after days out in the field. It was a chance to get cleaned up, put on a miniskirt, feel like a woman again. Life was comfortable in Saigon, with its excellent French restaurants and fancy villas. Indeed, some reporters rarely ventured outside the city limits. They were content to cover the war via the infamous "five o'clock follies." These daily military briefings were held in an air-conditioned amphitheater, where military officials invariably put an optimistic spin on the war. Afterward, journalists sometimes gathered for drinks on the roof of the Caravelle Hotel, where they could witness silvery flares and exploding bombs illuminating the distant sky. It was a clear reminder to everyone that even as we analyzed the war, drinks in hand, men were dying not far from the city.

In the bustling capital, the Vietnamese went about their daily lives as if the war were a thousand miles away. One day, a wealthy businessman invited me to go waterskiing with his family on the Saigon River. Mr. Vat slalomed effortlessly past huge cargo ships as his children waved at the sailors on the U.S. Navy river patrol boats. Afterward, sipping lemonades in the shade at the exclusive yacht club Cercle Nautique, we chatted about the war in French. *La guerre*, Mr. Vat said, had been very good for his radio company.

I lived in an apartment building on the rue Pasteur in a small room that had been vacated by the writer Michael Herr when he moved to a hotel. (He would later publish *Dispatches*, considered one of the very best books about the war.) Occasionally, a group of us would gather in Herr's suite at the Continental. There were other freelancers and photographers, like twice-wounded Tim Page (who would be gravely injured again in 1969), and Sean Flynn and Dana Stone, destined to mysteriously disappear forever in Cambodia. As the cassette player blasted the Doors' anthem "Light My Fire" over and over, we smoked cheap pot, drank too much, and danced in solitary ecstasy, obliterating the war and all its craziness, if only for a few hours.

Yet I never felt totally comfortable around that journalist fraternity. Most male reporters had the same attitude about a female correspondent in Vietnam as the military did. "What the hell is a woman doing in a war zone?" they would ask, either to my face or behind my back. "Why aren't you writing about widows and orphans instead of combat?" they wanted to know.

In the early days of the war, only a small number of women regularly went out in the field. Unlike male journalists, who partied together and occasionally partnered on patrols, we rarely socialized with one another and kept our distance while chasing stories. I felt there was almost an unwritten rule: With plenty of war action to go around, from the DMZ to the Delta, there was no need for two women to show up with the same unit, as if we were in competition for exclusive attention from the troops. Looking back, I regret I never got to know the other women reporters. Perhaps my periodic feelings of loneliness and alienation as a woman in a war zone could have been assuaged by someone who knew exactly how it felt.

Military officers had their own prejudices against a female reporter. They worried that I would be a distraction and that their men would be more concerned with my safety than protecting one another. "Your men are professionals," I countered. "They'll do the right thing. Besides, I can take care of myself."

Once, the 1st Air Cavalry Division went through an elaborate show to name a landing zone in the Bong Son plains after me—putting it on the map, broadcasting it over the radio. They called it "Landing Zone Kazickas." However, the paternal lieutenant colonel wouldn't let me get off the chopper to interview the troops at my LZ. "A lady should not be out there. It's too dangerous," he said, whisking me away to a less exposed site.

Another time, a commanding officer asked me to walk around the firebase and pose for pictures with his troops as "a morale boost." Seething, I demurred as politely as I could, explaining that I was a reporter, there to do my job and nothing more.

In July 1967, I went back to the DMZ when I heard reports of heavy fighting in the area. The men of the 1st Battalion, 9th Marine Regiment at Con Thien had suffered tremendous losses—more than 150 dead and 345 wounded. The battle earned them their macabre nickname "the Walking Dead." Con Thien was significant in the progress of the war because here the North Vietnamese used artillery for the first time in support of their infantry assaults.

But for me, Con Thien was my first encounter with war at its most obscene. What shook me to the core was the devastating sight of so many dead marines who had been lying in the sun for three days—their bodies bloated, their faces black as if charred by fire.

Trying to record the scene, I found myself caught in a swirl of emotions. I was horrified and achingly sad. At the same time, I felt the anger in me rise that anyone should have to die this way.

Capt. Troy Shirley was frantically issuing orders for loading these bodies on the APCs (Armored Personnel Carriers). The NVA was still harassing the troops with sporadic gunfire from the tree line. "Hurry up, let's go, spread it out. Give me some ponchos," the captain yelled. "Where are the body bags? Hurry! We gotta get out of here."

Overhead, the jets dived and strafed the area where we would be walking next. The stench of the dead was so overpowering that the men doing the policing wore gas masks, as if in some eerie sci-fi movie.

"It's getting so bad, I'm afraid to make friends anymore," said one corporal. "I talk to a guy one minute, the next thing, they bring him back in a poncho."

The tanks groaned and rumbled as they pulled away with the bodies of the dead. Sometimes I could see a muddy boot or a clawed hand as stiff as wood sticking out of the dark green body bag. It was all too much for me to bear when, suddenly, the marines in the back of the column were mortared again. Everyone scrambled for cover. Shouts of "Corpsmen, up!" filled the air along with the screams of the newly wounded.

Those sounds, those images of Con Thien have never left me.

In August, I joined up with the 101st Airborne for Operation Benton near Duc Pho. (The army, unlike the marines, did not insist on my having an escort when I went out into the field.) The area to be searched had been pounded the night before and in the morning by U.S. forces with bombs and heavy artillery in an effort to knock out enemy fortifications. It seemed impossible that anything could have survived that onslaught of firepower, but just minutes after we started across the rice paddies, enemy snipers opened fire as three NVA soldiers in khaki uniforms ran for cover. We threw ourselves into the trenches. I huddled as low as I could and listened to the whiz of bullets over my head. In the chaos of the firefight, which lasted for two hours, five enemy soldiers were killed while one GI died and three were wounded.

Daniel Moody, point man for his platoon, risked his life to rescue his friend Rob, who had been shot in the back in the fierce exchange of fire. When Rob called out his buddy's name with a wrenching cry, Moody ran, zigzagging through the paddy to avoid getting hit, and dragged him back to safety. He did his best to bandage the wound and covered Rob's body with his own until the medic came.

Moody and I had shared some C rations earlier. A thoughtful eighteen-year-old, he said he dreamed of going home to Maine and becoming a game warden like his dad. When I asked him about the war, he said, "It's worse than I thought it would be. But I'm a trained soldier. If you're lucky enough to make it through, it's a good experience."

Then, as if he had a premonition, he said, "I thought I might be able to save someone's life if I came to Vietnam."

Studying that earnest young face, I was struck that war, for all its brutality and horror, nevertheless offered men an opportunity like no other to be fearless and brave, to be selfless, to be a hero. It occurred to me that women had no comparable world of experience to prove their mettle, to give of themselves for another to the death. So often in Vietnam I struggled to make some sense of war's loathsome reality.

I once asked Reverend Ray Stubbe, the Lutheran chaplain of Khe Sanh and a military historian, if the men who lost their lives in Vietnam had died in vain.

"I don't think Vietnam was worth fighting for, but I cannot bring myself to say their deaths were meaningless. War is not about divisions and battalions of men. It is made up of squads and recon teams and your buddies in the bunker," Reverend Stubbe said. "These men did not die for Vietnam or Washington. They died for their friends— trying to save each other or giving of themselves to prevent others from dying. These deaths were not meaningless because the men died for each other."

My own doubts about the war began to surface that summer. As the weeks wore on and I spent more time in the field witnessing the casualties, the pursuit of this war became more and more depressing. I began to realize the futility of fighting a guerrilla war with massive firepower and trying to decimate NVA battalions that kept replenishing themselves from a seemingly endless supply of manpower. American soldiers were battling for possession of the same hill again and again, hill after hill, sacrificing so many lives for worthless terrain. Despite my loathing of communism and my belief that we could not walk away from the South Vietnamese who had asked for our help, I too began to feel the war was a terrible mistake, a sacrifice too great for any country, including my own, to bear.

The suffering of the Vietnamese people on both sides of the conflict was inescapable, even in the most remote corners of the jungle. Once, going through an area near the Laotian border that had been strafed by jets earlier that morning, we came upon the bodies of two North Vietnamese soldiers, curled up in the crook of a fallen tree trunk. I could have sworn they were sleeping. They looked like children—no more than thirteen or fourteen—in their khaki shorts and thin navy blue sweaters, their small hands tucked under their chins, their arms and legs so thin they could have snapped like twigs. There was not a bruise or mark on them that I could see. In their pockets, the Americans found notebooks of graph paper that looked like diaries and some photographs of beautiful young women, smiling demurely at the camera. Girlfriends, I supposed, or perhaps they were the mothers of these soldiers, these children. The men left the papers and pictures beside the bodies. I was grateful for that.

Another time, out with the 101st Airborne near Quang Nai after a firefight, we came upon a hastily abandoned NVA hospital complex. In a very low clearing of thick vines and brambles stood almost a dozen buildings including a mess hall, a supply room of medicine (from China and from the United States), and operating rooms. A body lay on a table in preparation for burial. Suddenly, we heard the groans of some wounded in a tunnel beneath us. The interpreter called down into the hole, pleading with them to surrender. A GI reached into the tunnel, trying to smoke out the North Vietnamese soldiers, but jumped back when someone below slashed at him with a knife.

The captain ordered the troops to move on. So we left the enemy to die there as we walked on for hours through a maze of trees to find a place to camp. All through the night, artillery pounded the hills behind us while I lay awake, curled up and shivering in my poncho against a steady drizzle, imagining the moans of the living dead.

The jungle war, as foreboding as it was with nightmares of bogeymen lurking in the shadows, was an easier assignment than witnessing the plight of villagers during search-and-destroy missions. The communal heartbreak was overwhelming as we marched through smoking, burned-out hamlets, where families were being ripped apart by the fighting, where sobbing women and terrified children watched the destruction of their plundered homes by an enemy that was supposedly their savior.

In early November, while I was on a patrol with the 3rd Brigade of the 1st Cavalry in Quang Nam province, several hundred Vietnamese had been given a twelve-hour warning to leave their homes so the huts could be burned. We'd heard reports that about seventy Vietcong had been in the area the night before. The Americans wanted to clear the village of civilians so that when fired upon, they could shoot back without killing any civilians.

After the soldiers set the flimsy houses on fire with torches, it began to rain, but the thatched roofs burned anyway. Women scurried around grabbing their possessions, meager bundles of clothes, family pictures, even some black lacquer coffins.

When a friendly GI tried to give a little girl a candy bar, the mother pushed the child's hand away, scowling at the American. The other soldiers were kicking down doors and knocking over big vats of rice. "No one has so much rice unless they're feeding the VC," one soldier remarked. Triumphantly, another soldier held up some khaki pants and shirt. "NVA!" he exulted.

"Not NVA," the interpreter said, shaking his head. "School uniform for children."

The old women were crying and calling out frantically to one another in high-pitched wails. Children in tattered clothes scrambled among the pigs and chickens. Standing by, taking notes but reluctant to use my camera, I felt a deep sympathy for the Vietnamese and a welling anger at the suffering of so many innocent people.

Suddenly, children gathered around me, their tiny hands grabbing at my fatigues. I doled out some lemon drops I had in my pockets. When a woman thrust her sickly baby at me, pleading desperately in words I did not understand, I assumed she thought I was a nurse. Unsure of what to do, I took the tiny child in my arms and begged the medics to care for it. They obliged.

While all this was going on, the battalion commander sat cross-legged like a swami in a sandbagged hootch, sipping coffee. As far as the eye could see, flames and barrel-shaped clouds of smoke filled the sky. The relentless rain added its gloomy cast.

"These people didn't believe us. We told them we were going to burn their village, that they should move to Que Son where they would be taken care of, but they didn't go. Why don't they understand that this is necessary?" he asked, gazing at the fires casting skittering red shadows in the dark sky. "We don't like to do things like this. I'm sure all my men regret that such things have to happen."

Then he shifted his weight and looked around the dimly lit room. "You know, I didn't even know the name of that village," he said. "I wasn't even curious about it."

While I preferred covering the U.S. infantry in the field, I also wrote a variety of other features, mostly for NANA, which paid $35 a story. The topics ranged from Vietcong women guerrillas to a sailor's life on the aircraft carrier USS *Intrepid;* a raid along the Cambodian border while defying gravity in an F-100 jet; and the quiet heroics of army nurses. I even did a piece on the poetry the GIs and the Vietnamese poured from their hearts.

American intelligence officers found this poem in a diary on a dead NVA soldier in the jungle:

> *How my hand trembled when I had to set a mine . . .*
> *And then I watched it do its work;*
> *Blasting human flesh and splattering a rain of blood . . .*
> *Whose blood, my mother?*
> *The blood of people like ourselves . . .*

I also discovered a new way of getting my stories into print—by doing "hometowners." If I met a GI with an interesting story while I was on a patrol or special mission, I'd write it up for his local paper. I reported on a Long Island sailor on the aircraft carrier *Bonhomme Richard* for the *Suffolk Sun.* I wrote about the sergeant who sang and danced in the mortar pits at Con Thien for the *Buffalo Evening News.* They were not big stories for major news organizations, but I always felt they were important to the servicemen, their loved ones at home, and the readers in the communities these men came from.

If I found myself in a serious firefight, after it was over I would try to get out on the first available chopper to the nearest press office in the rear and offer the story to the Associated Press. All reporters carried cameras, and photographs from a battle were another source of income. (Horst Faas, the legendary AP photo chief, gave me free Tri-X film with instructions to "shoot at f-8 and 250 and I will save you in the darkroom.")

In November 1967, I was the lone reporter on a significant action that took place in the Central Highlands. My exclusive AP photos of the men of the 173rd Airborne Brigade under fire on Hill 882 were reproduced on a full page of *Paris Match,* and the story made headlines.

The North Vietnamese had set up solidly fortified base camps in the dense hills near Cambodia. There were skirmishes every day for weeks on any one of the hundreds of knolls that dotted the ridges around Dak To, culminating on Thanksgiving Day in the infamous bloody battle for Hill 875. I had witnessed the fighting just days earlier on nearby Hill 882 when I choppered in with a resupply crew a few hours before the shooting began.

North Vietnamese snipers had tied themselves into the branches of some tall trees and were firing from everywhere. "Stay down!

Keep your heads down. They're all around us," shouted a para-trooper from A Company. Soldiers huddled behind any clump of bamboo roots or logs that would protect them.

A platoon headed by Lt. John Robinson of Orlando, Florida, had encountered a reinforced company of enemy troops. The fighting was at such close quarters, the men said NVA soldiers were hurling back grenades thrown by the Americans. While part of the company laid down a curtain of fire into the bamboo thickets, other men started to pull back with the wounded.

I crouched behind a tree in the middle of all this, trying to take photos of the frenzied scene. There was too much going on for me to feel afraid. I was an observer, a noncombatant, after all. I felt strangely detached, even protected, as if my journalist's mantle would save me.

Suddenly a rocket exploded in the middle of the chaos, tearing through the bunkers. Men all around, hit by the white hot shrapnel, lay bleeding and shrieking in pain.

"God, please don't scream," Spc. 4 Jerl Withers of Zanesville, Ohio, shouted, his eyes filling with tears. "It's boosting the goddamn North Vietnamese morale. Please don't scream."

He tried desperately to bandage the head of one of his seriously wounded buddies.

"Don't worry, man. You're going to be all right," he said. "You're going to be home soon, right? Can you hear me? Say something, man. Say something. Please God, please help."

I watched as Withers held his dying buddy in his arms. The moment was so intimate, so raw, so tender, it took my breath away. It was not the first time I had seen the unabashed love the men showed one another on the battlefield. Soldiers in Vietnam were not afraid to express their deepest emotions. They hugged each other and sobbed openly in the aftermath of a firefight.

"You cried when your buddies died. Yeah, we cried," a marine once told me. "It was tough. I mean, we were family. You felt the pain, but then you got all numb again. You had to move on."

Off to my right, a corpsman worked frantically on a soldier who had been wounded in the groin. His penis was exposed, and when he saw me, despite his pain and fear, he began fumbling with his clothes to cover himself up.

His embarrassment distressed me. I averted my eyes. I remem-

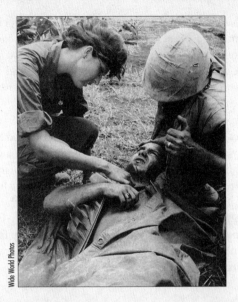

Wide World Photos

bered what one GI clutching his bloody leg in the muck and the mud of battle once said that hit me hard: "I don't want a woman to see me die this way."

I tried not to think of these things and focused on the fighting around me, straining to remember all I saw and heard. I scribbled furiously in my notebook, then focused my camera at the men crawling through the trees and firing their M-16s.

A young soldier nearby wrenched a grenade from his harness and lobbed it into the woods. "Damn motherfuckers," he shouted, then glanced at me. "Sorry, ma'am," he said with a grin.

Medics ran from one man to another, but there were too many needing aid. Everywhere I looked, someone was bleeding. I could no longer just watch without doing something to help.

I stuffed my camera in my pack and crawled over to a medic. "What can I do?" I asked. He shoved some pads of gauze in my hands and jerked his head in the direction of a group of wounded men huddled together. I fumbled with the bandages, trying to help a soldier with blood oozing through his shirt. Not knowing what to say, I asked, "Does it hurt?"

"Only when I breathe, ma'am," he replied. I didn't know whether to laugh or cry.

Later, back in Saigon, I was criticized by other reporters for deviating from my role as a reporter. One television correspondent taunted me, "Well, well, we heard you were playing Florence Nightingale at Dak To." I made no apologies. I could not imagine that there weren't other reporters who had helped out when the situation was desperate.

That night, as I lay on my clean, soft bed, a universe away from the misery of Dak To, terrifying visions of the wounded and the dead crowded my mind, but I steeled myself to push them away. In some ways, the stillness of my room was more frightening than the sounds of the jungle. Without the companionship of the men when I was out in the field, the sadness and loneliness I felt during those midnight hours in Saigon was wrenching, as if I had lost every friend I ever had. I had no one I could turn to and talk to about my fear and confusion. I could not make sense of this war, nor did I know why I still wanted to stay.

On January 30, 1968, the war took an unexpected turn. Known as the Tet offensive, this massive series of attacks by the North Vietnamese and Vietcong conducted during the traditional January holidays throughout South Vietnam caught the American military off guard. Several Vietcong sappers actually broke into the grounds of the United States embassy in Saigon before being killed.

As usual, much of the military action in Vietnam was to the north in I Corps, where the marines were stationed. I was soon drawn back to Khe Sanh, which had served as headquarters for Captain Bynum's ill-fated Lima Company in 1967. This dusty red-clay outpost was located a few miles south of the DMZ on a high plateau, ringed with lush hills that were shrouded in clouds of fog and mist during the monsoons.

Khe Sanh had leaped back into international prominence in late January when the NVA began the seventy-seven-day siege of the base with incessant shelling of the five thousand marines stationed there. Daily, hundreds of rounds from rockets and artillery entrenched in the Co Roc mountains in Laos, just ten miles away, pounded the base. There were reports that more than forty thousand enemy troops had massed in the area, and rumors swirled of an imminent NVA assault. The beleaguered marines hunkered down in their bunkers and waited.

I had secured a new assignment from WOR Radio of New York to interview the men of Khe Sanh from their listening area. I began looking for a ride into the base. It wasn't easy.

Because Khe Sanh was such a big story and the logistics of coming and going were fraught with so much risk and danger—smoldering carcasses of downed planes and helicopters lined the runway—the marines had instituted a quota system for reporters. No more than ten journalists were permitted to be at the base at any one time. Most of those slots were already assigned to the wire services and the TV networks.

Realizing that there would be a long wait for an extra seat on a transport plane, I resorted to my standard operating procedure in Vietnam: I lingered around the airstrip, looking for an empty chopper with blades whirring. One of the few advantages (or disadvantages) a women reporter had in Vietnam was high visibility. While male journalists in fatigues were indistinguishable from the masses of soldiers, a woman—even a scruffy one in combat gear—was noticed. More than once, the young hotshot helicopter pilots did not hesitate to oblige a "round-eye" American woman with a free ride to some forward firebase, even without official authorization. No one worried about getting in trouble. "What are they going to do?" asked one pilot. "Send me to Vietnam?"

Amazingly, I found a Chinook helicopter with space available heading for Khe Sanh.

I arrived on March 7, 1968, and reported to the information officer. He was furious that I had leapfrogged the waiting list of correspondents and somehow wangled my way to the base. Everyone was still badly shaken from the previous day's crash of a C-123 transport plane. All forty-seven passengers had been killed, including *Newsweek* photographer Robert Ellison.

"Are you the woman reporter they call Sam?" the press liaison growled. (Indeed, the unwanted nickname had stuck and followed me all over Vietnam.)

I was the last thing he wanted to see. Nevertheless, he gave me a flak jacket and helmet, and soon I was scouting the hundreds of bunkers to line up interviews with the dug-in marines.

The previous days had been relatively quiet, and there was a general feeling that perhaps the siege was ending. The monsoon, with its heavy rain and mists, was nearing an end. Without the cover of bad weather, the enemy was becoming more visible and airlifts might be less dangerous.

Several marines even started a pickup game of basketball. Rock-and-roll music blasted from the bunkers. A hand-lettered sign on a pole above one of the hootches read: "Home is where you dig it." The morale of the troops was more upbeat than it had been in weeks.

When darkness set in, we sat on a bunker and watched air strikes on the ridgeline, just a few thousand feet away. The men talked about the NVA, whom they referred to as "our neighbors." They laughed about some of the tricks the enemy used to make them nervous, such as pounding a drum so it sounded like the parting shot of a mortar.

"Some nights you can hear the NVA digging their tunnels, just coming closer and closer to the base perimeter," said one young marine. "Sometimes you can even see their tiny lights, bobbing up and down in the distance. It's spooky, man."

I spent the night in one of the bunkers, which had been constructed of logs, sand-filled ammunition boxes, metal scraps stripped off sections of the runway, and rows of sandbags. I felt safely sheltered. In fact, I worried more about the disgusting rats that had overwhelmed the base than an NVA attack.

The next morning, the fog slowly began to roll away and finally a crack of blue sky pierced the clouds. The sun felt good on our faces as we smoked our cigarettes and gulped steaming cups of strong coffee. Some marines, wearing only flak jackets against their bare chests, were washing their grubby uniforms in anticipation of a few hours of sunshine when their clothes could dry.

With my tape recorder ready, I began a search for New Yorkers to interview. I wore my flak jacket but dispensed with the helmet, as did most of the men around me. "Damn Yankees!" a southerner shouted when I asked who might be from New York. At last a small group of hometown boys was rounded up and we settled down on a pile of crates to talk.

Just as I flipped the on button of the tape recorder, the unmistakable high-pitched whistling sound of an incoming artillery round shattered the air. Frantic voices all over the base shouted, "Incoming!" The first shell flew over my head with a *whoosh* and landed about twenty yards somewhere off to my left.

Someone grabbed my arm and we started running to the nearest bunker. Another round exploded nearby; it was even closer than the first. Then I heard a clang—as if someone were throwing horseshoes that hit the target. Suddenly, I was knocked to the ground. I began stumbling toward a nearby bunker and then crawled the last few yards on my hands and knees until I collapsed inside the shelter.

"I've been hit . . . I've been hit," I heard my own voice call out. (Years later, I would sometimes replay the tape and listen to those startled cries.)

The bunker was as dark as a cave until someone lit a candle. Gasps and moans and sounds of clothing being shredded to locate wounds filled the stifling air. "Boy, this is some bad shit," someone exclaimed.

I knew something had happened to my legs because they were numb. When I touched my pants, my fingers felt sticky. It was blood. Oh, my God, I panicked. I'll never walk again. My hands flew to my face. My skin was dry, caked with dirt, and covered with little bumps the size of grains of rice. Apparently the high velocity of the exploding shells had spewed tiny fragments of metal, dirt, and pebbles into my cheeks.

Meanwhile, the bombardment continued with intermittent blasts. Four of us "damn Yankees" had been wounded by the incoming round. Lt. William Gay of Sunnyside, Queens, was badly hurt as chunks of shrapnel tore through his body. (Gay would have to spend six months in a Guam hospital to recover.) The shelling seemed to go on forever as we waited to be evacuated.

Finally, the pounding stopped and several marines arrived to load us on a small motorized flatcar. The last thing I saw of the 3rd Engineer Battalion was a group of very sad faces. I wondered if they thought I was seriously wounded. In any case, I smiled and waved to put on a brave front.

We were transferred through the base to Charlie Med, the central station for casualties. En route, someone placed a helmet over my face to protect me from more incoming. I caught a glimpse of a red scapular of the Sacred Heart taped inside. As a devout Catholic, I took this as a good sign.

I had no idea of the extent of my wounds. Nor did I know how many marines throughout the base had also been wounded during the morning attack. The recurring argument against allowing women in combat was that they would be a distraction. As we neared Charlie Med, I worried that my presence would be disruptive, that I would be nothing but trouble. The latent insecurity about being a woman in a war zone returned.

My arrival at the medical bunker did indeed cause a stir.

Upon learning that a woman had been injured, the staff hastily ordered the corpsmen to hang up some blankets to give me a modicum of privacy. But no one seemed quite sure what to do next.

Normally when a soldier is wounded, he is stripped of all his clothes to ascertain there are no hidden pieces of shrapnel that could cause complications. Even the tiniest metal fragment in the armpit could prove to be fatal. Whether the three doctors in the Charlie Med bunker, Ed Feldman*, James Finnegan, and Don Magilligan, were being chivalrous or could not think of a procedure to follow for their first female casualty, I never knew. Magilligan simply asked me, "Where do you think you've been hit?"

"My legs, my face, it's hard to tell," I said.

And then a squeaky voice somewhere from the back of the room piped up, "There's blood on the seat of her pants, sir."

The doctors told me to roll over and pull down my pants. A jagged piece of shrapnel about the size of a peach pit from a 152mm artillery shell, courtesy of the North Vietnamese, had lodged just a fraction of an inch from my spine. I was unbelievably lucky, for had it been any closer, I might have been seriously disabled. For now, I was merely mortified. A dozen eyes peered down at the wound.

"Is it below my bikini line?" I joked. The doctor laughed and assured me it was. As he removed the metal chunk and cleaned the wound, I asked, "Tell me, honestly, does my bottom look that much different from the hundreds of others you've seen in here?" trying to bring some pathetic humor to this embarrassing situation. In spite of myself, I was miffed when he replied, "Well, to be honest, not really."

It was not long before I was rushed by stretcher with the other wounded to the nearby runway and quickly loaded onto a medevac helicopter. Arriving and departing by aircraft was always dangerous at Khe Sanh since the NVA had bracketed their mortars and artillery to hit the landing area whenever they saw planes or choppers. However, not a round fell as my ride lifted off into the sky.

---

* But Lt. Feldman had courage when it mattered. Among his many heroic acts, in January 1967, operating by flashlight during a heavy enemy attack, he removed a live mortar fuse from the stomach of a wounded marine.

Once in the air, I could hear the familiar comforting clatter of the helicopter blades as we headed toward Dong Ha, the marine rear base about forty miles away. Perhaps I was still in shock, but I felt eerily calm.

After arriving in Dong Ha, we were transferred to a C-130 transport plane for the trip to the main hospital in Da Nang. The big aircraft was specially equipped to carry the wounded. Each stretcher was stacked one above another in two or three rows in the belly of the plane while troops in full combat gear were crammed in back. An air force nurse moved between the litters, checking IVs and tending the grievously wounded. Until my long hair spilled over the end of the stretcher, I was indistinguishable from the other casualties. But then, I could see some of the marine passengers nudge one another and whisper, "Hey, it's a girl."

Yet no one spoke to me. I squeezed my eyes shut and prayed, Oh dear God, please let everything be all right. I had no idea where I would end up or what would happen to me. I felt terribly lonely.

Meanwhile, back at Khe Sanh, there was a young conscientious objector named Jonathan Spicer, who had helped carry my stretcher to the waiting chopper. Spicer, who was much loved and extremely brave, was not very tall. He could never find a suitable size combat boot for his smallish feet. When Spicer came across my discarded size-nine boots, he was thrilled to put them on. He was wearing them later that day as he raced with his stretcher crew through enemy fire to load some wounded marines onto the helicopter. Just then, a piece of shrapnel from an incoming round pierced his heart. The Charlie Med doctors worked frantically to save him. Miraculously, he was still breathing when he was medevacked. But a week later, in a hospital in Japan, he died.

The story of "the little Marine and his new boots," written by John Randolph of the *Los Angeles Times,* was reprinted throughout the United States. (When the local paper in New Rochelle called my parents with news of my wounding, after the initial shock, all my distraught mother could say was, "I told her not to go to Vietnam.")

But I knew nothing of Spicer, the hero, at that time. I was in the Da Nang hospital, being shunted from room to room on a gurney. No one paid attention to me there, and since my wounds were not life-threatening, I didn't dare ask for help. Nearly ten hours had passed since I was injured, and I was still in my bloody fatigues. Fingering my face, I could feel the roughness. Yet I certainly did not want a mirror to see what I looked like.

At one point, a warrant officer with beer can in hand wandered by. "Hey, what happened to you?" he asked in amazement.

"Oh, just some incoming at Khe Sanh," I answered nonchalantly.

Peering down at my face, he shook his head. "Well, babe, your days in showbiz are over."

He thought I was an entertainer, and maybe I should have been flattered, but his comment undid me. After all, I was a girl lying there alone and hurt on the most vulnerable day of my life. In spite of myself, I began to cry—for the first time since I had come to Vietnam more than a year ago.

Even during the months of covering battles and witnessing the carnage of war, I had avoided tears. I had convinced myself that if I broke down, it would prove that women didn't belong in war. Now, however, I had reached the limit of my emotions. I cried and wished desperately that there were someone who would hold my hand, assure me that everything would be all right. I remembered an army nurse had once told me that mortally wounded soldiers in their last anguished moments would often cry out for their mothers. Though far from death, I too ached for the comfort only a mother could provide. The repressed sadness and weariness that had filled my soul for the last year in Vietnam suddenly surfaced in a painful flow of vivid memories. I thought of all the men I had seen die the loneliest and ugliest of deaths in muddy trenches or putrid jungles. It was all such a terrible waste.

At the same time, I indulged my self-pity with visions of a grotesquely scarred face that would serve as a perpetual reminder of my youthful arrogance in a war zone.

But once again, I was lucky. The only plastic surgeon in I Corps, Commander Martin Fackler, finally showed up at the end of that long day, took a look at my ravaged skin, and said, "Now, if you were a marine, I'd just take a Brillo pad and scrub that stuff out of your face." But instead he worked on me for an hour, painstakingly picking out each bit of dirt and minute shard of lead and carefully sewing up my face.

The shrapnel pieces in my legs, however, were deemed too deep in the muscles to bother removing. I stayed almost a week in the hospital getting my strength back and pondering my strange fate. I wondered why I had spent so much time going out on patrols with the infantry. As much as I wanted to be a respected war correspondent, perhaps what I really wanted was to experience what one writer called "the terrible ecstasy of war" and its horrific seduction.

It was as if war had a subliminal pull on my psyche. Having been too young to remember our World War II escapades, the air raids and bombings, I seemed inexorably drawn to be on the front lines, to see and feel the drama of the battlefield. And then again, hadn't my life been saved by a soldier? Even my first movie-star crush was a war hero—Audie Murphy. (When I saw *To Hell and Back* at age twelve, I was so captivated, I launched one of his first fan clubs in America, for which the highly decorated World War II veteran thanked me with a handwritten letter.)

Sometimes I wondered if perhaps I even wanted to *be* a soldier. Once on the plains of Bong Son, after a firefight when the men were gathering the weapons of the dead and wounded, I picked up an M-79 grenade launcher that was lying behind a palm tree. A young private offered to take it from me, but I waved him away. I wanted to know what it felt like to walk through the rice paddies bearing arms . . . like a soldier.

The gun felt heavy in my hands, but not uncomfortable. I knew about guns, how to load them, how to shoot them. I had been a hunter once, had tracked cape buffalo with my .375 Magnum for days through the bush in Tanzania.

The men eyed me strangely, and I snapped back to my senses. This was not Africa. The reality that if the shooting started I might have to fire the weapon and kill someone suddenly frightened me. That was not my job. I quickly gave the gun away.

But there was more to war than killing and death. The way men bonded in war fascinated me. The comradeship, the sharing of these intense moments under fire, was unlike any other human experience. Nothing seemed to bring men together to care for one another like facing almost certain annihilation: the danger, the risk, the intoxicating adrenaline surge of battle; walking up to the edge and cheating death. For so many men, war seemed to hold an irresistible attraction.

Women have no such cataclysmic experience in their lives. There is childbirth, of course. Women who go through pregnancies and the delivery room together form close, sometimes lasting, friendships.

But giving birth was about creation, life, joy, nothing at all like the hideous reality of battle, the finality of death.

"Well, she got what she was looking for," a colonel in the press office had commented upon hearing that I had been hit.

Would he have said that about a male reporter? I wondered.

After leaving the hospital, I continued to report on the war, even returning to Khe Sanh to cover Operation Pegasus with the 1st Air Cavalry Division.

But now, things were different. When we were mortared, suddenly I found myself trembling. Lying flat on the ground, clawing the dirt, I was paralyzed with fear. I couldn't take pictures. I couldn't take notes. Getting wounded had jolted me to the inescapable truth that I was just as vulnerable as any of the thousands of other GIs who were casualties of this war.

It was time for me to leave. But it was not easy to disengage. I knew I could not stay forever, but where could I go? I could not see myself in an orderly world with predictable highs and lows. I had become addicted to the surreal contrasts of a journalist's life in Vietnam—one day to be caught in a firefight in a rice paddy, the next to interview a navy lifeguard surfing at China Beach. And all the while knowing I was a witness to such an important part of my country's—and my generation's—history. What story could possibly involve me so profoundly again? How could a normal life hold my interest after all this? Further complicating everything, shortly after being wounded, I fell in love with a fellow journalist. He was very courageous and well respected. I had long admired him for his aggressive combat coverage. Suddenly, life in this alien world had a new meaning, and for a while, at least, my loneliness was lifted. The romance, born in the highly charged atmosphere of war, with nights spent in the sultry languor of Saigon, was probably doomed from the start but lasted off and on for many years.

In November 1968, I left Vietnam. Still longing for adventure, I decided to go back to Lithuania via the Trans-Siberian Express. I caught a boat in Yokohama for Vladivostok, where I boarded the dreary, lumbering train. For two weeks I traversed the vast, frozen Soviet countryside all the way to my homeland, where my long journey to a war of my own began.

When I returned to the States, my first months were difficult. Although passionate about seeing an end to the war, I could never bring myself to join the protest movement. I was deeply offended by the chants of demonstrators cursing American servicemen. My feeling of patriotism was simply too strong to march against my own country.

I locked away my Vietnam memories with a vengeance, not just the boxes of photographs, letters, and carbons of stories, but my nightmare images of firefights and the battlefield dead and wounded and the insanity of it all. Vietnam was a specter from my lost youth, a bizarre, singular event that seemed to bear no relation to where I went afterward in my life.

Yet as time passed, there was one memory of Vietnam that would never go away—Capt. Frank Bynum and Lima Company. Occasionally, when invited to speak publicly about my Vietnam experiences, I'd recount the story of that patrol as an example of my complex feelings about being a woman in a war.

If other Americans from all walks of life were enduring a collective guilt for what their country had done in Vietnam, my own private remorse was still hopelessly locked in the sad memory of that colorful and brave marine commander.

I stayed in journalism, eventually married and raised a family. But Vietnam had a powerful, twisted hold on my heart. In 1995, with a group of reporters, I went back to that country, peaceful now and even more beautiful than I remembered. It was a shock, though, to see the red-and-gold-star Communist flag flying over the Rex Hotel in Saigon.

I revisited the sites of some of the battles I had written about— Con Thien and Khe Sanh, now deserted, its red clay field ringed with coffee trees. There was nothing left of the place where more than two hundred Americans had died and two thousand had been wounded along with untold Vietnamese casualties. Only the eternal distant hills, the scene of so much fighting, looked familiar—the same hills that I had climbed with the men of Lima.

Back home in the States, years later, one frantic night I became obsessed about the fate of the men I had interviewed so long ago. Hoping they had survived the war, I wanted so badly to find them, reconnect, talk to them. I went down to the basement, where I kept the war in worn cardboard boxes, and found my old files and notebooks. They still smelled of Vietnam, a mix of smoke, piss, sweat. I rummaged through all my old photographs—hundreds of black-and-white prints of soldiers jumping out of choppers, patrolling rice paddies, firing machine guns. A picture of marines filling sandbags in Khe Sanh inspired me to try to locate the doctors of Charlie Med, and amazingly I did. Ed Feldman was now a gynecologist in California, Finnegan a surgeon in Philadelphia. Sadly, Magilligan had died from cancer in 1989.

Then, to my surprise, I discovered a picture of Captain Bynum. He was crossing that leech-filled stream, his shillelagh in his hand. It occurred to me that it may have been the last picture ever taken of him.

Suddenly, I realized I had to find out what happened on that patrol. Researching the 3/26 Marines via the Internet, I located a Lima Company veteran, Anthony Benedetto, who was twenty years old and a lance corporal in June 1967 when I had joined the patrol. I called him at his home in New Jersey.

He remembered me. "Yeah, we were all down by the river. You were splashing water on your head. We thought you were crazy to be out there with us," he said.

I laughed. We reminisced a bit about the awful heat, the elephant grass, the grueling hike, and then, afraid of what I would hear, I finally asked, "Can you tell me how Captain Bynum died?"

"We were back at Khe Sanh when we got the call that India Company was in big trouble on Hill 689. Bynum volunteered us to go right back out again. We weren't too happy, but we got in the choppers and—"

"You mean Bynum was not killed on our patrol?" I was stunned.

"No, ma'am."

Then Benedetto gave me the details. On June 27, three days after I left, Bynum and his men returned to their base at Khe Sanh. When the call came just hours later for a relief company to assist the men of India, who were under heavy shelling and sniper fire, Bynum ordered his troops to head out. In the ensuing battle, Bynum was shot. Even with a sucking chest wound, he continued fighting and giving orders. One of his men crawled through a mined area to rescue Bynum, but it was too late. He was dead.

I put down the phone. I had recounted the story of this patrol and my lingering doubts many times, and now, I could hardly believe it. At last I knew the truth.

But little else about Vietnam is that clear. The tangled memories of war come and go like the strange movements of that pea-size piece of shrapnel under the skin of my ankle. Some days it is so close to the surface that it hurts to the touch. Other times it recedes so deep into the tissue of my body, I hardly know it is there.

To this day, Vietnam taunts, haunts, and still mystifies me.

Edith Lederer

My First War

In my recurring dream of Vietnam, I am once again an ambitious young reporter, cocky but a little frightened, embarking on the greatest adventure of my life.

In the kaleidoscope that usually unfolds, I walk along an overgrown path, trying to find a family whose hut had been destroyed in a rocket attack. Sweating in the steamy Southeast Asian heat, I worry about straying off the road and stepping on a booby trap. The distant sound of gunfire grows closer, and AP photographer Nick Ut pushes me into a smelly ditch running alongside the path. We both crouch—I holding my notebook high in the air and he his cameras.

The sound of exploding artillery fades and the dream fast-forwards to Saigon, where I am racing into my apartment to change after finishing a story. Two long dresses hang ready on a hook in the bedroom, one fuchsia and one yellow, both perfectly ironed. I choose the yellow one.

In the next frames, I am in a cyclo heading to a diplomatic dinner given by my close friends Joe and Nancy Bennett. He is number three at the U.S. embassy, and their spacious house has a pool and a perfectly manicured lawn where all the guests are having drinks. As usual, I am late.

EDITH LEDERER, an award-winning reporter for the Associated Press, covered wars and political upheavals around the world for twenty-five years before returning to New York in 1998 to be the AP's chief correspondent at the United Nations.

The liquor and wine flow. The Vietnamese and Chinese food is sumptuous. After dinner, everyone returns to the garden, where music is playing, and I dance under the stars, which sparkle in the clear night sky, imbibing the scent of jasmine.

My date for the evening is a fellow journalist, and the scene shifts to one of the media's favorite haunts, the rooftop bar of the Miramar Hotel. It's raucous and noisy, aswirl with bar girls. The *mama-san* greets me with a kiss. We joke and drink too much. Just before curfew, my date drops me off at my apartment and I collapse in a deep sleep.

An explosion that sounds like a bomb going through the roof sends me bolting from bed, and that's how the dream usually ends, because the noise wakes me up.

Nearly thirty years after leaving Vietnam, I still have this dream, though not as often as when I first left Saigon. It is a microcosm of my life there. Today, as then, it reminds me of those mad, crazy, sometimes dangerous days that I lived with an intensity only occasionally matched in the wars I went on to cover.

Vietnam—in my dreams and in reality—was a place to work hard, play hard, and try not to worry about tomorrow.

Ten years ago, I discovered that I got there in a way I never suspected.

In 1971, a time of great turmoil in America, I was working for AP in San Francisco, covering antiwar protests, student unrest, and racial turmoil. An adventurer at heart, I decided to use a long vacation to travel around the world for the first time and convinced my good friend Nancy Goebner, a teacher, to come along.

Pan Am had the best deal, allowing stops everywhere it went—including Saigon. I wanted to see the war that had torn the fabric of America, and Nancy agreed. So we put Vietnam on our itinerary and never told our parents.

When we flew into Saigon, warplanes were revving their engines. Jeeps and soldiers were everywhere. The city was a jumble of noise and color, impossible to fully absorb. Thousands of motorbikes belched acrid exhaust. Lithe girls in flowing tunics of every shade brightened the drabness of France's onetime "Pearl of the Orient."

AP's bureau chief Richard Pyle and the rest of the AP staff became our instant guides. We saw the "five o'clock follies," the daily U.S. military briefing, and heard tough questions get evasive answers.

In an unexpected bonus, AP arranged for us to get a firsthand glimpse of the war.

On a U.S. Army helicopter reconnaissance mission over the Mekong Delta, we donned helmets for the first time and peered through the window at wisps of smoke from shelling in the tropical fields below. It seemed unreal from 1,500 feet—until the soldier seated in the open doorway shifted, training his M-60 machine gun on something he had spotted in the fast-changing landscape. The fighting was too far away for him to open fire, but the war was down there, somewhere.

Back home, I told everyone about being a war tourist and returned to work. For me, that meant covering more antiwar protests and the trial of black activist Angela Davis, who was acquitted in June 1972 of supplying guns for a deadly Black Panther courtroom shootout.

One day in early September, AP president Wes Gallagher, who was not known for small talk, called me and asked one question: Did I want to go to Vietnam for six months?

My initial reaction was shock.

I had joined AP in March 1966, and every year I had received a form asking what my ambition was. Every year I had written "foreign correspondent," though I must confess I wasn't sure I had ever included "war correspondent" in that definition.

But that wasn't the shock. What astounded me was that AP, which had been so fearful of sending American women overseas, let alone to war, was suddenly changing gears.

The foreign editor at the time, Ben Bassett, refused to let women work on the foreign desk—and that was a prerequisite for going abroad. He didn't think women could stand up to the demands of the world's backwaters and battle zones. But Gallagher's offer meant that I would bypass the foreign desk and go straight to Saigon.

Kelly Smith, a glamorous and talented reporter, had done a four-month special assignment in 1967, but I would be the first woman assigned full-time to AP's Saigon bureau.

I asked Gallagher for a few days to talk to my family, even though I knew my answer would be yes.

My sister, Alice, was living in Israel, another hot spot, and I knew my family would be upset if I went to an even more dangerous place. In a letter to my parents and my great-aunt Tillie, who helped raise me, I tried to answer their main fear—that I might die in a war that they and most Americans detested. I wrote in part:

> Perhaps the thing that is most difficult to explain to a person outside the news business is the challenge of covering a big story.
>
> There's almost a love-hate relationship about it, a feeling that often leaves you with a bottomless pit in your stomach. You are, in effect, writing history and it is through your eyes that millions of people all over the world will see a particular event. There is little doubt that the responsibility is awesome.
>
> But despite the responsibility and the accompanying nerves and anguish, this is what most reporters live for: the chance to be there to cover that unforgettable moment of history.

After sending the letter, I called Gallagher and asked when he wanted me in Vietnam. He said mid-October.

When I remember those hectic weeks before leaving San Francisco, I recall how panicked I was. I was an expert on the antiwar movement, but I knew nothing about combat.

While covering a visit of then–First Lady Pat Nixon to Moffett Field Naval Air Station, near San Francisco, I mentioned to the base commander, a Vietnam veteran, that I was going to Saigon. He asked what I knew about weapons, booby traps, and fighter aircraft.

"Nothing," I replied.

He invited me back for a day of briefings, a tour of the base's collection of innocent-looking devices designed to maim and kill, and a lesson on how to shoot both a .38-caliber and a .45-caliber pistol.

"You never know when you might have to shoot in self-defense, so you ought to know how to use a gun," the commander said.

I am five feet one inch tall and have child-size hands, but the sergeant on the firing range assured me that this was no barrier. There were plenty of child soldiers in the world. He was right. By late afternoon, I was hitting the target with both pistols (holding the .45-caliber with both hands).

I left the base feeling a little bit better prepared to cover combat.

But Gallagher, who had been a top frontline correspondent during World War II, deflated that prospect. In a letter, he made clear that as far as he and Pyle were concerned, I wasn't going anywhere near the fighting.

"Neither he nor I want you popping in and out of the fronts just to prove you can do everything that one of our veteran war correspondents can do. You are being sent there to do a job on special coverage, not to go into any combat zones. You are too valuable," Gallagher wrote.

It was clear that AP's underlying fears about women war correspondents hadn't gone away. So with Gallagher's marching orders, I left San Francisco—nervous, exhilarated, a little frightened, but above all determined to prove that I was as good as AP's male war correspondents.

I was twenty-nine years old, embarking on what I was certain would be the most eventful chapter of my life, and I wanted to remember my thoughts and experiences. So I decided to keep a diary for the first time since I was a child.

Too excited to sleep on the long Pan Am flight to Asia, I ended up at the bar (yes, there were bars on those early jumbo jets!), talking to a soldier, a pilot, and a U.S. government official. When I told them I was a reporter, they all blamed the press for turning Americans against the war. I argued that the press corps in Vietnam was reporting what was really happening—not just parroting the military's line—but I didn't win.

On October 20, 1972, I finally arrived in Saigon with 57 kilos (125 pounds) of baggage, wearing blue bedroom slippers (because I had tripped getting off the bus to board the plane, breaking a heel on my shoe). War or no war, Saigon was a big city. I'd worn a nice dress and had my hair done because I wanted to look good and impress my colleagues. Slippered feet weren't part of the image I'd had in mind, but nobody noticed.

After dumping my luggage at the Caravelle Hotel and putting on shoes, I headed across the street to report for work. The AP bureau on the fourth floor of the Eden Building—an aging French colonial edifice with offices, apartments, and shops facing Saigon's main square—was a gathering place for the media, and it was crowded. I remember looking at the portraits of the four AP photographers killed during the war as I walked in the door, a reminder of the price paid to tell the Vietnam story.

When I look back on what turned out to be an eight-month assignment, I realize how fortunate I was to be in Vietnam before, during, and after the pullout of the last American combat troops, and to have had the opportunity to write a small part of history.

I had arrived in Vietnam at almost the same moment as Henry Kissinger, then the national security adviser to President Richard Nixon. He had come from the Paris peace talks, fueling speculation that the United States and the North Vietnamese had reached a cease-fire agreement.

Kissinger left on October 23, still tight-lipped. The press corps started a peace pool anyway at 2,000 piastres (U.S. $4.50) a shot to guess the date of a permanent cease-fire. Not having a clue, I picked a date anyway.

UPI had a cease-fire being declared that day, and my male colleagues immediately began working their contacts to find out whether it was true. They discovered the deal hadn't been clinched. It was frustrating not being able to help, but watching them operate made me realize what a top-notch team I had joined. I was proud— and I must admit a little awed—to be the first female member.

There was Richard Pyle, dark-haired, bearded, passionate about the story, a perfectionist about reporting it right, and a superb editor who always backed his staff; George Esper, intense, curly-haired, always in motion, an acknowledged expert on using Vietnam's complicated phone system who never gave up trying to get a story and had a heart of gold; Richard Blystone, a rumpled ex-pilot with a mad sense of humor and a well-deserved reputation as the thinking man's thinking man; South African Holger Jensen, who looked like a Viking prince and was funny, generous, and a very good journalist; and Denis Neeld, a slightly balding, quick-witted British journalist regarded as the "ultimate" foreign correspondent.

The reason for Kissinger's mission quickly became apparent. He had negotiated a secret peace deal, but South Vietnam's president went on television to denounce it. Hanoi Radio then revealed the details and accused the Nixon administration of sabotaging the agreement.

With Nixon committed to ending the war if he was reelected, Kissinger held a news conference in Washington on October 26 while most of Vietnam slept, and declared: "We believe that peace is at hand. We believe that an agreement is in sight."

I woke up the following morning listening to a broadcast of Kissinger's words. During the night, I'd had the strangest dream that something big was going to happen. Elated, I kept thinking that I might cover the end of the Vietnam War.

I raced to the office, where Pyle already had a list of peace-related stories. I was assigned one on a family hit by war. Our office secretary, Tran Mong Tu, who had lost her husband in the war, knew a woman who had lost three sons. A photographer, an interpreter, and I piled into two taxis and headed to her nearby village.

Vo Thi Hai, emaciated, with sad eyes, and in desperate need of new clothes, lived in a one-room shack with five young children. The walls had rotted, and the roof rested precariously on the walls of the three adjoining shacks. It was as bad as some of the hovels I'd seen in India on my round-the-world trip.

Her husband was dead, and she had no adult sons to support her, so finding money to buy food was a constant struggle. Every night, she burned three sticks of incense on a family altar, one for each lost son. As she sat in the intense heat, recounting how each had been killed in battle, she insisted on cooling us with a paper fan. I felt uncomfortable, like some kind of colonial mistress.

Hai told me peace would make other mothers happy because their sons wouldn't die. But her sons wouldn't be coming home. "For me, life will just go on," she said. I gave her some money to make that day, at least, a little more bearable.

In those early days, I did lots of feature stories while my colleagues focused on cease-fire rumors. The American Forces Vietnam Network, better known as AFVN, had launched a campaign to get out the GI vote in the November 7 U.S. presidential election. The tourism minister already had plans for a postwar tourist paradise, including a Saigon-style Disneyland and fishing expeditions to B-52 bomb craters! Even then it sounded like wishful dreaming.

I also explored the city, starting on the verandah of the Continental Hotel, better known as the "Continental Shelf." It was the place where anything could be bought or sold. In my first five minutes there, a dozen Vietnamese, young and old, tried to peddle junk or get me to make a donation to something. Several were children, one with twisted legs, another with only one hand—the tragic human face of the war. A GI I started talking to took me to the black market, where he bought birdseed and fish food. The volume and quality of goods was amazing, everything from booze, canned goods, clothes, and appliances to monkeys, roosters, and snakes.

At work, I watched my colleagues operate and asked lots of questions. I realized that I had arrived at a critical time for AP's Saigon bureau. All my colleagues were combat veterans and still in muddy-boots mode, covering a war it seemed would never end. They weren't fully ready to shift gears to cover a possible cease-fire and an end to hostilities. I was. So I made appointments to meet South Vietnamese ministers, U.S. government officials, and foreign diplomats, and I accepted every party invitation to build up my own contacts.

Pyle liked my suggestion of going to an aircraft carrier to find out what American pilots and sailors thought about Kissinger's peace prediction. On Halloween, I flew to Da Nang and then to the USS *America* on a small plane. After a memorable short, sharp landing on the carrier deck in fifty-mile-an-hour winds that left my stomach in my mouth, AP photographer Neal Ulevich and I were welcomed by the executive officer and escorted down nine flights of stairs.

In his quarters, I was told I had to sleep in the isolation ward of the hospital, with a guard posted outside—for my own safety! Unlike today, at that time women did not serve on warships. It had been a struggle to get the navy to allow female war correspondents to spend the night on a ship. But I still couldn't believe the navy was so un-trusting of its sailors.

The following day, I interviewed several pilots in the room where they prepared for combat missions and relaxed afterward. Still hanging in the room from the previous night's Halloween party were two dangling skeletons—a woman with two big balloons for boobs and a man with two small balloons from his crotch. A calendar on the wall, sent by the pilots' wives, was also pretty raunchy for the time. The squadron commander almost had a stroke when he realized what I'd seen. I laughed it off and listened to the pilots speak of their hopes for peace—and the increased danger they faced because the North Vietnamese were firing every weapon they had, apparently believing there would be a settlement soon.

"All we're interested in is getting the job done, ending the war," said Maj. Lee "Bear" Lasseter, an F-4 Phantom marine pilot from Lake Wales, Florida, who had shot down a North Vietnamese MiG fighter earlier in the year. But "the rumors have got to affect people a little bit. You don't want to be the last one shot down."

These guys appeared so tough and so macho on the surface. But I was certain that underneath, this was the wish of every single squadron member. When I left, I hoped they would all make it.

Chick Harrity

Back in Saigon, I was again caught up in peace frenzy, the final days of the election campaign between Nixon and Democratic senator George McGovern and a social whirl that never stopped.

By election day, I had been in Saigon for less than three weeks, more hotly pursued by men—single, married, young, and old—than I'd ever been in my life.

I'd even been taken for a prostitute one day on the Continental Shelf. Perhaps I shouldn't have been so surprised. At one dinner, two American men—one working for the government, one a contractor—discussed the newswomen in Vietnam entirely in terms of whom they slept with or didn't. I kept interrupting, trying to make the point that some talented and courageous women reporters and photographers had produced memorable stories and photos, but it didn't seem to register.

One of the first single women I met was Lucy Guin, who was attractive and savvy and helped run the USO, the GIs' home away from home. She gave me a piece of advice I never forgot: "Don't expect that any relationship you have in Vietnam will ever translate into the real world."

I had already been through one passionate fling with a journalist who had come to Saigon. When he left suddenly, I wrote a rare poem.

Rereading it after nearly thirty years, I realize it revealed a lot of my anxieties about being in Vietnam, even though I hadn't yet been anywhere near combat. It said:

Waiting for tomorrow's yesterday,
For the phantom kiss of a mystery man who
touched and ran.

Was it real? The midnight melding
of two lonely forms,
catalyzing the inertia of solitude into
the protoplasm of life.

For those hours, there was no war.
Just an all-consuming peace that flooded
out the terror of death,
The fear of oneness against an onslaught of
multitudes.

I watch your half-filled glass,
Wondering where the lips are that only
yesterday gulped its searing brandy,
Where the soul is that shattered the
nonchalant phoniness of independence.

And I wait.
For tomorrow must come.

Tomorrow never came in Saigon, and when we met in Europe after I left Vietnam, Lucy's admonition proved to be absolutely right.

It was a memorable affair—and remains so.

My schizophrenic lifestyle went on, long days of work followed by nights of socializing with friends and other men. But I was never moved to write another poem.

After Nixon trounced McGovern, the cease-fire waiting game resumed: When would the president keep his promise to bring the American GIs home?

With virtually the entire media focused on the date of a U.S. pullout, I decided to focus on some of the war's forgotten victims.

During my six years as a reporter, I had covered murders and seen plenty of dead bodies, but coming face-to-face with Vietnamese kids and adults in the prime of life who would be forever scarred by war was far harder on the emotions.

Carrying about twenty colorful balloons, I arrived at the center for reconstructive surgery run by Dr. Arthur Barsky, an American plastic surgeon who had helped many women disfigured when the atomic bomb was dropped on Hiroshima in 1945. Youngsters of all ages, shouting with delight, almost bowled me over when they saw the balloons.

Though I kept smiling, I was distraught when I took a good look at the kids. Some were victims of napalm attacks, bombings, and shootings, and some had been burned in fires, usually from kerosene cookstoves.

The method of surgery used by Barsky made them look even more disfigured. To cover a burned area, attending doctors would graft an arm to a cheek, for instance, and let a tube of healthy skin grow in between, to eventually be cut and smoothed. The final result was not cosmetic—it always looked like a tire tube—and the lengthy process meant that youngsters had to remain in contorted positions for months. One boy I saw had a skin tube connecting his lower legs, but I was told that eventually he would be able to walk.

The lead to my story was about a young boy named Dien, who was shot in the spine and paralyzed from the waist down, possibly in an American helicopter attack. He made model helicopters from discarded intravenous tubing and sold them, hoping to earn money for a wheelchair. They became collectors' items. After the story ran, an Indiana congressman wrote to say one of his constituents wanted to buy a wheelchair for Dien. I gave money to help pay for a tutor for him, and I often wonder whether he survived the war and the Communist takeover in 1975.

My first real brush with the war came a few weeks after the election on my first foray to the Mekong Delta, where the Vietcong insurgency was born and still was strongest. Thousands of flag-waving villagers were demonstrating in support of the government along a fifty-mile stretch of Highway 4. It seemed so peaceful—ducks paddling in ponds, water buffalo meandering in fields, women in conical hats bent over in the rice paddies.

Suddenly, in the distance I saw smoke from air strikes and heard the booming of artillery. As the strikes got closer, photographer Nick Ut, who would shortly win a Pulitzer Prize, grabbed me and we jumped into a roadside ditch filled with six inches of muddy water.

I had no idea what to expect as I crouched over. I was frightened and very glad I was with Nick. Minutes later, the firing grew more distant again and stopped. We headed back to Saigon, joking and telling stories, relieved that the artillery was missing us. I laughed when I looked down at my feet. I finally had muddy boots and dirty khaki pants.

As December arrived, the cease-fire guessing game intensified, and so did the war.

At 7:40 A.M. on December 6, 1972, Saigon experienced its biggest attack since the 1968 Tet offensive. Tan Son Nhut air base was hit by fifty-two rockets, and I slept through it.

Apparently, nobody knew how to find me. I had just moved into a one-bedroom apartment overlooking an inner courtyard a few blocks from the office, and it had no phone. So I went to work oblivious to the bombing, wearing a dress to go to interview the foreign minister. Instead, I headed out with Neal Ulevich, one of AP's young, talented photographers (who later won a Pulitzer Prize), trying to find some of the villages hit by rocket fire. In my diary, I wrote about the search:

> We drove north of the base and then down all these muddy dirt roads asking police and military officials where all the damage was. Finally, we parked on the side of a road, walked down an alley and right into a pile of rubble. Loads of kids were picking through it—and there was one family of 11 whose roof fell in but survived. The only two things intact in the house were a picture of the infant Jesus and a statue of Jesus. The mother said she was saved by him.
>
> Then, we went off across the road down a muddier path followed by about 150 kids. They really are fascinated by American women—still a real novelty to them, I think. First, we came to a wrecked house where a young boy was still pouring water from a red plastic bowl onto smouldering ruins. The wrecked houses, where five people were wounded, were right beside a cemetery which was untouched.
>
> As we walked toward the next attack site, we came into a clearing and there was the airport. We really were close—less

than a mile away. The last house was the saddest. A 20-year-old woman had been killed and her body was laid out on a wooden bed, covered with a straw mat, with two candles and sticks of incense burning (near it). A big crowd had gathered outside the house and neighbors, crying and wiping their eyes, walked in to see the body.

I looked at the dead woman. She was a few years younger than I. Neighbors said she dreamed of marrying and having a family. I kept thinking to myself that she didn't deserve to die, and it brought home to me for the first time how cruel and random war can be. She was not part of the war, but now she was just another war statistic.

Speculation resumed about a cease-fire date, but the Paris talks collapsed on December 13. The following morning, I was awakened at four A.M. by a fantastic crashing sound that shook the windows of my apartment. Saigon was under attack again, I thought. But this time it turned out to be an ammunition dump exploding across the Saigon River. The noise and rumbling went on for hours, but it just got absorbed into everyday Saigon life. Motorcycles clogged the streets, and the food stalls and shopkeepers totally ignored the explosions.

According to historians, Kissinger warned the North Vietnamese that the United States would resume bombing if the peace talks broke down. So they knew the bombs were coming—but we didn't.

On December 18, the United States launched the most intensive aerial campaign of the war against the North Vietnamese—B-52s attacking around the clock in what became known as the "Christmas bombing." Nixon ordered a news blackout, and the five o'clock follies became a total joke, with enraged journalists, including myself, confronting the U.S. military spokesmen whose orders were to say nothing. Hanoi Radio, which AP monitored routinely, usually with little result, suddenly became a primary source of information.

With bombs falling in the North and fighting continuing in the South, Christmas was a time of uncertainty. I watched a GI Santa bring smiles to the faces of orphaned children, and comedian Bob Hope get a thunderous standing ovation from thousands of American soldiers in what turned out to be his last Christmas tour of Vietnam. Three days before Christmas, Hanoi Radio read out a list of captured U.S. pilots, and I wondered whether any were from the USS *America*.

I went to a Christmas party with an air force captain at the First Hotel near Tan Son Nhut airport, where his unit was celebrating. The hotel, I was told, was the unit's favorite watering hole. I quickly discovered why. There were a dozen guys and about twenty-five Vietnamese bar girls, all wondering about the new round-eyed competition. While I stood with the guys telling funny stories, the bar girls zeroed in on their targets for the evening. They tried to be nice. One told me I was attractive, and another said I reminded her of an American friend.

It was strange for a native New Yorker like me to be spending the holidays in a land of sunshine, sweat, fake Christmas trees, and wilting flowers.

On Christmas Eve, thousands of people swarmed the streets of Saigon, beeping motorcycle horns and throwing confetti, even though nobody knew if—or when—peace might come. On the way back from a dinner party, my magnanimous date, an air force major, handed out 500-piastre notes (about U.S. $1.15) to American GIs and smaller denominations to Vietnamese who looked hungry. It reminded me of New Year's Eve around Times Square.

For years, there had always been a huge "Light at the End of the Tunnel" party on New Year's Eve in Saigon. But this year there was none as the uncertainty of 1972 dragged into 1973. The Bennetts had a dinner party, then the air force major and I headed to the Miramar bar, and just before midnight we joined a small celebration hosted by AP correspondent Hugh Mulligan, a great writer and storyteller, and his lovely Irish wife, Brigid, in their penthouse suite. We toasted the New Year with champagne, watching yellow and red flares drift over a quiet city.

Once the Christmas bombing ended, peace talks resumed and cease-fire rumors intensified. The Saigon media was engaged in its own war, and scooping the competition was the equivalent of a battlefield victory. Success took cunning and sometimes money. South Vietnam's foreign minister Tran Van Lam headed to Paris on January 21, and George Esper decided we should both go to the airport to see him off and engage in a little subterfuge. I acted as a decoy, staying with the press pack outside the VIP lounge, while George slipped through a hole in the fence surrounding it. He got an interview with Lam, which outraged UPI's Tracy Wood, a tough competitor and old friend from California.

But CBS trumped everyone. The network purchased all the first-class seats on the Saigon-to-Bangkok flight, so reporters Bernie Kalb and Bert Quint had no competition flying with the foreign minister on the first leg of his trip—and they got an exclusive TV interview.

The following day, AP quoted captured Communist documents saying the cease-fire would be initialed on January 24, signed on January 27, and take effect on January 28.

This time AP was out on a limb—but the dates were right.

I awoke on January 24 to AFVN saying Nixon and North Vietnam's chief negotiator, Le Duc Tho, had scheduled press conferences.

The end of the war had arrived—at least for the Americans.

How strange are the ways of life and death that former president Lyndon Johnson—who dramatically escalated the U.S. military presence in Vietnam and saw his dream of a second term thwarted because of it—would be robbed by forty-eight hours of seeing a cease-fire declared. He died on January 22.

While I waited nervously in the office for the cease-fire announcement, I wrote a story with reaction to Johnson's death from Gen. Frederick Weyand, the U.S. military commander in Vietnam. Two hours later the announcement came, and after listening to two-thirds of it, I took off for Tan Son Nhut to get reaction from the GIs. At the PX, the first soldier I told didn't know and was ecstatic. Everyone else did, and the reaction was mixed. Some were unhappy about leaving their Vietnamese girlfriends, some about losing extra combat pay. Six black sergeants outside the PX were watching a Pan Am 747 take off and shouting to the world: "We'll be on the next one, baby!"

I also had mixed feelings about the cease-fire. The American public would be thrilled that U.S. troops and prisoners of war would soon be coming home. But I was certain the war would not end for the South Vietnamese, who would now be fighting alone.

The night of the cease-fire, I started on "Operation Bar Girl" with John Algood and Jerry Elliott (from AFVN), who had become good friends. The goal was to get the girls' reactions to the imminent departure of their GI boyfriends. The research—barhopping across the city from the sleazy joints near the airport frequented by enlisted soldiers to the classier clubs in downtown Saigon favored by officers—consumed two more nights.

Not surprisingly, many bar girls were in a sixty-day race against time to catch an American GI husband. Surprisingly, I found very little bitterness. Most of the girls were pretty stoic, though many wondered how they, and their half-American children, would survive. Perched on a bar stool in the down-market Lido Bar on Plantation Road near the airport, twenty-three-year-old Mai spoke wistfully about the GI father of her two children. "Before, he want to marry me and I say 'no.' I want to stay here," she told me. "Now, I want. But now be too late. He gone." My story—and Neal Ulevich's picture of a bar girl blowing smoke rings, surrounded by GIs—got smash play.

The Paris peace agreement, it turned out, was almost identical to the October deal: South Vietnam's president, Nguyen Van Thieu, would remain in power, North Vietnamese troops would stay in the south, the POWs would be freed, and the North would recognize the South.

A military commission comprising the four parties to the conflict was to oversee the pullout of the last fifty thousand American, Australian, New Zealand, and South Korean troops and arrange for the exchange of POWs. An international commission known as the International Commission of Control and Supervision (ICCS) would monitor the cease-fire and supervise the exchange of prisoners.

On the evening before the cease-fire, Frank Mariano, an ABC television correspondent and an old friend from San Francisco, threw a party for several departing colleagues. His wife, Ann, working as an AP stringer, had gone to cover the reaction in Pleiku. Denby Fawcett, one of the war's pioneering women reporters, whom I liked the minute I met her, was also at the party. The room buzzed with excitement. Everyone left early, knowing January 28 would be a big day—but none of us knew how big.

At seven A.M., an hour before the Vietnamese cease-fire went into effect, Tan Son Nhut was under rocket attack, and the Vietcong and North Vietnamese didn't let up all day. Whoever said a piece of paper could turn enemies into friends or end a war?

After the rocketing of Tan Son Nhut ended, I headed to the airport with Neal Ulevich. The North Vietnamese and Vietcong had been fighting and operating clandestinely in the south for years, but the arrival of their first legal delegations was big news. While trying to figure out exactly where their planes would land, we spotted a group of GIs dragging one of their screaming and kicking buddies toward the back of a truck loaded with green-dyed water. It was the base's last American combat squadron having a joyous cease-fire celebration—and it was a great picture and story.

At a time of such joy for most GIs, there was also a grim reminder that the fighting and the killing hadn't stopped. A U.S. military plane taxied in and two soldiers lifted down a body bag. One soldier almost dropped his end. It was probably the body of Lt. Col. William B. Nolde, the last of 45,941 Americans killed during the conflict, who had been hit by an artillery round near An Loc the previous day. Neal tried to get some pictures, but we were nabbed by an American sergeant and evicted from the base. It took half an hour of hassling to get back, and I kept thinking about his family, how happy they must have been when they heard about the peace agreement and how devastated they would be.

The Vietcong finally arrived from Bangkok, but the delegation wouldn't get off the plane because they didn't want to sign any customs or immigration forms. They remained on board all night. The next day I was back at the airport, waiting to see what happened with the Vietcong and the North Vietnamese, who were due to arrive from Hanoi.

A lot of journalists were getting kicked out. I ended up hiding in a cubicle with Fox Butterfield of *The New York Times,* part of the time under a desk with the military newspaper *Stars & Stripes* in front of my face. The only phone had loose wires, and to use it I had to sit on the floor or squat, holding two tiny wires together while trying to talk.

Neal was able to wander on the tarmac, wearing earphones like the maintenance crews and snapping pictures.

Two planes with the North Vietnamese finally arrived and I got my story, but they, too, refused to get off. Despite the day-old cease-fire, fighting continued, and two Italian newsmen were injured.

The "plane-ins" finally ended, and the Vietcong and North Vietnamese delegations were taken to their living quarters, chosen by the South Vietnamese. It was a prisonlike compound at Tan Son Nhut called Camp Davis, surrounded by a ten-foot fence topped with three rows of barbed wire.

Vice President Spiro Agnew arrived soon after. At a farewell news conference on February 1, he said he told the South Vietnamese that Congress would not give them all the money and military hardware they wanted to keep fighting. After filing, I went to investigate a report that U.S. pilots had flown in a Vietcong general and a bunch of other Vietcong from the jungle.

I ran into Lt. James Hodgson, the administrative officer for the U.S. Army's 59th Corps Aviation Company, who said he had just been in a plane that landed in a jungle clearing and picked up three American POWs. He described how the Vietcong had given them cigarettes and candy as a farewell gift. Hodgson said the Americans had been taken to 3rd Field Hospital in Saigon.

It was a great story—and it turned out to be one of the most painful lessons of my career.

Believing I had an exclusive on the first American prisoner release, I raced to the officers' club to call the AP bureau. Pyle decided to go with the story because the source was good, the report seemed credible, and the U.S. military spokesman was evasive, saying he couldn't confirm or deny it, a response the Americans often used to delay releasing information.

Unbelievably, the whole thing turned out to be a hoax.

The story hadn't made the AP news wire, but it had been used on the radio wire, so AP had to kill it—something never taken lightly. I was distraught and kept asking myself, How could this officer lie about such a sensitive issue as the release of POWs?

The next day, Pyle and I went to see Hodgson's commanding officer. He told us Hodgson had admitted it was all a lie. Hodgson then came in and told me it was a childish thing to have done, and he had thought it was such a wild story that nobody would believe it.

After he left, the commander said he thought Hodgson wanted to "put me on"—take advantage of my presumed naïveté—because I was "young and beautiful." If I had been old and ugly, he said, it probably wouldn't have happened.

That made me livid. It's a good thing Hodgson was gone because I'm not sure what I would have said or done. For my entire career, I'd fought to be taken seriously, and here I was being treated like the stereotype of the dumb blond sex object.

If the word *sexism* existed, it wasn't an issue in that era. Despite the arrival of the women's liberation movement, men were rarely slapped down for commenting on a woman's looks, and male superiority was almost taken for granted.

My predecessors who came to Vietnam in the 1960s had fought and won the big battles with the U.S. military over equal access for women journalists. But that didn't translate to equality of the sexes in the eyes of most men, especially in the military.

In the twenty-eight years since, this incident has served as a constant reminder to double-check and confirm reports, even from credible sources. And I have not been the victim of another hoax.

During the days that followed, I spent a lot of time covering the two commissions to find out when the POWs would be freed. To my surprise, the best sources on the military commission were the North Vietnamese. Because they were forced to live behind barbed wire, the media became their main link to the outside world. The Americans, by contrast, were simply uncooperative.

Media competition to cover the first release of American prisoners was fierce. On February 11, it seemed there was an announcement every hour about impending releases, but the sites kept changing.

AP had obtained names of the first POWs to be freed, and with help from Pyle's wife, Toby, I did a story on the oldest, the youngest, those with approaching birthdays, and the U.S. State Department officer who was also being released, Doug Ramsey.

I didn't get much sleep that night and was up before six A.M. and on the bus to Tan Son Nhut at eight A.M. The POWs were supposed to arrive an hour later. But there was a glitch, and it wasn't until eight-twenty P.M. that a line of blinking red and yellow lights appeared in the sky, strung out like a strand of Christmas tree bulbs.

As I watched the six helicopters circle gracefully, I tried to imagine what the men inside were thinking. They had been picked up in a jungle clearing and were about to take their first steps on friendly soil. Some had been prisoners for eight years. You could feel the emotion in the air and see it in the eyes even of the veteran combat correspondents. Some had tears in their eyes, as did I.

When the helicopters landed, the POWs peered through the windows, waving at us and about seventy-five American servicemen on hand to welcome them. The first off, a young blond man on a stretcher, was given a big cheer. When he heard the noise he sat up, waved one hand, then both hands, and his face broke into a broad smile. Then the twenty-six other POWs, emaciated and haggard looking, left the choppers. They walked across the tarmac, smiling broadly, to a waiting C-9 hospital plane. Their baggy pajama-style garb emphasized their gaunt appearance. Each one had a large nametag around his neck. It was almost as if they were packages being delivered, not people. Many carried black plastic bags with the few remembrances of their years in captivity.

That second sleepless night, I tried to imagine their years of suffering and how they felt, sleeping in a real bed with clean sheets for the first time in years without any guards hovering. Nothing came close to what I later read about the torture and suffering they endured in captivity.

Waves of releases followed.

A few days after the first POW release, the Vietcong attempted to give a cocktail party for both commissions and the press, but the South Vietnamese barred journalists and the Indonesians and Canadians on the ICCS from Tan Son Nhut. That night, the phone rang at AP and it was a VC delegate who asked if I was Tracy Wood. Of course, I said, "Yes"—as I said, the media competition was pretty ruthless. He gave me a statement and said he was sorry I (as Tracy) hadn't made it to their cocktail party. Pyle immediately said I could go to the next bash—the contest of the capitalist women journalists for the minds and hearts of the Communist men!

That soiree took place at the Canadian ambassador's residence in mid-March when Canadian foreign minister Mitchell Sharp came to Saigon. The Canadians were threatening to pull out the ICCS because it was polarized on East-West lines, unable to act against cease-fire violations. But that didn't stop Sharp from throwing a party—and what a party it was!

For the first and only time during the Vietnam War, the adversaries and their Communist and capitalist backers were at the same social gathering. The big question was, would they talk, or even look at each other?

At one point, the top Vietcong, North Vietnamese, American, and South Vietnamese officials were all in the same room. The Vietcong general, Tran Van Tra, asked the journalists around him about the tall, white-haired, impeccably dressed diplomat behind him. Pyle told him it was U.S. ambassador Ellsworth Bunker. There may have been some more eye contact among the adversaries—but definitely no words.

When I met Tra, he told me through his interpreter that he was glad to see "a very pretty journalist," and would I please come to his press conference a few days later. Then I walked over to North Vietnam's top official, Le Quan Hoa, who also commented about "lovely female journalists" and gave me his card. I was wearing a new long, flowered dress, and I guess they hadn't seen many Western women wearing makeup and nice clothes before.

With the deadline for the U.S. military pullout fast approaching, I flew to Da Nang on March 21 to see what had happened in the north since the cease-fire. Once a command center for major battles, the city was now quiet. It reminded me of a beach resort, with boats on the river and the last visitors (the U.S. troops) packing to leave.

The next day, AP White House photographer Chick Harrity and I drove over the Hai Van pass on a thirteen-mile road with blind corners and hairpin turns. It climbed 1,400 feet past lush tropical forest. An inviting beach shimmered in the distance. We then headed to the old imperial capital of Hue, stopping in An Loc, a rural village of ten thousand that straddles the main road.

On one side of the road, all houses were in ruins; on the other side, they were untouched. The village chief, Tran Tiep, said Vietcong attacked an hour after the cease-fire. In four days of fighting, five civilians were killed, fourteen were wounded, and four hundred houses were damaged.

It was clear that fear still stalked the rice paddies and vine-covered lanes. The attack had left many villagers even more skeptical about the cease-fire and understandably anxious. Tiep said he assumed there would be more fighting. "The Communists will create excuses to have a war," just as they did after the cease-fire with the French in 1954, he told me.

In Hue, it was chilly, a shock after Saigon's incredible humidity. We ate dinner at an outdoor restaurant overlooking the Perfume River and ran into several Canadians, who offered to take us to Quang Tri, scene of some of the war's fiercest fighting, to see an exchange of North Vietnamese and South Vietnamese prisoners. I accepted instantly.

The next day, we flew there by helicopter with a Polish colonel and a Canadian captain from the ICCS. From the air, the city resembled the World War II footage I'd seen of Dresden. Everything was rubble except the new compounds for the U.S. military and the two commissions. After landing, we walked past chunks of concrete, twisted metal, and fallen plaster for about half a mile. The only living things were large yellow squash flowers on vines, creeping up through broken masonry. I was overwhelmed to see so much devastation for the first time. As the Polish colonel said, "There is nothing more senseless than man's destruction of his world."

Eventually, we arrived at the Thach Han River, the border between North and South Vietnam. Several dozen North Vietnamese POWs were waiting to go home. They were squatting, and many covered their faces with their hands when they saw Harrity lift his camera. A few South Vietnamese women, in traditional flowing *ao dai* dresses, slit to the waist and worn over black pants, waited expectantly on the shore.

The ICCS had arranged for us to go to the Communist side by boat. We took off our shoes in the boat, hopped off two thirds of the way across, and waded ashore. As I walked up the metal ramp, pant legs rolled up and carrying my shoes, I could feel all the North Vietnamese looking at my bright frosted-pink toenail polish—and I imagined them thinking, What a sign of capitalist decadence.

The first South Vietnamese prisoners were waiting to cross, and Barry Kramer of *The Wall Street Journal* and I tried to talk to a few of them, but they were too frightened. When they were led into boats, they smiled with the realization that their journey home had begun. Several, however, decided at the last minute to stay in the North and were led away.

Soon after, we saw the first group of North Vietnamese POWs run down the ramp on the other side of the river, peeling off the clothes and shoes the capitalist southerners had given them. They got into boats, but halfway across many jumped out and started running toward more than a dozen North Vietnamese soldiers who had waded into the river and were clapping and cheering them on. Several injured POWs were helped by their buddies. A few were carried on stretchers.

There was a noisy celebration with lots of embracing as the POWs arrived on the northern side of the river, clad only in underpants. They were given white shirts, khaki pants, sneakers, tea, and cigarettes while they waited to be interviewed by senior officers.

As I watched the exchange, I felt some of the same emotions that I had watching the American POWs. These soldiers were probably going to see loved ones who might have spent years wondering whether they were dead or alive. But unlike the Americans, these men might still be facing war. With the fighting continuing, I was sure at least some would be on the front lines again—and then what would their fate be?

We flew back to Hue to file and then headed to Da Nang, where the city threw a big "Good-bye, America" party two days later—complete with speeches, medals, and banners saying "thank you." Afterward, we drove to the beach near the Hai Van pass. But every time I tried to go to sleep, a barrage of artillery fire woke me up. It was pretty close. The ceaseless fire . . . and from what I had seen I was certain the firing would continue long after the Americans were gone.

Back in Saigon, the last American GIs were waiting to leave. At Camp Alpha at Tan Son Nhut, the staging point for the withdrawal, soldiers were ecstatic as they saw their names going up on the plane manifests. I would have loved to start a story with the U.S. Army's instructions to soldiers to start their processing out of Vietnam with a trip to the "Pee House of the August Moon" and deposit a sample in a "golden yellow bottle." But alas, that lighthearted takeoff on the movie *The Teahouse of the August Moon* would never have made it onto the AP wire.

On March 29, the final American POWs were freed in Hanoi and the last GIs flew home, although the American military was still keeping a large defense attaché's office at the U.S. embassy in Vietnam, headed by Maj. Gen. John E. Murray.

Minutes after the last U.S. military police left Tan Son Nhut, about two hundred South Vietnamese raided the mess hall and walked off with everything that wasn't nailed down. South Vietnamese military police helped shovel the loot through the fence, and private guards, paid by the U.S. government, did nothing to stop them.

General Weyand said the United States accomplished its purpose, but to me the North Vietnamese and the Vietcong looked like the winners seeing off their defeated enemies.

The last American freed by the Vietcong, Capt. Robert White, wasn't released until April 1, three days after the deadline. I spent hours at the airport, waiting with General Murray. Finally, a helicopter arrived and White got off, leaning heavily on a gnarled walking stick with a bouquet of plastic flowers on top. He seemed dazed as he walked the one hundred feet to a C-9 medevac plane, but he came to when he saw Murray at the foot of the stairs. He smiled and saluted, and I thought to myself that that was probably the moment he realized he was really free and finally heading home.

It was my thirtieth birthday on March 27, but the celebration was postponed until after the American pullout. The Bennetts hosted a joint party in their garden for me and Barbara Treaster, wife of *New York Times* correspondent Joe Treaster, who shared my birthday. By the fate of timing, the huge bash was in many ways an end of the American war party, too. Dozens of journalists, diplomats, and South Vietnamese dined on spaghetti and toasted us with champagne. The inscription on the chocolate cake, which I designed, read, "Happy Birthday, Barbara and Edie. You're Never over the Hill."

As I looked forward to the year ahead, I also looked back. Despite the Hodgson debacle, my confidence had grown. In just a few months in Vietnam, I'd learned a lot about war, even though I hadn't been in combat.

Writing the daily war wrap-up was no problem—I knew the places, the equipment, the military lingo. For someone who hadn't known the difference between an F-4 Phantom and a prop-driven A-1 Skyraider, I could now identify them in the air, and I could distinguish the sounds of incoming and outgoing artillery. More important, I had cultivated very good diplomatic contacts for AP, which was crucial as the story turned from war to what Art Buchwald called "warce," somewhere between war and peace.

I had worked with some of the top journalists in the world and gotten to know them over steak and wine. I'd shared a mango with James Jones, author of *From Here to Eternity*, who came to Saigon on assignment for *The New York Times Magazine* but liked to hang out with the AP staff.

Vietnam had already turned me into a real "foodie." I was fascinated by everything I ate and drank—cracked crab, fish soup, vanilla-based liqueur, papayas, a coconut drink with big pieces of coconut floating in it, curried lamb, and stuffed lobster, to name a few of my favorites. The best cheese soufflé I've ever eaten was at the Hotel Royale at a lunch in November to celebrate the return to Saigon of Horst Faas, AP's legendary Pulitzer Prize–winning photographer whose keen observations and friendship added a special, extra dimension to my Vietnam assignment.

Days after his return, Faas took me antique shopping for the first time, for old Vietnamese ceramic elephants, which got a new name

Chick Harrity

from the American GIs. It supposedly came from a mail sergeant who had to ship hundreds of new models of these large elephants to the United States as GI souvenirs. They have flat tops and make great cocktail tables. When one too many fell on the sergeant's foot, he supposedly shouted: "These bloody useless fucking elephants!" So BUFEs, or "buffies," were born.

I tagged along with Faas on several other antique expeditions, never buying anything. After months of looking, I found an old blue-and-white plate I liked that cost a dollar. Faas turned to me after I paid for it and said: "You're hooked." He was right. I still love collecting Oriental antiques.

There had been no letup in my mad social life. The air force captain turned out to be married and said he was going back to his wife. The air force major left Vietnam in January. But there were still plenty of dinners and parties and men to dance, drink, and dine with, though the Saigon press corps was quickly shrinking.

With the Americans officially gone, the war story shifted to Cambodia, where fighting had intensified even though the Paris accords had called for an end to the conflict there as well.

George Esper, who took over from Pyle as AP's bureau chief in mid-April, sent me to Phnom Penh to help out.

The Cambodian capital retained its old French colonial beauty, with wide, tree-lined streets and aging but graceful buildings. Because gasoline was rationed and expensive, there were no taxis and few cars, and it was quiet.

The AP office was at the Hotel Le Phnom, which boasted almost constant electricity, a swimming pool, and an outdoor restaurant that was conveniently the main hangout for the press corps.

Immediately after arriving on April 24, I went to a briefing on the shortage of rice, the staple of the Cambodian diet. Writing the story was easy. Filing it, I discovered quickly, was not. Every story had to be approved by government censors, who worked set hours but liked to sneak out for a drink or food and sometimes had to be dragged back—if you could discover which bar they'd gone to. There was always time pressure as well, because of a ten P.M. curfew.

After finally getting my story cleared and sending it to Hong Kong, I had dinner, talked to a few of the veteran journalists on the terrace, and went to sleep.

I awoke to a loud rumbling and felt my bed and the whole room shaking. The hotel was being bombed, I thought, throwing on some clothes.

I opened my door but didn't see anyone else in the corridor. In the lobby, the desk clerk acted as if nothing had happened. You could still hear and feel the loud rumbling. I then headed toward the pool and outdoor restaurant. A group of journalists and photographers were sitting around telling war stories. I joined them and somewhere in the conversation nonchalantly asked about the noise, which hadn't let up.

It was the B-52 bombers, someone said, on their regular late night bombing runs against Khmer Rouge targets across the Mekong River. In other words, no big deal.

Eventually the bombing stopped, and everyone on the terrace went to bed.

I hardly slept because I had received a phone call from the Ministry of Information minutes after I arrived, inviting me to be at their office at five-forty-five A.M. the following morning to take a trip to cover "a senior government official." We headed to the airport and flew by military transport to Kampot, once a fashionable holiday haunt for the French elite near the southern coast but then just eleven miles from enemy lines.

The VIP turned out to be President Lon Nol, making a rare appearance outside Phnom Penh. Leaning slightly on a carved wooden cane, he told about two thousand people in the sleepy fishing town that bringing his three chief political opponents into a new council would unite the country "for the last round of fighting against the enemy."

That night and for the next few nights the bombing runs woke me, but then, like much of the press corps, I slept through everything.

U.S. warplanes came during the day, too, and I joined hundreds of Cambodians standing on the banks of the Mekong, watching them swoop down and drop their bombs on the other side.

It was the greatest show in town. It reminded me of the old B movies I saw as a kid, only this was real war. Hundreds of people were still being killed, and thousands of refugees trying to escape the conflict had flooded into Phnom Penh. Lon Nol's prediction of a last battle seemed optimistic.

Back in Saigon, the war was also far from over.

A helicopter from the military commission was shot down. Colleagues returning from the north said everyone was waiting for the next Communist offensive. The Vietcong held a news conference and accused the United States of bombing inside South Vietnam for a month along the Cambodian border near Loc Ninh. The U.S. planes were supposedly targeting VC bases.

Nonetheless, the South Vietnamese were also thinking about peace.

They had just chosen twenty-seven firms to bid on offshore oil concessions and were even planning to revive horse racing, so I discovered.

My successor, Tad Bartimus, one of AP's talented young writers, arrived from Miami on May 8, and watching her initial reactions brought back the frustrations of my early days in Vietnam. Walking into a new environment, especially one like Saigon, is tough because you don't know how to operate. But after a while, all the pieces fall into place. They did for me, and I was sure they would for her.

After showing Tad around Saigon for about ten days, I took her to Phnom Penh, which seemed even hotter. The Hotel Le Phnom was full, so we stayed at the Hotel Monoram, which had its own generator. At least there was air-conditioning to make it easier to sleep, but there were water shortages, which meant keeping the bathtub full at all times.

I was supposed to be working on several longer pieces on the state of the war, the political situation, and the inflated figures the Cambodian government was giving for the size of its army. But AP's correspondent Lee Rudakewych decided to go to the beach for a few days, so I had to run the bureau and do the daily war reporting as well, with Tad's help.

We joked about AP women finally taking charge of the war coverage. Frankly, it had taken far too long, and I was determined to prove we could do it as well as the guys.

Early one evening, a rocket missed its target near the port and landed around the corner from our hotel. Tad and I hit the floor. Then several more crashed nearby. More than a dozen people were killed and injured. The blackouts were so bad that we ended up writing the story by candlelight and flashlight. Even the candle makers were complaining. The electricity went out so often, they couldn't run their candle-making machines.

Tad went back to Saigon after four days, but I stayed—and every day the fighting seemed to be getting worse. Two American planes were shot down, and there were reports that the Khmer Rouge carried out a massacre in an outlying village.

On several days, I drove a short way out of Phnom Penh to try to get a sense of what was happening in the countryside. Nothing happened to me. But soon after I left, a Japanese correspondent went off on a similar reporting trip and never returned. He had been so excited because his wife had just had their first child—a daughter he never got to see.

Everyone was waiting for the monsoon rains to begin, which usually slowed the fighting, and to see whether Congress would approve a bill to stop funding the U.S. bombing in Cambodia.

There was such a rice shortage by then that the entire city was fixated on the arrival of a ship convoy bringing food and other supplies from South Vietnam. As the convoy headed up the Mekong River on May 28, four ships were hit by Khmer Rouge fire, including a tanker, which started burning. I arrived at the dock just in time to see the bodies of two Filipinos who died in the attack being lifted off one of the damaged ships that managed to limp into port. Despite the losses, enough rice got through to avoid an immediate crisis.

The next day, I flew to Laos for the first time. The United States had been bombing there for years in an attempt to destroy the Ho Chi Minh Trail, which supplied Communist forces in South Vietnam—and to keep Laos's own Pathet Lao Communists at bay. The so-called secret war had been unmasked, but the bombs were still falling.

The capital, Vientiane, a deceptively sleepy-looking French colonial city, was a hotbed of spies and diplomatic intrigue, one of the few places in the world where almost every Communist and capitalist country kept an embassy.

Plunked down in the tropical foliage on the outskirts, incongruously, was a sprawling enclosed community called Kilometer 6, which looked just like a piece of American suburbia. The majority of Americans in Vientiane lived there, in large modern houses. There was a school, a snack bar, a community pool, and an unofficial mayor named Harry Carr. I couldn't find anyone who objected to living in an American "ghetto."

In Vientiane, I also talked to many diplomats for a story on East-West secret contacts and the spying game. One young Western diplomat who looked like the actor Omar Sharif invited me to dinner, and we made a date in Bangkok for mid-June, my first stop after leaving Saigon.

When I returned to Saigon in early June, I was suddenly counting the days to my departure. The farewell dinners and parties began almost immediately, capped by a final bash hosted by Nancy and Joe Bennett. On June 17, coincidentally my sister's birthday, I left Saigon in bubbles of champagne. Flying to Bangkok, I wrote a letter to my family, trying to put into words what my Vietnam assignment had meant.

Dear Mother, Dad and Auntie,

Eight months is not a very long time—but in many ways this eight months has changed my life.

That's a very dramatic statement but there is really no drama. There are just subtleties—the way you look at a flower, or a cripple, or a gourmet dinner.

In many ways, Vietnam was probably one of the best things that happened to me. Professionally, it was the kind of challenge you dream about and fear at the same time. And I loved that about it.

I loved the people and the places and my colleagues and

that indescribable level of excitement that you live with day in and day out—to the point that it becomes commonplace.

Perhaps most of all, I proved to myself that I could compete in the so-called big league. And you never really know that until you walk into a strange country and after a few days know what's important and what isn't. That's what I loved about Cambodia—the challenge of covering the only "hot war" in Asia—and doing it alone. And in the final test, doing well competitively.

Of course, there are tragedies. And much as you would like to ignore them, you never really can. I worry about how the few crippled beggars I helped to support will survive. I worry about the street children who've never known childhood and are often hardened at the age of five. One of the great frustrations is that as much as you do, you only dent the surface.

I donated my television to a hospital for paraplegics through the only woman senator in Vietnam. And being the cynic that one becomes very rapidly, I wonder whether it will ever get there—and if it will be used properly, or if it will be ripped off.

When I left San Francisco I cried for two hours at the airport. Today, I cried only when I got on the plane and was alone. I cried for all those fantastic times that can only be recaptured in the portals of your soul—and for all the wonderful people that I came to know and left behind.

In the United States, life is so complicated and there is so much that uses up your time that it's hard to get really involved in the lives of other people.

But in Saigon, you live and work so closely with your colleagues that you become part of a very large family. And breaking away leaves you almost rootless in a strange way.

It's the most wonderful feeling to arrive in Cambodia, Laos or even Thailand and know that you're going to find somebody from the family in town. We eat together, laugh together, get drunk together—and compete like hell against each other. And that's just the way it works.

I don't really know if I wanted to stay. But on the other hand, I worry about returning to 9 to 5 days, weekends, and that old lifestyle which was getting a little rusty. . . .

Right now, I'm very nostalgic, but I wanted to write and tell you what I was thinking—and that I love you all.

Edith

———————————

Vietnam taught me a lot about war and peace, about life and death, about relationships—and about myself.

It launched my career as a foreign correspondent.

In 1991, I finally learned how I got my Vietnam assignment.

Richard Pyle and I were working together again, this time in Saudi Arabia during the Gulf War. Reminiscing about Saigon over dinner, Pyle told me that he had started lobbying to add a woman reporter to the Saigon staff in 1971. After he met me on my round-the-world vacation, he told Gallagher: "I'd like to have Edie Lederer."

I was stunned because I realized a snap decision to stop in Saigon—really on a lark—had played such a key part in shaping my career.

I remained overseas for twenty-five years for the Associated Press and covered many other conflicts—in the Middle East, Asia, Africa, and Europe. After my current assignment reporting on the United Nations in New York, I hope to be posted overseas again.

Though far-flung, the Vietnam journalistic family still retains a very special bond. That bond has been reinforced at reunions large and small around the globe over the years, and it will remain a bond for life.

In 1993, I returned to Vietnam and Cambodia for the first time in twenty years, with Horst Faas, Nick Ut, and several other friends. It was my fiftieth-birthday present to myself.

As we drove from Phnom Penh to Saigon and then on toward Hanoi, I realized for the first time how beautiful Vietnam was, with its lush jungle foliage and pristine beaches. But the beauty was tempered by memories.

We were passing so many roads and battlefields where our colleagues and thousands of soldiers had lost their lives.

I thought about their friends and families—and the children they never saw grow up.

Once again, I realized how fortunate I was to have survived all the wars I had covered, and I said a prayer for those who had not.

Tad Bartimus

In-Country

I lead a life estranged from myself . . . I am very wild at
heart sometimes. Not confused. Just wild—wild . . .

—Robert Frost

Vietnam returns to me in snapshots: a boot with a foot in it, sitting
upright in a road; a child's angelic eyes shining out from squalor; my
own unlined face in a mirror, reflecting no trace of the mysterious illness that would turn my tongue the color of road tar and send me
home from the war.

"Life," John F. Kennedy said, about the time he committed the
first American troops to Vietnam, "is not fair."

It's one of the two truths Vietnam taught me. The other is that
life is always surprising. Which is why I'm never able to imagine, or
remember, more than I can bear.

When I was first asked about my most vivid Vietnam memory, I
stood silent and slack-jawed, trying to choose one image over another. I couldn't, so I just said, "The children," and moved on.

That answer was true.

I don't have famous battles to relive or fields of dead to forget. I
was not at the siege of Khe Sanh or on Hill 881. I was not in the Ia
Drang valley or a witness to Tet 1968.

My tenure coincided with the "decent interval," a relatively
peaceful hiatus following the United States's pullout in March 1973,
but before the final North Vietnamese offensive in early 1975. No
bookend battles anchored my twelve months in-country. Mine was a

TAD BARTIMUS writes books and the weekly syndicated column "Among Friends"
(www.tadbartimus.com) and is a radio commentator. She lives in Hawaii with her husband.

pentimento war, each layer enriching the whole: dawn mists rising from the jungle, almond-eyed widows gliding by in the white silk of mourning, braided rivers on fire from the setting sun, dazed amputees cadging cigarettes. And children—children everywhere.

From May 8, 1973, until May 8, 1974, I pushed beyond the boundaries of my own inhibitions to love passionately, risk completely, and learn we're all capable of the best and the worst. Half a life later, Vietnam is still my phantom limb.

Unlike many of my contemporaries, I have not returned to Saigon for anniversary celebrations of our ignominious involvement and disgraceful departure. If I ever go back, it will be quietly, unobtrusively, to see the trees. In my time they were cut down for firewood; now I would thrill to find tender green leaves arching over the boulevards. Birdsong would surely make me weep.

I don't expect to sort out Vietnam's curses and gifts, but to write this chapter I sat down with a pen and a legal pad and under "Positives" I listed: dear friends, perfected craft, professional cachet, appreciation for life, heightened compassion, adventure, love.

As for the "Negatives," I wrote: weakened health, no children, loss of innocence, and blind faith in government.

In my youth I thought I was invincible, that if I didn't get shot or visibly maimed, I'd get away clean. But surviving a war doesn't mean you escape being its victim. Something in Vietnam—perhaps Agent Orange, perhaps some other toxin—got me as sure as a crippling bullet.

When I met my future husband four months after I left Vietnam, he told me I was "a grenade with the pin pulled." Some days I still am. My war experience remains for me an emotional minefield that even now explodes if somebody trips the wire.

Nothing about Vietnam turned out the way I'd imagined it.

For years I'd thought I would write about American soldiers and nurses and social workers from Kansas City and Kalamazoo, folks who looked like me, grew up like me, thought like me. But when I got there, I almost never did. By that time, the war wasn't ours anymore. My dead answered to Nguyen and Cai and Duong, and died in twos and threes, or as peasant-boy platoons lost in all-Vietnamese operations that barely rated a couple of paragraphs stateside. The GIs were gone; there was no "Big Story," only small, random ones.

No American military infrastructure meant no helicopters to hop on, no briefers or public information officers to track down, no inside sources to tap. I was mostly on my own, both in the office and in the field, and initially this made me feel insecure and adrift. Soon, however, I discovered that independence suited me; no minders meant more freedom. I started to trust my instincts, to look left when my competitors looked right. I learned to listen to my conscience and have no qualms about putting down my notebook to pick up a suffering child.

I knew then, and believe now, that I would never regret going to Vietnam. I tasted real fear under fire in a ditch in the Mekong Delta. I witnessed courage in a Saigon prison cell while interviewing a condemned Vietcong girl surrounded by her torturers. I trembled with wonder as I faced down a tiger on a Laotian mountainside. Those life lessons have helped me find my way.

When I was in Vietnam, I kept close to the ground. My world was rice cooked in the street, shit beside the road, babies born in fields. If I was hungry, I ate whatever was in the pot. If I needed to sleep, I found a bed or lay down in the mud. There were no department stores, no gift wrap, no personal shoppers. If I needed dishes, I went to the kiln. If I wanted a dress, Mr. Minh whipped one up before dinner. If I wanted sex, it followed me home. If I wanted out, I paid the policeman at the terminal gate and the flight attendant at the door of the plane. Everything was possible; I knew the rules.

What I miss most about Vietnam is knowing the rules. In-country, I had a clear understanding of what I could or could not do. I learned fast that love, honor, and friendship were all that mattered. I lived in the moment because it was all I had. I almost never worried about dying, though I was constantly terrified of snakes. Life was verbs: eat, sleep, hurt, hold, love, work, surrender, leave.

Now I live in, but not of, a world that overwhelms me. I often turn away from its complexity, speed, and surfeit of information. Because I learned in Vietnam that the worth of a life isn't measured in money, power, possessions, or status, I am out of step with most of the people around me. I distrust authority. I am not a team player or a go-along-to-get-along gal.

War radicalized me, turned me into a loner. Take away my designer scarf and sensible shoes and I am barely housebroken. But I've become a good actress and keep up a facade to stave off questions. If someone misses my vibes and asks, "What was Vietnam like?" I reply, "Interesting," and walk away.

As a child, I preferred the company of animals to people. Old photos show me clutching a pet chicken, hanging on to the neck of a liver-spotted pointer, being followed by a black Angus calf.

While I was growing up, my nuclear family was the center of my universe, but disagreements over Vietnam split us apart and we never recovered from the fallout.

My father, a brash fighter pilot in North Africa and Sicily during World War II, flew cargo to Vietnam as early as 1963 while telling us he was on U.S. Air Force missions to the Philippines. In 1964, we picked up a local newspaper to find him in a feature story that disclosed his true destination.

My mother, a vocal Democrat, grew increasingly worried that her soon-to-be-draft-age son might get drawn into the quagmire. That year, she voted for Barry Goldwater, hoping he would end the war. When Lyndon Johnson won, she vacillated between wanting him to drop an atomic bomb or just unilaterally declare victory. The hell with honor, bring the boys home.

My brother, two years my junior, was graduated from high school in 1967 and joined ROTC at the University of Missouri. He eventually served unscathed aboard an aircraft carrier; by then he and I couldn't spend five minutes talking about Vietnam without shouting at each other. Now we don't speak at all.

My defining trait has always been curiosity. I absorbed Vietnam through *Life* magazine and *The CBS Evening News with Walter Cronkite,* sitting cross-legged on the living room floor every evening watching CBS correspondent Jack Laurence's "Charlie Company" and Morley Safer's report of American troops using Zippo lighters to set peasants' villages on fire. As a high school junior, I started telling everyone I was going to become a journalist so I could go to Vietnam.

It was osmosis, rather than epiphany, that set me on my course. My family was verbal and visceral, all four of us type As hell-bent on winning the others to our point of view. We ate dinner together nearly every night, and our friends were always welcome—"I'll just cut the pork chops in smaller pieces," Mom would say—and admission to the table was paid in intelligent conversation about current events, ours and the world's. Nothing was off-limits.

By 1964, Bartimus suppers had become passion plays, especially when my father was home. The war was no longer just on television, it was passing the meat and potatoes at the head of the table. My friends could get low draft numbers; with some of them already in uniform, Vietnam was dominating our lives.

I repeatedly challenged Dad to explain why America was there. I no longer remember his answers, which probably meant he didn't have good ones. Much later, I came to believe—perhaps because I wanted to—that my father grew morally opposed to the war after he saw it firsthand. I'm also fairly certain his sense of loyalty to those who fought it, as well as his patriotism, kept him silent.

But my dad was nobody's fool. He knew that old men sent young men to die and that sometimes old men got it wrong. A military pilot from 1942 to 1967, he knew a bad war from a good one. He never spoke Defense Secretary Robert S. McNamara's name without prefacing it with "that sonofabitch." I'm sure it caused my father great personal anguish to follow orders he didn't believe in, but besides being a wonderful dad, he was also a brave and good soldier. He did his duty.

After he died, I found out that he'd flown hundreds of corpses home from Saigon, that he could never bring himself to watch the loading or unloading of the flag-draped coffins, and that he'd refused to enter the cargo bay while they were there.

By 1967, my sophomore year at the University of Missouri, several of my Belton High School classmates had been killed or wounded. My fondest wish was that the war would end; my second fondest was that it would wait till I got there.

That spring I resolved to drop out and go to Vietnam as a free-lancer.

Then I met Larry Burrows.

Burrows was a hero to me through his photo stories in *Life* magazine, which often took up six or eight pages. He was an Englishman who'd paid his dues for twenty years photographing European royalty, politicians, movie stars, and Old Master paintings. When he went to Vietnam, his brilliant "eye," acute intellect, and meticulous technical skills captured the war in classic compositions and breathtakingly powerful images.

When Burrows came to the university to accept the 1967 Magazine Photographer of the Year award, I wangled an introduction. After hobnobbing politely with the grown-ups, the honoree invited a few journalism majors back to his hotel room. Instead of bragging about "bang-bang" or holding court as a world-famous shooter, Burrows spoke quietly, with deep melancholy, about Vietnam. It was clear he was exhausted and had hoped for an early night, but he also wanted to share, so he passed around some of his photos. Their power stunned us into silence. As he talked about the war's toll on the innocent—particularly children—his voice grew stronger and his passionate commentary carried the conversation well past midnight. He believed the United States was losing the war.

It is hard now to remember how invincible I felt, how sure I was of myself, when I spoke up and said I intended to quit school and go to Saigon to work for anybody who'd hire me.

Burrows gave me a scathing look.

"You will not!" Each word was perfectly enunciated. "The last thing this war needs is another stringer getting killed for twenty-five dollars a day."

I was stunned, mortified, and completely cowed.

In gentler tones, Burrows explained that reporters and photographers needed legitimacy and credibility, "otherwise you've wasted your time and you're just in the way. You might even get somebody else killed."

He'd delivered a stinging slap of reality and a body blow to my pride, but he hadn't said a word about my gender. I seized on that omission as a good omen.

At the airport the next day, Larry put a hand on my shoulder and promised to do everything he could for me "when somebody sends you to Vietnam. I'll make sure we all try to keep you alive. Drop me a line once in a while."

I promised to graduate and get on with a wire service. He seemed pleased by my spontaneous decision; impulsively, I hugged him. When he disappeared through the aircraft door, my chest tightened and my head felt heavy. I waved until the plane was out of sight.

I wrote Larry often, and once in a great while a letter would come from Hong Kong or through *Life* in New York. He'd answer a few of my many questions, include a sentence about his latest assignment and a little encouragement, then close with "Happy Days."

A month after the January 1968 Tet offensive, I flew to Hawaii to see a friend whose ensign husband was on a destroyer in the Gulf of Tonkin. By then I'd persuaded *Columbia* (Missouri) *Tribune* editor Hank Waters III to hire me as his paper's MU campus correspondent. Waters became my first mentor and a friend for life when he advanced me $281 for a round-trip ticket in exchange for my promise to write a series about American soldiers enjoying rest and recreation—R&R—in Honolulu.

I expected to find happy, vacationing couples reuniting for a relaxed week between the first and second halves of a Vietnam tour. Instead, I witnessed traumatized men and distraught women valiantly trying to act normal.

One night, as fragrant plumeria blossoms filled an open-air Waikiki nightclub with their intoxicating scent, singer Don Ho and his rowdy bar band yelled, "Suck 'em up!" for the twentieth time and swung into the Hawaiian ballad "I'll Remember You." Drunk and sentimental, the men wept as their stricken wives sat beside them, unable to comprehend what had transformed the boys they'd married into these grim-faced soldiers returning to war.

I was a nineteen-year-old cub reporter who didn't know any better, so I asked the soldiers straight out why they cried. I think the directness of the question prompted honest answers. Vietnam, they said, was a hellhole, the generals were fucking it up, the cause wasn't worth it, America ought to get the hell out and go home. Their stories became my first Vietnam reporting, as pure and true as any I'd do five years later in-country.

My last day in Honolulu I sat on the beach, acutely conscious of being halfway to Vietnam. I spent hours staring out to sea, trying to imagine what those men had tried to describe to me. Only my promise to Burrows kept me from following them back to Saigon. That night, aboard a navy medical ship that had just delivered hundreds of casualties to a military hospital, I listened to President Johnson announce he would not run for reelection. When loudspeakers broadcast the stunning news, some sailors cheered.

Now, I thought, it will finally end.

It didn't.

After Robert F. Kennedy's assassination that summer I plastered MCCARTHY bumper stickers all over my dad's car. He got mad, but he didn't make me scrape them off. Not even after Eugene McCarthy lost the Democratic nomination to Hubert H. Humphrey. Not even after Richard M. Nixon beat Humphrey. My dad drove the "peace-mobile" past the lockjawed salutes of military guards at the gates of Richards-Gebaur Air Force Base as long as he owned the car. He never explained why he kept the latex daisies, and I never asked.

I was graduated from MU on January 2, 1969, and went to work for the AP in Topeka, Kansas, three days later. Within six months I was a full-fledged Associated Press staff reporter in Miami, badgering AP general manager Wes Gallagher to send me to Vietnam.

A gruff chauvinist who'd competed against—and been beaten by—Marguerite Higgins of the *New York Herald Tribune* during World War II, Gallagher had little respect for women war correspondents and made it clear he thought they only got in the way. For a year, AP's personnel department responded to my entreaties with: "Your letter has been received and put in your file."

As two more years passed, seasoning me into a journeyman journalist, I often tore front-page bylines by UPI war correspondent Kate Webb out of *The Miami Herald,* scrawled across them in red grease pencil, "If I was in Vietnam, this would be AP's!" and sent them to Gallagher.

He grew increasingly annoyed. "I will never send a woman to Vietnam," he once answered.

"Never say never," I responded. I had nothing to lose. Working overnight broadcast shifts, covering hurricanes and hijackings, and being a gofer for the Apollo missions at Cape Canaveral and for AP's White House correspondents when Nixon vacationed on Key Biscayne was wearing me down.

On February 10, 1971, a helicopter carrying UPI's Kent Potter, Keizaburo Shimamoto of *Newsweek,* Henri Huet of AP, and Larry Burrows was shot down just inside Laos during a disastrous South Vietnamese offensive. All aboard were presumed killed, though evidence confirming their deaths wouldn't be recovered until 1998.

It was the greatest journalistic loss of the war, and at first I couldn't take it in. Larry had seemed invincible; correspondents in the field had treated him as a talisman. The superstition went that if you stuck with Burrows, you'd be safe, because no matter how bad it got, Larry always came through.

War's eternal mystery is that some humans die and some don't, and nobody gets to choose. We can say that Larry Burrows's luck ran out or that it was his time or any number of mumbo–jumbo–isms humans fall back on when we don't have answers to cosmic questions. The only thing I knew for sure was that he was gone, and my image of him would remain that of a tired man with haunted eyes, raising his hand in farewell.

Despite losing my Vietnam fulcrum, I continued to press Gallagher to send me to war. When he replied, "If you got killed, what would I tell your mother?" I fired back, "What did you tell Henri Huet's?" He did not respond.

On an ordinary Monday in April 1973, Gallagher's deputy in New York, Keith Fuller, arrived in Miami and I was summoned into the bureau chief's office.

Leaning back in my boss's chair, his feet on the desk, Fuller slid a green plastic credit card toward me.

"What's this?" I asked.

"Your ticket to Vietnam," he replied.

By sundown on that joyous day, I had used my new AP international air travel card to book my ticket, sold my 1966 Mustang to a delighted co-worker for a hundred bucks, given away most of my clothes, told my boyfriend to have a great life, and arranged a rendezvous with my parents in San Francisco in a week.

Fuller's mandate was brief: Get to Saigon to replace Edie Lederer, who'd been sent with other AP reinforcements the previous October when Henry Kissinger had prematurely believed that "peace is at hand." Edie had stayed on to cover the real cease-fire and prisoner exchanges.

Fuller promised I would have "complete freedom" to report throughout Vietnam, Cambodia, and Laos and would be "treated like any other staffer," with no restrictions or special benefits just because I was a woman.

Later, I learned that Gallagher had ordered Saigon AP not to let me go beyond the South Vietnamese capital and had decreed I was to be sent only on "safe" assignments. Fortunately, like so many other headquarters edicts, those two were ignored.

I was ecstatic as I shed the trappings of my Miami life. Pictures taken of me reuniting with my family in San Francisco show us during our last "happy days," hamming it up for the camera and holding on to one another in affectionate solidarity.

My brother, by then a navy ensign based in Alameda, was handsome in his uniform as his beautiful young bride stood proudly beside him. Though my mother was often caught lifting her hand to her throat in a nervous habit that symbolized her many fears, she smiled broadly into the camera lens. I looked impossibly young in my Sears polyester pantsuits and jaunty straw hat. My dad—the war veteran, the survivor, the only one who knew what I was flying into—frequently had his arm around my shoulders.

His was the last face I saw as my Pan American World Airways 747—*Clipper Intrepid*—pulled back from the gate. Through the terminal window, he gave me a thumbs-up: "Good-bye, and good luck." I choked on tears as I waved back.

By the time the jet's wheels had lifted off the runway, I'd dried my eyes and ordered my first ever cocktail in first class, those being the expense-account glory days when AP reporters were allowed to ride up front on any flight lasting more than five hours. Turning to the 3M executive sitting next to me, I announced: "I'm going to Vietnam."

My transition from domestic bureau drone to foreign correspondent was complete. My destiny had caught up with me.

At noon on May 8, 1973, I was standing in the door of another Pan Am plane, trying not to choke on humid air saturated by jet exhaust at Tan Son Nhut airport, when I heard my name being yelled across the tarmac and saw a man waving his arms.

With the dexterity of a veteran traffic cop, my new boss, George Esper, extricated my duct-taped Samsonite suitcase and Dad's battered World War II footlocker from customs, then steered me out of the terminal and into a waiting AP car at the curb.

My first impressions of Saigon were of waves of people trying to get somewhere else and of being so hot that I wanted to unscrew the top of my head and let the steam out. Both images stayed constants throughout my tour.

By the time we arrived at the AP office in the Eden Building half an hour later, I was firmly under Esper's ever flapping wing. George, I learned, was dedicated to the AP and devoted to his fellow correspondents. He was easy to love as a friend, if not always as a supervisor. We would argue frequently over approaches to my assignments, but George never tried to hold me back.

Rarely did I encounter resistance in Vietnam because of my gender. When I did, it was from American and South Vietnamese military brass. Soldiers in the field, as well as my own colleagues, expected me to haul my own gear and pull my own weight. In Vietnam, my performance was judged strictly on merit. The man I fell in love with there said he initially was attracted to me because I did my job well.

Those first twenty-four hours in Saigon, I met people who became as important to me as any I would ever know. Besides my future lover, I was introduced to three women who became dear friends, and I caught a first glimpse of an orphan boy I would help become an American citizen.

Minutes after my arrival, I was also staring into the faces of the maimed and the lost, of abandoned children and displaced old people, of skinny teenage whores from the countryside and plump matrons living high off their military husbands' corruption. I sensed that first day that I'd find my best stories in the streets, not on the battlefield.

I also gagged on Saigon's motorbike pollution, ate my first salt-and-pepper-fried cracked crabs, had an inaugural ride in the AP's "flying coffin" elevator, took beginner's notes at the "five o'clock follies" military briefing, wrote an immediately forgettable three-paragraph story on an Army of the Republic of Vietnam (ARVN) firefight, and went to a party honoring a colleague's departure and my arrival.

Careers are built on excellent timing and good fortune. That extraordinary first day became one of my luckiest. Horst Faas and Peter Arnett were passing through town. The war's most enduring photographer-reporter team had been in and out of Saigon since 1962, and each man was an international journalism star. Gallagher took a personal interest in their assignments and sent them anywhere on the globe from which he wanted an in-depth report.

Horst was then living in Singapore, while Peter had moved to New York; they were back in their old stomping grounds to see friends, eat favorite foods, and check out Asian antiques. They were supposed to go on to Australia together, by way of New Guinea, but the Vietnam story continued to sidetrack lesser adventures.

Their schedule was "loose," as they put it, much to the laughter of old friends who knew that trying to keep track of Horst and Peter was like trying to bottle lightning.

The two old Vietnam hands invited the office to lunch on Gallagher's expense account at a restaurant around the corner where hot sauce, chili flakes, rock salt, rice vinegar, and peanuts were staples in the center of the oilcloth-covered table.

Horst and Peter—along with Neil Sheehan, formerly of United Press International and then with *The New York Times;* Malcolm

Browne, formerly of AP and also with the *Times;* and David Halberstam, who'd left the *Times* to write bestselling books—were the most famous journalists of the war. All had Pulitzer Prizes, all had established towering reputations reporting stories that contradicted the official line, and all had driven presidents and generals crazy with their unflinching honesty in words and pictures.

Meeting Horst and Peter at the same time left me barely able to speak, which was fine, because Edith Lederer was doing most of the talking.

A tiny woman with big hair, baby wrists, and perfectly lacquered red nails, she was conversing with me while typing eighty words a minute in the AP office. She set the permanent pattern of our friendship by telling me to sit down and wait. I did. Within ten minutes I'd agreed to rent her apartment when she left, use her hairdresser, and copy-edit the story she was pounding out on deadline. I realized this take-charge woman's professionalism in Saigon during the past seven months had persuaded Gallagher to give me my shot, so I loved her instantly. I still do.

At lunch, Horst and Peter held court. Peter was the loud, cocky one, while Horst ordered the food and made sure everyone got served. He didn't seem to mind being the grown-up.

Peter was short but wiry, with thinning hair he wore long. His angular face was dominated by a nose broken in his younger days back home in New Zealand. As he told nonstop stories, he would feint and parry with his words, and when he stood up he did the same thing with his body, as though he were plugged in to an alternating current. He punctuated his tales, many of them off-color and at the expense of absent colleagues, with guffaws. His good humor was infectious, and I guessed, rightly, that he would be fun to be around, but only in small doses.

Horst was more reserved, but when he had something to say, the Vietnamese photographers leaned forward to hear it. He had a leonine head of thick chestnut hair, and the more wine he drank, the more he ran his hands through it. His soft mouth was often drawn into an amused smile, but his wide brown eyes were half-hidden under hooded lids; he was hard to read. He didn't engage in idle chatter as Peter did, but he could convulse a table of correspondents with a few succinct phrases in his German-accented English.

Later I found out he'd been heavyset nearly all his life, but when

I met him he was so thin that his hipbones poked against his tight jeans and his broad chest looked too big for the rest of him; the top two buttons on his plaid cotton shirt wouldn't stay closed. I guessed, correctly, that a woman could find a safe place to lay her head on that chest.

He smiled at me. I smiled back.

At the end of the meal, Horst paid the bill, then suddenly turned to photographer Dang Van Phuoc, who'd lost an eye covering combat, and pointed to me.

"Keep her alive," Horst said for no apparent reason. I thought of Larry Burrows's promise and had a premonition I'd be seeing more of Mr. Faas.

Phuoc saved me at least twice. The first time, I stood silhouetted too long in the doorway of a South Vietnamese army helicopter as it hovered over a dike in the Mekong Delta. He pushed me out, then jumped on top of me in the mud a millisecond before Vietcong bullets began to fly. His second rescue was halfway through my tour, when we'd stayed out too long on assignment and been caught on a dark Saigon street after curfew. He talked the trigger-happy policeman—of the infamous "white mice"—into letting us go. I'm sure there were other times I never knew about.

My Vietnamese colleagues earned a pittance compared to my salary, took more chances than I ever would, spoke several languages to my English, and were unfailingly polite about my cultural gaffes. Besides Phuoc, there was young Nick Ut, who won a Pulitzer Prize for news photography for his famous 1972 photo of Kim Phuc, the napalmed little girl running down a road with her back on fire. Huynh Minh Trinh was the office "fixer" who knew how to reach people in key places and who helped AP get countless scoops. Thai Phuc Ly was a highly educated young reporter and translator who could do it all; he frequently was my guide through the bureaucratic and linguistic maze. Tran Mong Tu—whom we all called TuTu, a term of endearment meaning "little one"—was a lively but modest young widow who'd gone to work for AP after her Vietnamese bridegroom was killed in battle. As the office secretary, she was paid less than $200 a month to hold us all together. By the time I left Vietnam, I loved her like a sister.

All my co-workers taught patience, endurance, and courage by their example. They opened generous hearts to us interloping round-eyes galumphing through their beautiful, war-torn country, and I was instantly, and permanently, indebted to them for their kindness.

After the leisurely lunch with Horst and Peter, Edie took me on a minitour of Le Loi and Tu Do streets, the heart of the refugee-clogged city that fanned out from the centrally located AP office, which was within a few blocks of the presidential palace, American embassy, Roman Catholic cathedral, legislative assembly building, and some of Saigon's best hotels and restaurants.

This became my neighborhood, where I bought a pine tree on Christmas Eve, cherry blossom branches for Easter, a yapping dog on my birthday, sling-backed shoes that took me dancing, Marlboros I smoked, a gold ingot I tucked into my boot heel in case I was captured, and just about everything else I needed to live day to day.

My favorite stops were tarp-covered tables where Hemingway could be had for eight and a half cents and Faulkner cost a dime. Like weather-beaten friends huddled together against the storm, these street stalls sheltered thousands of English-language paperback and cloth-bound books waiting to be recycled into fresh American hands.

The monsoon had long ago streaked their colored covers and pasted together many of their pages. Some had no beginning, others no end. Their original owners had cast them aside in haste, dumping them in alleyways where peddlers salvaged them to sell for a few piastres. Over the years, the piles had grown, paperweights of unread wisdom holding down the city's edges.

Napoleon's battles hid under Grimms' fairy tales, Bambi protected Darwin, *The Rise and Fall of the Roman Empire* leaned against Churchill's memoirs. Cockroaches built nests in *Europe on $5 a Day*, and fat rats nibbled at *The Joy of Cooking*. Bar girls bought Bibles because they liked the pretty plates, *Webster's Unabridged* made fine fuel for cooking fires.

But nearly every volume had a middle, and when I reread a familiar passage, it anchored me to find the story reassuringly the same: Gatsby still loved Daisy, the snow leopard still roamed the high mountains, Sacajawea still guided Lewis and Clark up the wide Missouri.

Like previous owners, I started out caring for my books. I dusted them, dried them in the tropical sun, supported them on new shelves. Initially, I guess, I hoped to find new truths in old company, but the longer I stayed in Vietnam, the less I looked for answers. After a while I stopped reading.

I assumed, correctly, that after I left, my books went back to the street. Hidden in one was Henry Kissinger's admonition that "we must learn from history." Another contained Ho Chi Minh's exhortation to fight on because "you are hard and proud, my friend, not soft and long like the tongue: together we have shared all kinds of bitterness and sweetness. . . ."

On that first day, at dusk, I heard my first *clickety-click, clickety-clickety-clack*. The sound, made by a boy striking together hollow bamboo sticks, became as familiar to me as church bells, a street anthem heralding the comings and goings of my life.

Already I'd observed old men and women lumbering behind pushcarts, their cheap pots clinking together, mingling odors of rice and dried shrimp, vegetables and pungent fish oil. The boy with sticks was sent ahead, to advertise.

Most of the nearly two million refugees who'd crowded into Saigon by 1973 to escape violence in the countryside couldn't afford the *pho* seller's soup, but the white-shirted bureaucrats, shopkeepers, soldiers, and most other workers with a job could buy a cheap bowl of noodles and broth dished up in the street.

Squatting flat-footed on the pavement, their skinny hips balanced a mere inch above the detritus in the gutter, diners summoned by the boy with sticks cradled a cracked porcelain bowl in one hand and dexterously moved wooden chopsticks back and forth with the other.

They had no finesse, these hungry Saigonese; greasy juice dribbled down their chins as the chopsticks went *snap!* like a clothespin on the noodles, out-up-into the mouth, back down into the bowl, *snap!* like a clothespin on the noodles, until the last drop of liquid was slurped, the tiniest morsel of meat consumed, and the bowl handed back for the dirty washpan. With a loud belch, a muffled fart, and a brief grunt, the satisfied customer relinquished his place to another.

All the while, the boy with sticks kept up his *clickety-clack, clickety-clickety-clack,* alerting passersby with his compelling cadence. The noise, especially in the evenings, made me want to tap my toe in time, softly clap my hands in accompaniment. I'd close my eyes and revel in the strangeness of it all, the *clickety-clack* blending with the honking of the little blue-and-white taxis, the whirring of chopper blades, the nasal singsong of Vietnamese TV.

There were many little boys with sticks, but their music, clothes, and cart smells were all the same.

"Oh look, here comes the boy with sticks," somebody would say, and we'd all lean over a terrace, sunset cocktails in hand, to watch as a dark head rounded a corner and bobbed down the boulevard. Wearing a shirt with missing buttons, torn shorts handed down from older brothers gone off to war, rubber slipper–clad feet moving in time to his hands, the stick boy always stepped lively to his own music, oblivious to the smiling round-eyes gazing down from their lofty perches.

Stick Boy's world was far removed from ours. He lived in a refugee camp or a nearby hamlet or a riverfront shack. Because he got a little food for his labors, he wasn't as skinny as the other urchins prowling the streets, but like them, he didn't go to school, didn't own a pair of shoes, probably didn't have a father still alive. If the war went on long enough, Stick Boy, too, would die on a battlefield or leave parts of his body there.

The boy with sticks became a touchstone, something to count on in my unpredictable world.

It was the same with Jasmine Girl. She was born about the time the flower children found Haight-Ashbury, the elder of two girls and the prettier one. Her baby sister had a mangled leg and couldn't wear shoes, but never mind, said Jasmine Girl, the sidewalks were warm on bare feet.

Every night this child of seven, eight, or nine—malnutrition made it hard to guess the right age—raced up and down the slimy cobblestones, hugging tight to a red plastic dishpan, scattering cockroaches and hungry-eyed hookers in her wake. Her long black hair swayed against her bony shoulders and never looked dirty, but her clothes were rags. Her eyes were bright as chocolate drops; her smile rivaled that of a Botticelli angel.

I was perfect prey for this little girl who depended upon the kindness of strangers.

"Please buy, please buy these flowers, Number One," she'd singsong in her memorized English, all the while rubbing her nonexistent belly.

Then she'd offer up hundreds of delicate jasmine blossoms she'd strung on a thread, their sweet, intoxicating fragrance drifting toward me on the evening air.

In the beginning, I bought as many leis as she had left in the red dishpan at curfew. But soon she claimed me as a friend, lying in wait to leap out of the shadows and grab my arm. To her there were two kinds of people, customers and friends. By and by, friends didn't have to pay. One night, when I reached for my wallet out of reflex, her oval face crumpled and her doe eyes dulled.

"For you, from me," she said, touching her heart, then mine. "Please."

My professional detachment began to unravel. Jasmine Girl wanted to give me the only thing she had. Why was that? It got harder, night after night, to watch her as she danced merrily away in search of an empty doorway, crippled little sister hobbling along behind, confident Jasmine Girl would find them a place to sleep before the whistle blew.

Jasmine Girl changed everything. Battlefield victories and defeats no longer seemed important; it was the suffering that mattered. Hers became the story I wanted to tell.

Exhausted and drenched in sweat in a riverfront Majestic Hotel room with fifteen-foot ceilings, I relived every minute of that inaugural day and knew, without a doubt, that I wasn't the same person who'd stepped off an airplane that morning. I was finally in the river, the current had me; it didn't matter where it took me.

Beyond my hotel window's iron grates, Saigon dozed fitfully, like a beautiful woman forced into slumber at sundown. Fishermen's twinkling lanterns reflected off the river. Floating restaurants bobbed at anchor. Passing cargo ships threw black shadows on the wall. Gunshots throughout the night testified to nervous sentries, reminding me that no matter how good the wine and pâté, I now lived in a city at war. Distant rumblings echoed from along the border in Cambodia. Towering cumulus clouds occasionally lit up the western sky—probably B-52s hitting their targets, I thought. I fell into a fitful sleep.

"Boy, that was sure heavy bombing last night," I said to Edie over coffee the next morning. I tried to sound nonchalant, a seasoned pro.

Breaking apart her hot croissant with her elegant fingers, she grinned as she gently put me in my place.

"That wasn't bombing, my dear, that was thunder."

A week later, in Phnom Penh with Edie on a "fact-finding tour" that also was her Cambodian shopping swan song, I was again jolted awake by *boom-boom*. Staring hard out the window, I tried to see the coming rainstorm. I was unconcerned, remembering my first breakfast conversation with Edie. Tucking a pillow under my cheek, I drifted off again.

"Boy, that sure was heavy thunder last night," I remarked to Edie the next morning.

Breaking apart another hot croissant, she grinned.

"That wasn't thunder, my dear, that was bombing."

I bought an umbrella, a poncho, and a helmet at the central market; Edie pronounced me ready to cover the war.

The noose had tightened around the Cambodian capital as Khmer Rouge guerrillas infiltrated to the edge of the international airport's two-mile runway. Pilots put commercial jets into sharp left-hand banks to avoid rockets fired by fourteen-year-olds who couldn't read. Terrified passengers wildly applauded every landing.

The capital's infrastructure was disintegrating: power was intermittent, the water seldom ran, refugees were everywhere. Beggars without legs trundled around in wagons made from American ammo boxes, their tiny wheels swiped from fake leatherette executive chairs at the U.S. embassy.

At the Hotel Royale, renamed the Hotel Phnom when Prince Norodom Sihanouk was overthrown and fled to China, there was no ice but plenty of gin. Fresh limes grew in profusion next to a pool where, if you held your nose when you dived in, the algae didn't bother you too much.

Beckoning like a cool cloth, the dim lobby still held traces of its elegant past. I thought of all the expatriate rubber planters and beautiful Eurasian women, diplomats and Corsican drug czars, and even of Jacqueline Kennedy, who'd glided past the tall porcelain vases now standing empty. Like their cultivators, flowers had become casualties of war.

What a sight this city must have been before Nixon and Kissinger launched their secret war in Cambodia. Even on that very day, southbound traffic still flowed unimpeded along the Ho Chi Minh Trail to Communist infiltrators in Saigon. Khmer Rouge child-soldiers less than ten miles away ate their victims' livers in the false belief that doing so made them invincible. Meanwhile, the Cambodian legislature debated whether to choose a cymbidium or a phalaenopsis as the national orchid. Debate dragged on for weeks; like so much in Cambodia, no decision was ever reached.

Edie and I were at the hotel to cover for AP correspondent Lee

Rudakewych, whose garden-suite office was also his home and a crash pad for a motley parade of photo stringers. After working two months without a break, Lee had reluctantly been persuaded to join other correspondents for a day at the beach at Kompong Som on the Gulf of Siam, a three-hour drive. They planned to be back by dark, when it was too dangerous to be on the roads.

"Can you handle it?" Lee asked dubiously.

"Of course," Edie replied, sounding slightly insulted. "You just take that Mercedes and go."

Every morning a handful of reporters, photographers, and TV crews sauntered down the hotel steps to a fleet of white Mercedes-Benzes parked under an ancient banyan tree. Neat little drivers in black patent-leather shoes with pointy toes awaited them patiently, polishing gleaming chrome bumpers to pass the time. Twenty-four waxed doors stood open to let butter-soft leather upholstery breathe.

In three minutes, the drivers had loaded up correspondents' picnic baskets full of Brie, baguettes, and wine; thermoses of coffee; portable recorders with Janis Joplin and Jimi Hendrix tapes; first-aid kits with plenty of morphine; flak jackets; and photo gear. As the air-conditioned caravan drove out of the hotel compound, pretty women in bikinis—French schoolteachers, girlfriends, and wives, groupies lured by the thrill—waved farewell as they deepened their tans. One woman became famous among correspondents after her fiancé showed up unexpectedly from Hong Kong and asked the hotel desk clerk which room his lady was staying in.

"Twelve, eighteen, and twenty-three, sir," came the straight-faced reply.

Most days, correspondents climbed into their limousines to go "up the road" to cover the war. But not that day. That day was for play, a rare and precious occasion for men and women who worked 24/7 long before anyone thought to invent the term.

Edie and I were joined in the AP office by Christine Spengler, a tenacious Belgian photo stringer who was making a name for herself in Indochina. We giggled together at the idea of cabling Gallagher that three women were in charge of his Cambodian war coverage but decided he might retaliate by firing Lee.

The day drifted on through the relentless heat. Edie and I wrote a roundup about scattered fighting and sent it off by motorcycle messenger to be passed by the censors and cabled to New York. We lunched, had a swim, took a nap. At twilight there was still no sign of our friends.

Then Christine burst into the suite.

"It's very bad, the Khmer Rouge have mined the highway, a small patrol got blown up. A few survivors were trapped in burning jeeps. We arrived just as reinforcements came. There was a lot of shooting. Somebody got nicked in the arm, but everybody else got out all right. I got very good pictures, and I can—"

Crash!

"Incoming!" Christine yelled. We crowded under the old iron bed's sagging mattress. The rockets were aimed at some oil tanks but were far wide of the mark. Christine mumbled about painting a bull's-eye on the tanks to help the Khmer Rouge, then buried her head in her arms as more rockets crashed down, each closer than the one before.

Finally they stopped: two minutes, four minutes, six. May's play-mate smiled coyly down from the wall. Bees buzzed around the honeysuckle bush. Not a hair on Edie's head appeared out of place.

Christine bolted for the door, yelling: "I'll count the dead."

Edie found a map and hunted for a ruler. Failing to locate one, we agreed a Tampax would do. Carefully marking off quarter inches along its length, we used it to plot the rockets' progress and the Khmer Rouge advance toward the heart of the city. Today they were closer than yesterday. Tomorrow they'd be closer still.

Christine reported back that three civilians were dead and eighteen wounded just a block away. Edie dictated and I typed on Lee's portable with the bloodred ribbon. The motorcycle messenger arrived, knowing rockets meant overtime. Half an hour later the story, with art, was on its way to New York.

During the rocket attack, the seventy-year-old bellman had delivered tepid tea by pushing his silver tray ahead of him as he inched down the hall on his stomach. This time, upright, he brought us dainty tinned-chicken sandwiches on china plates and apologized for the lack of mayonnaise. We tipped him the equivalent of his monthly salary.

Eventually New York AP cabled, "Good job," and told us we'd made *The New York Times* with our rocket story. Christine's photo ran, too. Edie and I cracked open a bottle of French red wine, and I sat back and reflected on a letter written to me years before by AP's Wes Gallagher.

In response to another plea to be sent to war, Gallagher—the father of three daughters—replied that the AP hadn't sent a woman to Vietnam because there was no safety anywhere. Acknowledging that his attitude was old-fashioned, he explained that AP staffers in Indochina had to do everything; in other words, a woman would have to cover combat. He softened the blow by adding that he never ruled out anything because as soon as he did, the AP went ahead and did it anyway.

Lee and company made it back at dusk the next day with broken lenses, flooded cameras, two wounded, all scared. They'd been caught between Khmer Rouge snipers and government armored personnel carriers. One Mercedes rode home on four flat tires—those pointy-toed drivers didn't earn their pay just to haul thermoses and bathing suits. If they weren't blown up, they were expected to get the boss home.

It didn't take courage to go "up the road" the first time, but it did ever after. Cocktail conversation swirled around whether it was worth risking your life for another picture of another dead soldier, another story about another orphaned child. A plaque fashioned from melted-down 105mm brass shell casings hung over the hotel bar:

GOING UP THE ROAD

If nothing happens, you don't have to be there.
If something happens, you don't want to be there.

When I left Phnom Penh, I took the grid-measuring Tampax with me as a souvenir. Stranded out in the field on an ARVN operation two weeks later, I used it for its original purpose. Sentimentality had become a luxury I couldn't afford.

All AP correspondents were expected to hit the ground running, so I was immediately writing about economics, refugees, maimed veterans, stalled peace talks between the Vietcong and President Nguyen Van Thieu's government, American missionaries, land reform (mostly a lack of it), and anything else that fell on my plate. The International Commission of Control and Supervision (ICCS), charged with monitoring the cease-fire (and failing miserably), offered the press corps rides on its helicopters and planes if there was an extra seat, and I jumped aboard every chance I could get.

Indochina was relatively quiet as I hitchhiked to provincial capitals, villages, and hamlets, from the demilitarized zone in the north to the mouth of the Mekong in the south, and west toward the Parrot's Beak, close to the Cambodian border.

In those early weeks, I began to notice a subtle shift in my energy level, sudden bouts of exhaustion when my legs filled up with fluid so that, by nighttime, I could hardly move around. Listening to friends complain about diarrhea and parasites, I chalked up my dwindling endurance to a delayed adjustment to daily 105-degree temperatures and alien internal bugs. I knew if I couldn't work seven days a week, I'd become a liability. If anything, my fatigue galvanized me to push harder.

Several times I was downright stupid, like when I rented an old Chevy in Vientiane and drove with three friends to Luang Prabang, the old Laotian capital. It took us three days to navigate the mined, bombed-out track of Highway 13; when we arrived in the most beautiful of all Laotian cities, nobody believed we'd come by road. As late as 1998, insurgents were still ambushing travelers who ventured overland.

From Luang Prabang we took a leaky boat up the Mekong River, in search of God knows what. I was following my nose then, and a hunch, and wound up shivering through a cold night in the mountains, sharing a precious orange I'd brought from Saigon with a seventeen-year-old Pathet Lao soldier.

"Cold wind from China tonight," he said in the halting, broken English he'd learned from listening to the BBC in the jungle.

The Communist guard should have taken us prisoner, but because our boat had strayed into his territory at sunset, we had lots of food, and we weren't armed, he allowed us to spend the night on his riverbank. Together, we counted falling stars.

At first light, my friends and I backtracked in search of the Hmong people who, trained and financed by the CIA, were fighting the Pathet Lao. I wrote about what I found:

"This," said the old Hmong man, "is not my home." He pointed toward a dusty road snaking through a cluster of ramshackle lean-tos offering more protection to the rats in the rafters than the people huddled on the dirt floors. It was a place where the number of grimy water pots, dented kerosene cans and threadbare burlap bags separated the poor from the poorer. The camp's richest man earned his title by owning an oilcloth for his table and a hoard of canned Ovaltine.

"The Americans feed us," Shong Yi Tho said angrily. "Anything you raise here halfway up this mountain dies—the pigs die, the chickens die, the rice dies, the opium is no good. The children think rice comes from the sky because airplanes bring it to us. . . . I don't care who wins the war, the Americans or the Pathet Lao or the North Vietnamese or [Laotian general] Vang Pao. . . . I want them to leave me and my mountain alone forever."

When I returned to Saigon, Esper was incredulous at my chutzpah. The trip remains one of my best memories.

Another is a three-day respite at a leper colony on the beach at Qui Nhon, the most peaceful place I visited in Vietnam. The Canadian nuns who'd run it since the early days of French colonialism said that because of the lepers, the compound had always been avoided by armies. However, injured soldiers who made it to the gate were always carried inside and treated, irrespective of their politics. The nuns had many stories of would-be enemies healing together and of their being reluctant to leave the tranquillity they'd found behind the much feared walls. Every night the nuns hung an antique lantern in the window, a beacon to anyone lost in the dark.

"All knocks are answered," said the Mother Superior. "If we have to, we go out and carry the wounded in. God does not discriminate."

When Esper sent me to Hue to chronicle the rebuilding of the old imperial city mostly destroyed during the 1968 Tet offensive, I found a young pianist playing a grand piano in the rubble, a painter posing a seminude teenage widow in front of an emperor's tomb, an optimist promoting his cheesy hotel as an international tourist destination (I wonder if that nice guy lived long enough to see his dream realized?), and the wizened Queen Mother of Vietnam living behind the doors of a weed-choked house, reading her Bible by a single dangling lightbulb.

It was on those assignments that I found my journalistic voice and the confidence to use it, and learned how to spin such gold into stories.

All AP staffers worked every day for three months, then got a week's R&R. But we weren't drudges; there was time to go out for a quick lunch or grab a nap on a desk. Occasionally I went to embassy soirees, hoping to pick up story leads, and I had friends in for dinner.

I'd inherited Edie's maid, Kim, who had a sister, Sue, who had a mother, Madame. They turned my spare room into their family headquarters, and I was glad to have them to come home to. They were discreet and unobtrusive, and if I couldn't actually converse with them, we nonetheless understood one another. Or at least they understood me.

On Sundays, they went to see relatives in Cholon, Saigon's Chinatown, but always returned on Mondays. Madame had cooked at the French embassy in Hanoi before fleeing to the South with her family after the country's partition by the 1954 Geneva Accords. She prepared elegant, elaborate dishes for my infrequent dinner parties, while her two daughters cooked my everyday meals, did all the grocery shopping, and kept my clothes clean and my home spotless. The "see no evil, hear no evil, speak no evil" trio also protected my mongrel dog from a Chinese stew pot, where most strays wound up.

My friends were other correspondents, a couple of diplomats, and a few civilians. Besides radio reporter Laura Palmer, I was closest to Jolynne Cappo, who'd first visited Saigon as an antiwar protester from Michigan State University in 1965. The following year, she returned as an English-language editor for the Vietnam Press Association and eventually fell in love with Corsican rubber planter and

Aterbea restaurant owner Pierre d'Ornano. They were married the day before the 1968 Tet offensive began.

With her midwestern accent, ready laugh, baby son, Olivier, and great-hearted Doberman pinscher, Roscoe, Jolynne lent me a sense of belonging, if only peripherally, to an American family. Being with her was comfortable, familiar, and fun, and I stopped in at least once a day at Aterbea's, where she and Pierre took most of their meals at an oversize table next to the bar.

Unless I was with Laura or the d'Ornanos, or Faas was in town, I was usually by myself, craving sleep. A perfect, though very rare, night was reading a book or reviewing interview notes, then going to bed at nine o'clock.

As the swelling in my legs and lymph nodes worsened, I sought help from the hospital at the U.S. naval base at Yokosuka, Japan, where my brother was stationed, and from specialists in Bangkok and Hong Kong. Returning to Saigon with different diagnoses—parasites, a virus, an unidentified tropical disease—and a medicine cabinet full of antibiotics, I continued to grow weaker. The medical mystery deepened.

Because my biggest fear was professional failure, I made up my mind to live on Lomotil to control diarrhea, put my swollen feet up every chance I got, and keep my mouth shut. I was determined to tough it out and decided a more active social life would help me forget my troubles.

Vietnam was not a place where too many Westerners had actual "dates," but casual sex was easy to come by. So, thankfully, was deep affection and even love.

My first romantic encounter was with an aging television correspondent headed home to New York, where his career would soon end. He was sweet and I was bored, so he became my first fling as I became his last. As he left for the airport the next morning, he realized he didn't have a present for his wife. I took off my heavy Cambodian silver bracelet and gave it to him, not so much out of guilt, for at twenty-five I was too self-absorbed to consider the consequences of marital betrayal, but because, cavalierly, I knew I could get another one.

Within weeks of arriving in Saigon, I'd shed inhibitions I'd spent a lifetime acquiring. Nobody from my past was around to pass judgment or put the brakes on my behavior, so nothing held me back from my own impulses. That is one of the great intoxications of war—if you want something, you take it, consequences be damned, because you might not be there tomorrow.

My second lover was just passing through, a former army doctor on a trip around the world who'd stopped off to visit his best friend. He was sexy, sophisticated, funny, and divorced from a journalist, so he knew the territory. I promised to adore him for three weeks if he'd do the same. Deal! We ate good food, had great talks, enjoyed each other's bodies, and vowed to stay in touch. We remain comfortable friends.

Three months into my tour, I took my first R&R and tacked on some vacation, too. I was unattached, had $2,000 in salary burning a hole in my pocket, and wore a size ten. Life was good. I'd visited only Mexico and the Caribbean before my transfer to Asia, so I had a whole new slice of the world to explore. After three months in Indochina, I'd become a blithely confident traveler, writing to my parents: "How can I get lost if I haven't been there before? Besides, on vacation, nobody's shooting at me!"

I went to Bali for a week because of its beaches, then went to Bangkok for a week because of its big-city room service. At the beach, I enjoyed my own company. When I got to the big city, I was ready to knock somebody dead.

I picked the wrong guy.

A mutual friend had urged me to look him up; when I did, he invited me to dinner. I asked him to stay for breakfast. Within two days, he'd carried me down a moonlit street, tossed me into a fountain, and made love to me on a balcony. He was tall, dark, and handsome. He also had a wife and kids back in the States.

When I returned to Saigon, friends saw I'd fallen hard for somebody, but they thought it was Horst Faas. He'd returned to Vietnam twice since our initial meeting, once presenting me with a beautiful silver elephant in full view of the AP office. I'd done nothing to deserve such a gift, but everybody gossiped anyway.

The first time Horst took me to dinner at the old Hotel Royale, where he kept a permanent room, he spent the evening talking about his old friend Larry Burrows. When we got to my apartment it was almost curfew, but we stood another hour at the front door before a tentative, chaste good-night kiss. From that evening on, we were friends.

Our relationship has mutated often, but because we started as friends it has been easy to continue that way. For a time we were devoted lovers, in our fashion. We've also been creative collaborators. The book *Requiem* came to life in my Colorado living room in 1990 during a third bottle of wine, long after my generous husband had gone to bed and left us to bicker about how to properly honor and remember photographers killed in Indochina.

The book, which originally was meant to be only a catalog to accompany a traveling exhibition of those photographers' best work, became a labor of love for Horst. His Taurean temperament bulldozed the project past all obstacles—some of them seemingly insurmountable—until *Requiem* finally was published, to great critical acclaim and astounding popular success, in November 1997. As he compiled and edited the photos, I labored over how to make nine thousand words of text relevant and moving in a coffee table–size photo book. We continually reassured and supported each other even though we were separated by ten thousand miles. Blessings on the founder of the Internet and the inventor of e-mail.

Requiem brought us closer than ever, and working with Horst over those seven years brought me great joy. The book, as much as his own renowned body of work, is his legacy. The humility and dedication he invested in honoring his fellow war photographers guided him in making sure his friends' and colleagues' lives, as well as their art, was not lost.

From those first enchanted Saigon days with him more than a quarter of a century ago, until yesterday, when we had our weekly phone chat about creaky knees, AP bureaucracy, and another unwelcome birthday, Horst and I have cherished each other. Next to my husband, he is the dearest person in the world to me. Our emotional connection transcends time, distance, and very different lifestyles. Because of Horst, I look back on Vietnam not just as a war story, but as a love story.

I'm chagrined, now, that I used him as camouflage while continuing to see the other man for the next several months. Horst once got off a plane in Saigon as my R&R lover was boarding it, and they greeted each other in customs.

Laura Palmer, who witnessed the encounter, was greatly amused but made it clear to me from the outset that she thought Faas was by far the better fellow.

"He's kind," she said, recognizing his greatest attribute before I did.

Laura was the sort of soul mate we're all lucky to find once in our lives. Office proximity threw us together on my first day, when she wandered in from NBC next door to check the wires for war action.

Laura had done exactly what Larry Burrows had ordered me not to do—she'd turned up unemployed in Saigon and managed, as a freelance radio stringer, to support herself well enough to stay on after the boyfriend she'd come with had returned to the United States.

She was sanguine, worldly, athletic, and stylish. We each had a nice apartment, acquired Ming porcelain together as much out of respect for its survival as for its beauty, preferred being in the field instead of the office, and wanted to make a difference with our reporting.

I was superstitious about going on an operation without Laura, but increasingly I had to, as she focused on the more lucrative freelance reporting in Cambodia.

Our friendship grounded me. She became my best sounding board, and we loved each other no matter what. We could screw up, be silly, be sad, and act stupid in front of each other without having to justify our actions or moods. When our stories were tough, Laura baked bread and I made meat loaf. We were, at heart, two good middle-class midwestern girls who also happened to be independent, strong-willed, feminine, vulnerable, tough, and oddities in an alien place—no contradiction there, right?

The beginning of the end of my Vietnam tour occurred on March 11, 1974, when a single 82mm artillery shell blew up a schoolyard in Cai Lay, in the Mekong Delta, and shredded twenty-three children. Eighty-six more were maimed by shrapnel. It was my last big story.

The South Vietnamese government immediately went into propaganda overdrive, blaming the Vietcong. The Communists countered that President Thieu was so desperate his soldiers had fired on their own school to gain more American aid.

Most Saturdays, I spent three tedious hours listening to diatribes from a small group of alleged Provisional Revolutionary Government (PRG) negotiators living in a compound surrounded by concertina wire and sandbags at Tan Son Nhut. The colonel in charge wasn't really a Vietcong colonel, though we didn't know that then. Instead, Vo Dong Giang was a four-star North Vietnamese general who later became deputy foreign minister of a unified People's Republic of Vietnam.

Vo Dong Giang loved Mozart and Belgian chocolates, read Camus in French, and, during the weekly press conference's tea break, enjoyed tweaking reporters with double entendres that his interpreter could barely translate. Listening to his rhetoric week after week, I'd learned to pay attention to the undertone, the message within the message.

The Saturday after Cai Lay, I drew him aside: Did the Vietcong fire the shell, yes or no? I'd heard all the goddamn propaganda I wanted to listen to, now I wanted a straight answer from him, a military officer who professed to live by a code of honor. Did his troops kill those kids? I was so angry, I could feel the blood beating in my temples.

"No, Miss Bartimus," he replied. It was the first time he'd addressed me in English. "No. It wasn't us. I give you my word. It wasn't us."

Eighteen years later, over more hot tea in a chilly room, Vo Dong Giang repeated his denial. Together, we lamented war's waste.

I'd accompanied a U.S. congressional delegation to Hanoi aboard a White House plane. The now venerated Vo Dong Giang had been part of the welcoming committee on the tarmac.

When I'd appeared in the plane's doorway, he'd called out: "Missy Tad, you get fatter!" Then he'd startled me by embracing me against his rough wool overcoat, and I'd found myself in the incongruous position of introducing American VIPs to their Vietnamese hosts.

I was inordinately glad to see the old warrior. I'd brought chocolates and Mozart, just in case, but had never dreamed we'd actually connect. That afternoon, in a formal reception salon at the Foreign Ministry, he carefully turned the pages of a photo album in which he'd collected snapshots of his time at Tan Son Nhut. As Vo Dong Giang spoke, it was clear his days as a soldier had been more successful and less complicated than his subsequent tenure as a politician. Shortly after our meeting in Hanoi, I heard through State Department friends that he'd "retired."

After Cai Lay and the onset of the scorching Vietnamese summer, my health nosedived and my reporting lost its corresponding energy. By then I could hardly drag myself out of bed in the morning. I'd racked my brain trying to remember when I'd first gotten sick, and narrowed down the onset to a trip to the Mekong Delta, where farmers had been burning defoliated fields. As I'd researched the story on a new rice crop and how South Vietnam was managing to feed itself, I'd developed a bad cough while breathing in the smoke. I'd never gotten over my hacking.

In April, I collapsed in the office and Esper put me on a plane to the Swedish Clinic in Bangkok. I have only two memories of my three-week stay there. One is of excruciating gold injections into my liver; the other is of Australian photojournalist and independent cameraman Neil Davis, who became my hospital roommate after being wounded in Cambodia. The liver shots were horrible; Davis was terrific. The rest is a blur. I'm told all I did was sleep.

By May Day, Wes Gallagher was berating me down a phone line from New York that I had to come home "before you die like Maggie Higgins." Gallagher's old nemesis, who'd shared a Pulitzer Prize for her reporting of the Korean War, had contracted a tropical disease on her tenth fact-finding trip to Vietnam in 1965 and died a few months later in Washington, D.C.

I couldn't walk across my hospital room without falling; I was no longer of any use to the Saigon AP bureau. Devastated, I was certain that what I considered a temporary physical problem would be blamed on my gender and used as an excuse to not send any more female reporters to cover wars.

That didn't happen. It's now commonplace to see women covering all news events around the globe. Edie Lederer went on to many more wars, and I eventually reported on sectarian violence in Northern Ireland and guerrilla movements in Latin America.

But I was also wrong about having a temporary sickness. When the AP's doctor had examined me before I went to Vietnam, he'd pronounced me in "excellent health." Treating me at University Hospital in New York upon my return, he was baffled by a plethora of seemingly unconnected symptoms.

So were more than fifty physicians I consulted during the next eighteen years. In 1992, desperate to find out why I kept getting pneumonia and was struggling to walk, I again turned to the AP's same doctor. In the intervening years, he'd become a specialist in autoimmune diseases, particularly HIV and AIDS.

He put me through a battery of tests that hadn't even existed when I returned from Vietnam, and almost two decades after I first fell ill, he concluded I had "acute onset of autoimmune disease" resulting in "infertility, muscle joint pains, severe fatigue, skin sensitivity to sunlight, low grade fevers, and severe dental problems."

A year later he pronounced me "incapacitated," effectively ending my twenty-five-year AP career. Denied long-term disability by the AP's insurance carrier on grounds I couldn't prove I'd been exposed to toxic poisoning so long ago in Vietnam, and refused early retirement benefits by the AP, I was given a Hobson's choice: trade my pension to keep my health insurance or lose all benefits within two weeks. Sick at heart as well as in body, I acquiesced.

I know that nobody gets away clean.

Life certainly wasn't fair to the nearly fifty-eight thousand American soldiers killed in Vietnam. Millions of Vietnamese—fighters and civilians, North and South—also died. Land mines continue to maim, and birth defects plague new generations; Agent Orange is our lasting legacy in Vietnam.

My health problems remind me that thousands of veterans in this country still fight the Vietnam War every day in their own bodies.

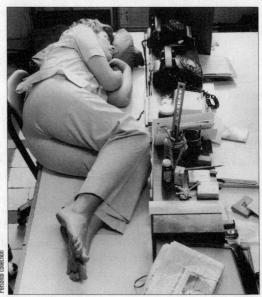

Personal collection

Following the AP doctor's diagnosis and my subsequent fall from corporate grace, I went through a time of "Why me?" Eventually, I realized nothing was really lost: I could still think, I could still write. With the help of dear friends, of Horst, and of my beloved husband, I moved on.

I'm glad that during my last days in Saigon I had no inkling of the long road ahead. Instead, I believed I'd soon return to my life there, to my job, and to my friends. All I needed, I thought, were a few weeks of sleep and my mother's home cooking to cure whatever ailed me.

While Esper handled the paperwork and Laura assumed responsibility for my household, I packed a few small pieces of blue-and-white porcelain and a couple of changes of underwear to carry back to America, sure I wouldn't require much else for a quick trip.

On my last day in Vietnam, I made the biggest mistake of my tour; I did not say good-bye to Trung.

When he'd come into my life he'd been about ten years old, though he looked barely six or seven. He'd spent half his life sleeping on Saigon pavements. He said his family was dead, and the way he said it, I believed him.

Laura and I had been walking back to the AP office after dinner at Aterbea's one balmy twilight in early September when a familiar-looking orphan fell in behind us, imitating our striding gait and making us laugh with his pidgin-English wisecracks.

We knew the kid on sight; he'd been working the streets for months, begging money, cadging cigarettes—just one of thousands of orphans surviving on their wits, quick fingers, and fast feet. Trung, though, had seemed the bravest, the boldest, the Artful Dodger of his gang of thieves.

He'd never followed me so far before, all the way up the three flights of stairs and into the bureau. That night he sat in Esper's big swivel chair, picked up a *Stars & Stripes* newspaper, and began to read it—upside down!

"Me number one!" he said, poking his little finger into his bony chest. "You take me to movies? We get ice cream? *You* number one!"

Laura, who had watched in faint dismay as my apartment had filled up with Kim, Sue, their mother, and assorted strays needing a place to sleep "just for a few days," read my mind.

"Don't do it!" she warned. But even as she wagged her index finger at me, I knew I was about to play God.

Why that child? Why that night? It didn't matter. I took Trung home. The first time he held a toothbrush, he tried to comb his hair. Then he put the toothpaste on his face. He tried to eat ice cream with chopsticks. When he accompanied me as a paying customer to Givral's, the restaurant where he'd hawked newspapers and begged, he calmly tucked the napkin under his chin and stuck out his tongue at the waiter who'd chased him away with a soup ladle the day before.

The waiter did not bring the big bottle of soda for half an hour; he also did not get a tip.

Trung stayed three months, filling my airy apartment with his laughter. His lice went down the drain, the cracker tin became a cookie jar, and the stubborn little hustler got to sleep in his own bed.

But the ways of the street can't be banished by a hundred baths and a new teddy bear. And Trung needed to learn to read and write, to go to school. The afternoon our little blue taxi backfired at the orphanage gate, Trung screamed and begged for another afternoon of kung fu movies:

"Please no no thank you *no no* I love you *no no no!*"

Wiggling away from the nice orphanage director trying to coax him into the building, Trung aimed himself at a concrete corner and rammed the wall again and again. I fled into the street, trying to convince myself I was doing the right thing but believing in my heart that I was not.

At three A.M., Trung went over the orphanage wall and disappeared for three weeks, four days, and five hours. Then the AP office door opened and he was back. His bright new clothes were gone, traded on the black market for food. His shoes had disappeared. His gaunt cheekbones offered mute testimony to his struggle to stay on his own.

Slowly he walked toward me; we were both exhausted when his tear fell on my outstretched hand. The whisper was so soft, I wasn't sure I'd heard it as I bent my lips to the dirty head buried in my neck:

"Please thank you I love you me go school yes?"

He gained four pounds in two months. One Saturday he asked if he *had* to go back to my plant-filled house to be coddled, a weekly habit around which I'd built my days. His friends from the orphanage were going to a kung fu movie and he wanted to tag along. And so the umbilical cord was cut and Trung began to live his own life.

All that last day in Saigon, I told myself I simply didn't have time to say good-bye, even though I'd promised—*promised*—never to leave without telling him. Besides, I rationalized, I was coming right back.

In truth, I broke my promise because I didn't have the courage to face a child who'd put his total trust in me and whom I felt I'd abandoned. On my last day of war, I was a coward.

Trung, however, was not. When the North Vietnamese launched their final offensive on Saigon, he had the courage to save himself with the help of George Esper, the late AP photographer Jim Bourdier, and a trail of helping hands stretching from Alaska, where I was then AP's bureau chief, to Saigon and back through the Philippines to Los Angeles.

Traveling under an assumed name because the desperate South Vietnamese army had banned any male above the age of ten from leaving the country in case they were needed to fight, Trung somehow got separated from his volunteer American escort during his evacuation plane's refueling stop in Honolulu.

After bluffing his way aboard another jetliner, he arrived in Los Angeles with two telephone numbers in his pocket. One was mine. The other belonged to David Seltzer, a Hollywood director whom Trung had met in Saigon while David was filming *Green Eyes*, a documentary about the war's orphans.

David's phone number was a local call. Trung dialed, David answered, and by the time I tracked Trung down, he was living in Beverly Hills with a new mom and dad, new sisters and a brother, and his own bicycle.

Well-meaning friends persuaded me that Trung would be better off with the Seltzers than with a then single mother in Anchorage. David, who subsequently adopted Trung, suggested through intermediaries that I not contact the boy for ten years. I agreed, though later I wondered: Why ten years? Why not five? Or two? What harm could it do?

In 1985, Trung and I nervously met in a Chinese restaurant on the beach in Santa Monica. He ate with a fork; I used chopsticks. In fluent English embellished with idioms and slang, Trung at last was able to tell me his harrowing story and I was able to explain why I'd left Saigon.

If anyone asks, "What's the best thing you've ever done in your life?" I can answer, without hesitation, that it was taking a little boy home on a sultry Saigon night a long time ago.

But that feeling of satisfaction was far in the future when I boarded the airliner that lifted me away from the war. On that sad evening, no one was there for me to kiss or to hold or to tell me good-bye. Stretched across seats 1A and 1B, shivering under three blankets, and facing the bulkhead, I was too weak to raise my head for a last glimpse of Vietnam. I fell asleep before the jet's wheels left the ground.

May 8, 1973, to May 8, 1974.

It was over.

Ed Bassett

Tracy Wood

Spies, Lovers, and Prisoners of War

In Vietnam, May 1972–February 1974

March 30, 1972. Holy Thursday in New York. Halfway around the world in Vietnam, already Good Friday. Easter week. The week North Vietnam proved to the world one more time that it had the manpower, the firepower, and, most of all, the willpower to launch yet another full-scale offensive against the South.

"We're sending someone to Vietnam to beef up the bureau," UPI foreign editor Bill Landry told me as NVA troops raced south toward Hue. "You're next on the rotation."

It wasn't supposed to be this way. I was in New York, working on the foreign desk at UPI, at that time one of the world's largest news organizations. I was studying Chinese with the promise that when Peking opened its borders, I would be on the first team in. In the meantime, there was the excitement of New York, a sometimes diffi-cult boyfriend, and a job I loved.

And not Vietnam. Everyone at UPI was clear on that. The war was winding down, and so was the UPI Saigon bureau.

Part of me—a big part—was relieved. The war was so old, it seemed it always was a piece of my life. Stuey Burns, the quiet older kid who lived a block or so away in the New Jersey town where I grew

---

Tracy Wood, the only woman ever elected president of the Association of Foreign Cor-respondents in Vietnam, later was an investigative reporter for the *Los Angeles Times* and investigations editor of the *Orange County* (Calif.) *Register*. She currently is editor in chief of *Ms.* magazine.

up, died there. Johnny Biddar, whose mom had been friends with my mom since high school, was a helicopter medevac pilot there.

I'd read books on the war, covered demonstrations against the war, listened to endless debates about the war, and, for the past seven months, edited daily stories from the Saigon bureau about the war.

I'm not violent by temperament and don't enjoy violent or even scary books or movies. I'd never known violence in my personal life, and frankly, the idea of going to Vietnam frightened me.

But the minute the invitation left Landry's mouth, the other part of me, the decisive part, knew I was going.

"When do I leave?"

Landry looked out over the newsroom. "There's something I need to tell you."

UPI's executives had debated whether to send a woman to Vietnam. Editor Roger Tatarian and news editor H. L. Stevenson wanted me to go. Landry, my immediate boss, didn't.

"Why not?"

Landry was a veteran foreign correspondent who'd covered the world's major conflicts and glamour spots, from the savagery of civil war in the Congo to the luxury of Paris. He's a mild, fatherly personality with no children.

"I don't believe women should cover wars," he said, the glare from the fluorescent lights on his glasses hiding whatever was in his eyes.

I didn't know how to answer. There were more than one hundred reporters and editors in that huge UPI world headquarters. But the only sound I heard was the clacking banks of Teletype machines that streamed stories across the wires from Europe, Latin America, the Middle East, Asia, and the rest of the United States. For the first time in my life, someone in a position to decide my future was telling me that because I was a woman, I wasn't good enough.

Kate Webb, one of the finest combat correspondents of the Vietnam War—male or female—worked for UPI. In fact, right then she was covering the South Vietnamese army's flight from Quang Tri, the provincial capital south of the DMZ.

A year earlier, she'd been captured by North Vietnamese troops in Cambodia, held for three weeks, and nearly died of malaria before being released. Was that what spooked Landry?

"If anything happened to you," he continued, "I'd feel bad."

Stop. Right there. Landry had just articulated the problem that for generations held women back. Not overt sexual discrimination. Not conviction that women couldn't do the job. Something much harder to fight: well-meaning men in positions of authority who honestly believed it was more important to protect women from risks than encourage them to reach for the stars.

"Wouldn't you feel bad if a male reporter got killed?" I wanted to argue, but I kept silent. I was going. Tatarian and Stevenson had decided that.

Less than a year later, I was sipping coffee with North Vietnamese diplomats in Vientiane, Laos, all alone and chafing with uncertainty, negotiating the final details for U.S. press coverage of the release of American prisoners of war. Outside, Walter Cronkite and more than thirty other journalists from major U.S. newspapers and television networks waited for the results.

In the months between New York and Vientiane, I learned, as had thousands of unschooled Americans before me, how easily the human body is shredded by small bits of steel. I discovered that a child raised in the midst of garbage and death still will smile at a glimpse of his mother's face. I looked into the blank eyes of American prisoners of war, nerve endings battered and souls too fragile to risk revealing even a toehold of hope.

I drank and sparred with cold war spies, the real kind who slide from persona to persona and late at night whisper in confidence the terrors of their childhood. I witnessed, over and over, a love and gentleness between men for each other that I never knew existed.

I fell in love myself.

ARRIVAL

In the rush to leave, I took all of my shots at once: plague, typhus, polio booster, and I've mercifully forgotten what else. Most people at that time spread the shots over a few weeks to avoid the flulike side effects. But the war wouldn't wait. The day after the shots, I woke with a high fever.

Stevenson and UPI president Roderick Beaton were taking me to a farewell lunch at one of New York's private men's clubs. I had to make it. I feared that if I couldn't handle the simple consequences of inoculations, they'd change their minds about Vietnam. They joked later that I fainted facedown in my soup, but that's not true. I made it to the ladies' room before I fainted. Okay, I made it *most* of the way to the ladies' room.

Stevenson sent me home in a cab, handed me $20 for the fare, and reminded me—twice—to bring him the change. UPI was like that.

I dressed carefully for my Saigon arrival. My new boss, Arthur Higbee, had spent nearly three decades filing stories from some of the most exotic datelines in Africa, the Middle East, and Europe. He spoke fluent French with a Parisian rather than provincial American accent, he loved classical music (at least we had one thing in common), and he was known to disdain the ordinary.

I wanted his first impression to be a good one. My long hair was wrapped into the most sophisticated knot I could manage. A tailored yellow-and-white dress—short, but not the then-fashionable miniskirt—panty hose, and white heels made my rail-thin body look, I hoped, professional. As it turned out, I'd made a mistake that would haunt me for months.

But on that day, my only concern was getting to Saigon. I tried not to let the other Air Vietnam passengers see me clutch the seat arms when we took off from Hong Kong's old Kai Tek airport. I've always been afraid of flying, something I carefully didn't mention to the UPI execs in New York. I also didn't tell them I had a heart murmur that doctors said probably was fine as long as I kept checking on it. I found out later that compared to the weight, alcohol, and psychological problems—not to mention drugs, malaria, hepatitis, venereal disease, and dysentery—that afflicted some other members of the press corps, I was in peak physical condition.

My first preconceived idea about a war-devastated nation was pushed aside before the runway at Tan Son Nhut airport came into view. As the 727 began its descent, I pressed my nose to the window. The ground below was green, as green as Hawaii or the northeast United States in summer. Green. My favorite color. Peaceful, calm, reassuring. The color of childhood backyards, the friendly woods where we played cowboys and Indians, the cool soft grass where we ran barefoot at dusk to catch fireflies.

BASIC TRAINING

"During a rocket attack," my instructor said between sips of bourbon, "throw yourself down as flat as you can. Find a dip in the ground, a gully, even a slight indentation, and get *down*. The explosion will spray up. So unless the rocket lands right on top of you, you should survive." It was advice that would prove itself over and over.

Welcome to Combat Correspondent 101, or as I called it, "Barney's Basic Training."

One thing nearly all beginning Vietnam War reporters had in common was a total lack of military experience. We were mostly in our twenties, the men either draft exempt or, as happened to UPI's Pulitzer Prize–winning photographer David Kennerly, already combat veterans when their draft notices arrived. A few had done military tours in Vietnam, either with the military newspaper *Stars & Stripes* or, in the case of one of our stringers, with the Green Berets. But they were the exception. This was on-the-job training.

My instructor was the late Barney Seibert, a fifty-two-year-old UPI reporter who chain-smoked Salems, was at least one hundred pounds overweight, sweated sitting still in the oppressive Vietnam humidity, and knew more about military history and strategy than many generals.

He was a combat correspondent in Korea, and now was on his second tour in Vietnam. He also was a private, gentle man who tended colleagues through hepatitis, dysentery, and other ailments that hit despite the best precautions.

But Barney was no pushover. He had a temper, and it could roar. Show him disrespect or let him see someone picking on an underdog, and his rosy complexion turned purple. When that happened, no one, not the U.S. ambassador, not the most aloof general, not, I thought, God Herself could avoid his thundering wrath.

"It's up to you whether you carry a weapon," he continued, hitching himself more comfortably onto the stool in the CORDS bar, a U.S. government–run refuge in Hue.

"But the most important rule, the one you can *never* forget, is this: We're only reporters. What happens to us, what we think, what we feel, what we experience, doesn't matter. We're here to cover the war. Anytime we get too scared, too sick of it, too tired, we can hop on a plane and go home. The military and civilians can't do that. They're stuck. *They're* the story, not us."

It was my first day in Hue. I'd flown north packing my new, tailor-made marine fatigues, new combat boots, a 35mm Nikomat, and—the latest in communications technology—a seven-pound tape recorder with a handheld mike.

The fatigues were from a Saigon black-market tailor who catered to the news media. Reporters weren't allowed to buy military-issue fatigues and, catch-22, many unit commanders wouldn't let reporters travel with them *unless* they wore the appropriate garb—paratroop fatigues with the airborne, standard green camouflage with the army, tiger stripes with the marines.

There was one other catch.

Saigon bureau chief Higbee ordered me to stay away from combat.

"You're too feminine," he said a few days after my arrival. Blame that yellow-and-white dress. Higbee was candid. He liked seeing a Western woman in a dress. He wasn't saying the few other female reporters who had worked for any length of time in Vietnam *weren't* feminine.

But most non-Asian women spent their time in jeans and T-shirts or baggy fatigues—the same work clothes worn by their male colleagues. Rarely did female journalists wear dresses other than to an embassy function.

"Don't become like the others," he advised. "Stay feminine."

And, he insisted with the full authority of my boss, I was not to cover the fighting. Political stories, diplomatic receptions, refugees, and hospital stories. No war.

I couldn't let that happen. I was a full reporter, not a partial reporter. This time I didn't have executives in New York to take the decision out of Higbee's hands. I'd have to figure it out on my own.

A helicopter tour to get a sense of the geography seemed a reasonable initial compromise. Just north of Hue, between the outskirts of the city and the DMZ, Vietnamese marines, supported by what remained of U.S. Marines and American air strikes, were fighting to reclaim territory overrun in the past few weeks by the North Vietnamese. I'd check it out from a safe distance and decide the next step from there.

It was a disaster. The flight was arranged by the American province adviser, a cheerful, steady personality who gave you confidence just standing still. Accompanied by his Vietnamese counterpart and a U.S. military observer, we were picked up by a helicopter based in Da Nang, fifty miles to the south.

Everyone knew I'd just arrived in-country, so it seemed okay to ask obvious questions:

"Where are the doors?"

"You don't want anything to obstruct their field of fire," the American adviser said, pointing to two Vietnamese door gunners, their bodies wrapped in ammunition belts, who stood guard at the doorless entry to the helicopter.

We climbed into our seats and greeted the two smiling U.S. pilots. The door gunners casually took up their positions on the floor, one on each side of the helicopter, facing out, legs dangling into space.

First they showed me the beaches, long, wide, lovely stretches of deadly, mined sand. Then they demonstrated flying techniques. Skim so close to the water that the helicopter skids almost touch the wave tops, then up, up, up, and a hard sideways turn that left me staring straight down at the earth through the missing doors. Next the treetops. Heading dead straight for a line of tall trees, the pilots pulled up just in time to keep the skids from pruning the upper branches.

"Cowboys," shouted the U.S. adviser over the roar of the helicopter's engine. He grinned happily and nodded toward the pilots. "Good practice. When they fly like this in combat, the North Vietnamese don't see them until it's too late."

Right arm locked around camera and tape recorder, left fingers aching from my death grip on the seat rim, I tried to turn a grimace into a semblance of relaxed understanding.

Before I was forced to respond, the inside of the helicopter turned to chaos. The door gunners simultaneously opened fire, legs braced, faces grim, M-60s aimed directly at the ground, the constant din of machine-gun fire overriding even the racket of the engine. The helicopter began a series of sharp twists and turns that even the greenest newbie like me knew had nothing to do with stunt flying. Too scared to close my eyes, I let the camera and tape recorder swing wildly from the straps around my neck while I clung to the seat rim with both hands, praying that whatever was happening, it would end *now*.

"We got lost," the American adviser said matter-of-factly when we were back on the ground. Lost indeed. The Da Nang pilots, unfamiliar with the battle lines north of Hue, strayed not just into North Vietnamese territory, but clear up into the DMZ.

I've wondered what the North Vietnamese on the ground made of that lone U.S. helicopter stunt flying its way north. Whatever their mystification, they'd radioed the alert to be ready for the return flight. And while we innocently headed home over the heads of hundreds of expectant NVA soldiers, they opened fire.

"It's difficult to bring down a helicopter with ground fire," the adviser assured me later. "They have to hit it just right. The tail rotor, maybe."

Or the pilots, I told myself.

"But they did hit us," he continued. "Here, let me show you."

There were the bullet holes. A couple near the tail, two or three closer to the front, and one right through the empty seat directly behind me.

"Well, we can't tell Arthur," Barney said thoughtfully when we met that night at CORDS for predinner drinks. "He'll have a fit you didn't follow his orders."

I took a deep swallow of my own drink.

I was tired and shaky and going to have a fit myself if I didn't find a way to change Higbee's policy.

And then Barney did something for which I will always love him. Starting right then and over the next two weeks, he showed me all he could about covering combat.

If I'd been a new male reporter, the training would have been the same but done openly, with war stories to share with the staff back in Saigon and more tips and encouragement from colleagues. Barney and I kept quiet.

By the time he returned to Saigon, I knew as much as any new reporter. It certainly wasn't West Point, but it was enough simple survival to allow me to do my job. For example:

- Forget what you learned about basic car care in the United States. When you see a pothole in the road, aim straight for it. The NVA learned early that Americans treated their cars well and swerved to avoid deep ruts. NVA soldiers mined the ground next to potholes, and a lot of soldiers died.
- Military jeeps overturn easily. Under fire, never swerve sharply.
- Always carry an ice chest of cold Coke and a carton or two of cigarettes. Humans in war appreciate the smallest courtesies.

Barney took me to a remote area and we practiced shooting a borrowed handgun, although I decided I wouldn't carry one. I was a civilian news reporter—a noncombatant to all sides. If I was captured, I didn't want there to be any confusion about my role. Some reporters said they did carry weapons. A few said they'd rather shoot themselves than be captured.

Arthur had to know I wasn't obeying his rules. There were no stories about nurses, few about refugees. The detail in stories I filed, if nothing else, had to give it away. But I never said anything, and neither did he.

Barney also covered for me when I went to increasingly vulnerable firebases, the hilltop outposts that were the major line of defense through much of the war but now were being made obsolete by the NVA's new long-range artillery. And he never told Arthur when I hooked up with a unit that let me stay with them for a few days in the field. Or about the day I was ambushed.

AMBUSH

The puff of dirt shot straight up from the embankment. Strange. What quirk of physics causes dirt to leap from the ground?

Our military jeep was headed south from the Quang Tri battle zone to Hue on Highway 1, the main artery that connects Vietnam's coastal cities from the Chinese border to the deepest delta.

Normally, I would be driving the military jeep that UPI rented in Hue. We never went alone into the field. Safety demanded the buddy system, usually a reporter from one of UPI's client newspapers, but occasionally a photographer.

We always left word where we were headed so people would know where to start looking if we didn't come back on time.

And we strictly obeyed the "daylight rule": Never go out before eight A.M., and *always* be off the road before dark—*well* before dark. South Vietnamese government troops might control the main highways during the day, but the situation was wide open after sundown.

Today I'd left the jeep in Hue and gone with a U.S. Army major to look over the embattled troops he advised. Not a pretty sight. While the bulk of the fighting was in the hands of the highly competent South Vietnamese marines, scattered South Vietnamese army units reinforced—more or less—parts of the perimeter.

"It's the corruption," the major complained. "Everything, every decent assignment, every promotion, everything requires a bribe." No money, no results. As we started the drive back to Hue, he said bitterly that he was counting the days—less than two months—until he was out of there for good.

Another half hour and I'd be at the Hue post office, taking my place in line with dozens of Vietnamese, each of us waiting to make a long-distance telephone call. Once I'd screamed my story notes across the static to the UPI bureau in Saigon, I could head to the small, cinder-block-walled guesthouse that served as the UPI head-quarters in Hue. A hot shower, change of clothes, and I'd be ready for dinner with an army captain who'd been shoved into my life a few weeks before and was now as reluctant as I to let go.

Another dirt puff gusted from the ground, just behind us this time and a bit higher on the embankment that separated the blacktop highway from the weedy, abandoned rice fields below. I turned to watch the dirt clods dissolve in the still afternoon air.

Bullets.

War lore says events sometimes transpire in slow motion. This was one.

Driving south through the hot, humid air, I lost all sensation, in-cluding fear. I saw nothing of what others in the jeep—the U.S. Army major at the wheel, the two South Vietnamese soldiers in the cramped backseat—were doing. I felt nothing, not even the jarring crash of the jeep's wheels slamming through potholes. I heard no sounds, not the rush of wind through the open jeep, not the racket of combat, not the shouts of my compatriots. Only curiosity re-mained. My eyes took in every detail of those mesmerizing puffs of dirt.

The next burst was right beside the jeep, but too far down the embankment for the red dirt spray to reach us. Beautiful.

Ambush Alley. It's a nickname given countless vulnerable stretches of highway in war zones all over the world. Like this straight, unshel-tered section of Highway 1 that for months was a contested zone in the battle for Quang Tri. Some days the highway was firmly in the hands of the South Vietnamese marines and U.S. support troops. Other days, the warnings went out early. Avoid Highway 1 today. And sometimes, like today, you just didn't know until you got there.

We were speeding now. I don't know at what point the army major at the wheel shoved his combat boot flat to the floor, but the jeep's engine groaned toward its top speed of eighty miles per hour, and the empty blacktopped highway stretched straight ahead. One embankment dropped to the right, another rose a few feet above our heads on the left, and there was nowhere to take cover or turn off the road.

To my right, the North Vietnamese crouched in the weeds and bushes, firing AK-47s, one meticulous single shot after another. Not ripping ribbons of automatic fire, but carefully aimed single shots. Target practice. We were sitting ducks. The NVA were confident, unhurried hunters, certain their game had no escape.

Another spray, big this time. Mortars. Deadly shells spraying earth and stones high into the air. And much closer.

Other reporters and photographers had been shot at in almost exactly this spot. A few weeks later, ABC-TV cameraman Terry Khoo and his film crew would die barely a mile away.

Only a couple of weeks before this, the first dead body I'd seen in my life crumpled with a bullet through his brain not far up this road. I remember standing spellbound.

Death.

I'd come to Vietnam afraid that I would be afraid. Too afraid of death to be a good reporter. Too afraid to do anything. Would I fall apart? Run home?

What about inside? How could you see violent death and not be crushed? How did you prepare to learn firsthand about human beings deliberately killing one another?

I didn't know. And those questions I was afraid to ask even Barney.

And then I was staring down at a young Vietnamese man who minutes before had been alive and now was a washed-out grayish parchment.

"That's it?"

Death was supposed to be a cosmic earthquake, a churning tornado of blackness, a soul-screaming pain that broke you forever.

Now I knew. Fear disappeared, along with spirituality. Something hard inside took their place. Death was nothing huge or dramatic or frightening. It was small and absolute.

I didn't want to die. But once the mystery was gone, I took comfort in its finality. Or at least, for years afterward, that's what I believed.

Sounds broke through my defensive bubble. In the tight backseat, the South Vietnamese soldiers trained their American M-16s in

Ed Bassett

the direction of the attack and opened fire, the din drowning out all else.

Except the pounding. I have no idea when it started, but suddenly I was aware of a massive hammering in my head. My steel helmet was pulled down almost to my eyes. My neck, turtle fashion, was tucked as far as possible into my flak jacket. Still, my arms and legs were unprotected, open to whatever the NVA shot through the open side of the jeep.

I knew I should do something, but the awful pounding in my head made it impossible to think. Slowly I turned toward the driver. His left hand was on the steering wheel. His mouth was wide open in a shout lost to the racket of war. One word seemed to come faintly through the clamor. Down! I read it on his lips more than heard his voice. Down!

Suddenly, the pain raining down on my head had an explanation. His right hand balled into a fist, the major was pounding with all his strength on my helmet.

"Down! Get down!"

Jeep designers may disbelieve, but it's possible for a five-foot-seven-inch woman to curl into a ball and scrunch into the kneehole between the seat and the dashboard. I know.

KILLERS

"How far away were the mortars?"

The question was the professional one. Back home, if someone narrowly escaped a terrible accident, the obvious question was, "Are you okay?"

Now I was learning the military equivalent. Soldiers in combat didn't ask one another, "How do you feel?" To an outsider, "How far away were the mortars?" sounds impossibly cold and clinical. It's not. Tell a soldier the details and he or she will fill in the emotions: The mortar hit less than twenty feet away, easily close enough to kill, but somehow it didn't. Men of war know what that means. They know how frightened they were and how afraid you must have been.

Some bull through their fears with bravado, alcohol, drugs, or all three. Others close themselves off, just shut their emotions down.

But some—watch for it—treat one another with extraordinary tenderness in those moments. Outsiders need to learn the codes. An extra second of eye contact. A quiet, unusually detailed debriefing that requires the teller to get it all out in the open—nothing held back to add to the nightmares that will inevitably sneak out of the dark. A careful studying of each individual, staying alert for signs of trauma. A million and one little signals of caring, of trying against impossible odds to make sure that fellow human beings stay human.

Stay human in war. A true oxymoron. The purpose of war is to kill, maim, and dehumanize your opponent. Armaments purposely rip bodies into jagged pieces. No matter what fear and common sense scream, soldiers move out on patrol again and again. Some lose touch with humanity altogether. Like the serial killer.

A college graduate, he was, as far as anyone knew, a reasonably normal man until he found his calling on long nights of reconnaissance inside suspect villages and behind enemy lines. By the time I met him, he terrified everyone, including his colonel.

I'd stop by his unit's base every few days, hoping for bits of information to help sort out the accuracy of the often wrong official government statements issued by all sides.

His unit was spies. The goal was to come and go silently, leaving behind no trace of their presence. The work was done only at night. If they were in danger of being caught or having an alarm raised, they were authorized to kill—quietly. But the main idea was to avoid detection. A dead body left behind was the spy world's equivalent of a brass band announcing, "Reconnaissance has been here!"

To protect themselves, the men in that unit carried garrotes, metal wires that are pulled tight around an opponent's neck until he strangles. Some in the unit never had to resort to the garrote, others once or twice. But the serial killer somehow was in danger of being caught almost every time he went out. Again and again his wire jerked tight around a Vietnamese neck and a body was left behind for the NVA to discover at sunrise. And he enjoyed it. Over and over he would report how necessary each killing was, his voice alive with relish.

Like everyone else, I was civil to his face and scared to death of him.

"He's a killer," his colonel told me. "Avoid him as much as possible." The serial killer was due for promotion. He didn't know it, but his colonel said it wasn't going to happen. If he wasn't promoted, he would leave the military.

And become what? The last I heard, he'd volunteered to fight in the Middle East, but that was twenty-five years ago.

LOVER

"Too close," my captain said quietly as we discussed my encounter with the NVA ambush. I think sometimes if we are very, very lucky, we meet someone and know each other instantly. This was such a connection.

I'd needed a ride from Da Nang to Hue a few weeks back, and calls to military acquaintances turned up an army captain on temporary duty in the area and his jeep. Halfway up the Hai Van pass, locked behind a diesel-spewing, barely crawling truck convoy, we'd looked at each other, and he has been part of my life ever since. He knew me and I knew him.

He was a stable personality, sensuous, intelligent, gentle, and well educated, with a fine sense of humor. I can still picture the lively light in his eyes. Can you tell I was very much in love?

He meant commitment, children, giving up my career, staying around the house, and the PTA. This at a time when my own life was just opening up, the whole world was out there, and I wanted to see and learn about it all.

His colonel approved. Hell, *everyone* approved. He was turning down his promotion to major, giving up his military career, and planning to go to law school when he got home.

"He's seen too much," said his colonel. "He's everything the army needs, but he's too sensitive for this war."

Could we make this relationship work?

HOW PLEASE?

Beat AP. If it sounds like a high school cheer, well, there's truth in that. The UPI-AP rivalry was one of the greatest competitions in U.S. journalism.

Each day UPI's New York headquarters sent out the "logs": How many major newspaper front pages used UPI stories, and how many went with AP? Serious business. Vietnam was one of the longest-running front-page stories in U.S. history, and the goal was to beat AP. Every day. Every story.

To convince newspapers that the UPI story was better than the AP version, reporters always were expected to file breaking news before the competition. "Beats" were measured in seconds. Honest.

But you had to be right. No mistakes. If the AP reported twenty killed in fighting and we said there were eighteen, New York was sure to fire off a Teletype message asking for an explanation. In the old days, long before my UPI experience, those New York queries typically ended with a chilling, "How please?" In other words, explain yourself.

The New York editors were more polite when I was in Vietnam, but the unspoken message was the same: "How please?"

Fast. Accurate. Well written. The three requirements of a top wire reporter. And it was *fun!*

I literally used to remind myself that all this was real. I was traveling the world, covering the most exciting—and most frightening— story of the decade. And they were paying me!

UPI was privately owned and expected to turn a profit, although I don't know that it ever did. AP is a co-op. Newspapers, television, and radio stations that want the AP news wires are assessed membership fees based on their size. That made AP the more financially stable of the two. In years when wars, assassinations, elections, or natural disasters decimated the news budget, AP could ask its members to increase their payments. UPI was locked into contracts.

The financial setup meant that in addition to covering the news, we were constantly reminded to "downhold expenses," a phrase we heard so often that UPI retirees to this day call themselves "downholders."

The word originated one hundred years ago or more when stories were sent from around the world by expensive cables, not the kind that link computers, the old-fashioned kind like telegrams. Cables were paid for by the word. To cut costs, reporters and editors developed their own language, cablese, which abbreviated some words and combined others. "Hold down" became "downhold."

One of the most famous cables was the World War II resignation of a South Pacific reporter: "Hours too long. Pay too low. Life too short. Upstick job assward." Or at least that is the legend passed along to those of us who came later.

Beating the AP was so ingrained that there was little a reporter or photographer would refuse to do, short of bodily harm. UPI legend Merriman Smith, riding in the press pool car in Dallas four cars behind President John F. Kennedy, grabbed the car's only radio-telephone and dictated the news that stunned the world:

"Three shots were fired at President Kennedy's motorcade today in downtown Dallas."

Instead of hanging up, Smith earned himself journalism immortality. While the press car careened in pursuit of the wounded president's limousine and the AP reporter screamed in frustration and beat on his head and shoulders, Smith bent over with his head between his legs and refused to give up the phone.

At the hospital, he was first again to another phone and flashed the news:

"Kennedy seriously wounded, perhaps fatally, by assassin's bullet."

And on it went . . . Kennedy's "limp body cradled in the arms of his wife" . . . Vice President Lyndon B. Johnson on board Air Force One taking the oath as president.

AP Teletypes were silent for a full seven *minutes* after the first UPI report and never caught up. Smith last saw the opposition through a window on Air Force One. The plane was taxiing down the Dallas runway. On board were the new president of the United States, the body of President Kennedy, and Merriman Smith. Outside, running across the taxiway, was the AP reporter. Too late, again.

In Vietnam, the tradition thrived. AP and UPI reporters rarely socialized. We ate at different restaurants, drank in different bars.

When a UPI stringer reached the only phone in a remote corner of the airport, he surreptitiously pocketed the mouthpiece, leaving his rival to shout futilely into the receiver.

But tricks were useless unless you had the facts. And in Vietnam, that meant doing everything in your power to learn more and more.

When presidential adviser Henry Kissinger announced on October 26, 1972, "Peace is at hand," I was packing for a stint in Cambodia.

American military personnel weren't allowed to travel to Cambodia, at least not officially. That meant separation from my captain right as he was coming to the end of his tour of duty.

We still hadn't resolved our basic impasse. I'd grown up in a stable household, was well cared for, and lived in the same house in the same small town most of my life. Summer vacations we traveled, and I had been encouraged by both parents to choose the career that interested me most, regardless of apparent barriers.

In the days before I left for Vietnam, my parents interrupted a trip, drove a thousand miles to have dinner with me, and took me to the airport.

They were concerned about my going to Vietnam, but they never tried to talk me out of it. We'd spent years sweating through my brother Scott's draft status. Just when it seemed he was safe, I was on my way.

I'd known ever since I was small that I was lucky. I wanted the same for my own children. And I knew I wasn't ready.

My captain was. He craved permanence and a family with a hunger that was almost visible. When he spoke of the future, his eyes sparkled at phrases like "mortgage" and "lawn mower."

And he was such a good person, such a decent and personally exciting man. When I thought of him, nothing seemed impossible.

By the time I returned to Saigon near Christmas, he would be a real short-timer with only days left in-country. R&R, we reassured each other. We'd put up with our brief time in December and then give ourselves a real reunion on my next R&R. We'd meet . . . somewhere. He would be out of the army by then. We'd figure it out.

So, as Christmas approached, I covered the roads outside Phnom Penh by day and studied biographies of North Vietnamese leaders, among other issues, in my hotel at night.

If the war truly was coming to a close, the U.S. prisoners would be released. How could I get to Hanoi?

PEACE WITH HONOR

"We today have concluded an agreement to end the war and bring peace with honor in Vietnam and in Southeast Asia," President Nixon announced to the world on January 23, 1973.

At *last!*

No one—including, it seemed, top newspaper editors—understood why there was no celebration in South Vietnam.

The tubercular old cyclo driver who stationed himself outside the UPI office each day, reading his newspaper and waiting for the fares that would send him gasping down Tu Do Street, told me what it meant: The United States was getting its prisoners back and abandoning South Vietnam. It was only a matter of time until North Vietnam took over the whole country.

"The people of South Vietnam have been guaranteed the right to determine their own future, without outside interference," Nixon's announcement continued.

"The United States is forsaking us," translated Vietnamese in cafés and soldiers shopping on the black market.

Beginning reporters are taught that no matter how hard they try to be impartial, they always will have biases. It's a normal part of being human. The goal isn't to rid yourself of all feeling and opinion, but to be conscious of those attitudes and alert to the ways they can creep into stories.

The hardest struggle I had with my own convictions occurred in the days immediately after the cease-fire announcement. I loved my country, and I'd grown to love the Vietnamese. Vietnamese and Americans are a lot alike—fiercely independent, stubborn in defense of their ideals, and blessed with a wonderful sense of humor.

Like many Americans who spent any length of time in Vietnam, I was sickened by the pervasive corruption and the apparent willingness of South Vietnamese leaders to sacrifice their homeland for their own greed.

The beauty of the country captivated me. Despite everything that the war had done to the land—defoliation, bomb craters, eroded hillsides—it still was stunning, from the long, magnificent coastline to the exotic hill country jungles.

And now I looked at the Vietnamese men and women who worked for UPI and those I'd come to know outside the company and was embarrassed: Yes, the United States was going to collect its prisoners and go home. Republicans and Democrats alike had had enough.

Thousands from my generation killed and wounded. Thousands—maybe millions—more from both sides in Vietnam dead, permanently injured, and economically ruined.

In my heart, I celebrated the end of this war that dominated my coming of age. In that same heart, I mourned for a Vietnam that different leadership might have created.

And I was excitedly curious about the future: within days, Vietcong and North Vietnamese delegates would arrive in Saigon. What were they like, these soldiers who'd sacrificed so much to fight first the French and then the United States? What would the future bring?

Shortly after dawn on January 28, 1973, Saigon was blasted awake by one final rocket attack against Tan Son Nhut airbase. The NVA message was clear: We're close by. Hours later, North and South Vietnam began a nationwide cease-fire.

HANOI

The surly Aeroflot stewardess checked my passport, pushed it back at me, and turned disagreeably to my two companions, Pulitzer Prize–winning AP photographer Horst Faas, who was West German, and Chris Callery, a British cameraman for NBC.

She was no more polite to them than she was to me. At least her attitude apparently had nothing to do with the fact that I was the only American on the nearly empty flight from Vientiane, Laos, to Hanoi.

Virtually every Western reporter in Saigon and dozens more throughout Asia and in Paris and Washington had petitioned the North Vietnamese and American military for permission to cover the POW releases. Only the three of us were told, "Take the Aeroflot flight from Vientiane. Your visa will be waiting in Hanoi."

And I was the only U.S. reporter.

I'd started working on it back in December when I got myself included on the manifest for a trip that Representative Pete Stark, a California Republican, was planning to Hanoi.

Stark's trip never came off, but it started me on a journey that ended with the North Vietnamese allowing me to make two trips to

Hanoi to cover prisoner releases. For the second trip, they gave me a visa to bring along about thirty other journalists.

But first we'd tried to convince the U.S. military to let a small group of reporters and photographers fly to Hanoi with the official delegation from Clark Air Base in the Philippines. Initially the military seemed willing, but then a range of officials told us that Nixon vetoed the idea.

According to the information we got in Saigon, Nixon supposedly said something like "No U.S POW ever will be photographed behind bars."

Why he opposed the coverage never was made clear. But documents among the Nixon papers in Washington indicate prisoners released sometime earlier through Germany said they felt harassed by the news media. Whatever Nixon's reason, I couldn't find a way from Saigon to change his mind. I even tried contacts from an earlier UPI assignment, asking Nixon's old friend Health, Education, and Welfare Secretary Robert Finch, for help. Word came back: Forget it.

Me? Forget it? Not a chance. If the U.S. government wouldn't help, maybe the North Vietnamese would.

The problem was, whom should I talk to and how? The Saigon government was less than thrilled to have the Vietcong in town. Thumbing their noses at both the VC and the Americans, they housed the Communists in barracks without air-conditioning on Tan Son Nhut air base. The old, barbed wire–ringed compound was called Camp Davis, named for Spc. 4 James Thomas Davis, killed in 1961, the first U.S. casualty of the war.

Communist delegates were allowed outside only to attend official meetings. In the first few days, reporters, photographers, and television crews jostled for position at every meeting, shouted questions in English, French, and Vietnamese, and shoved business cards into the hands of anyone who would accept them. There had to be a better way.

If the Vietcong—officially the Provisional Revolutionary Government, or PRG—didn't get out much, they did have telephones. And if there was one thing that UPI reporters did extremely well, it was work the phones. Phones were a lot cheaper than airfares and hotel rooms.

Every night, sometimes for hours, I was on the phone with translators or whoever in the PRG delegation could speak English. I learned that even supposedly hardened Communists get bored and lonely.

They were reluctant to talk about their personal lives and not authorized to say much about the political situation, so we talked about what was going on in the rest of the world, current uses of English slang, anything impersonal enough not to cause trouble. One night we spent nearly an hour discussing the appropriate uses of Mrs., Miss, and Ms. And gently but persistently, I'd put in my plug to cover the POW releases.

After the PRG phone session, I'd head to my next resource, an Eastern European Communist member of the four-nation peace-keeping force. We'd met within a day or two of his delegation's arrival to police the cease-fire and now had drinks nearly every night. Almost immediately someone from a Western consulate warned Barney: "You and Tracy be careful. He's a spy."

I'd learned quite a bit about spies in the past few months. They seemed to be everywhere. There were Americans who ostensibly were travel agents, antiques dealers, civil engineers, and economic consultants. In reality, I was told, they worked for the CIA.

Probably half of those who supposedly were CIA agents really weren't. And others, whom no one suspected, probably were. Life in Saigon could be pretty confusing.

In addition, the military in past years had given press credentials to intelligence officers, a practice that ended when the press corps loudly protested that it endangered lives and ruined their credibility.

Most pervasive of all were the Vietnamese themselves. Who was really rooting for the Vietcong? There was no way to know. And as long as the journalists did their jobs accurately, it didn't matter. At least that was my attitude.

Now we had an Eastern European Communist who supposedly was a spy. Well, why not?

One memorable night, Barney and I went out drinking with the CIA station chief and the Eastern European "spy." Does the CIA guy know the Eastern European is a spy? Do the CIA agent and the Eastern European know that Barney and I know that they're both spies? My head was spinning. *MAD* magazine in real life. Spy vs. Spy.

What counted was that the Eastern European might help me get to Hanoi.

He was an intense man, lonely, loyal, an idealistic risk taker who drank too much. One night, when the bar was mostly empty and the bartender was wiping the tables and looking at his watch, the Eastern European began to talk.

He always needled me about Appalachia and poverty in the United States. Now he told me why—really—he was a Communist. It had nothing to do with economics. It was personal.

He told about the boy (himself) during the Nazi occupation of his homeland whose father was in the Resistance, a Communist because it was the Communists who stood up to the Nazi occupiers. And then his father was captured. And the boy who still lived in the eyes of the man who was sitting across the table from me was the one who found his tortured body crumpled in a ditch.

"You want to know why I'm a Communist?" he demanded. "The Communists were the only ones doing anything to stop the Nazis. Not the English. Not the Americans. Not until they had to. How would you feel if it was your father in that ditch?"

POWS

The prisoners in their gray and faded red-striped baggy pajamas stood at the iron-barred windows of the cell doors. A few were outside, walking between cells.

Callery, Faas, and I were too far away to see the expressions on the prisoners' faces, but something in their posture made me uneasy. They were only a day away from freedom and I'd expected them to be energized. Instead, they were droopy and something else I couldn't identify.

It was the same later in the day when we were closer. It wasn't entirely their eyes, blank, deliberately emotionless, avoiding eye contact. It wasn't just that they wouldn't talk to us. The guards had told us not to talk to the prisoners, and I assumed the POWs had been given the same instructions. When we thought no one was watching, we tried quietly to communicate, but the POWs were steadfast. Until they were certain that they were being freed, I doubted they would break the rules.

There had been rumors for years that POWs were tortured and forced to make public statements denouncing the war. No wonder they were leery of anyone with cameras, including Callery with his handmade NBC logo.

But there was something else. Something bigger. What *was* it?

Most captured Americans were fliers, air force and navy pilots, navigators, and B-52 crew members shot down on bombing raids of military installations, factories, and highways.

Once all of the prisoners were released, they talked about the torture.

Those who parachuted into the hands of Vietnamese villagers were seen as evil personified: enemy devils who impersonally dropped the massive bombs that killed men, women, and children and flattened military targets along with civilian homes.

Furious villagers vented their rage on the dazed and sometimes badly injured Americans. They were stripped of their clothes, beaten severely, spat on—battered and humiliated in every way short of death. In fact, some may have died at the hands of the first civilians to rush to the site of a downed parachute, but most were turned over to government officials and taken to Hanoi.

And there the torture was systematic—and far worse. Prisoners were singled out seemingly at random. They were beaten, had their limbs stretched and twisted until they lost consciousness, were deprived of sleep and food, and kept in isolation, sometimes for years.

I didn't know those details as the three of us waited for the U.S. prisoners to board camouflaged buses for the trip to Hanoi's bomb-wrecked Gia Lam airport.

But I was nagged by something terribly wrong that I couldn't place.

Then I began to understand.

They had no identity.

Even from a reasonable distance, I can identify friends, including those in the military, by the way they walk and hold their shoulders, their general posture.

These men had no posture.

Or they all had the same posture.

They were unidentifiable, taller and shorter, darker and lighter versions of the same man. Their faces had the same lack of expression; they walked the same, stood the same. No one stuck out in the crowd.

Only long practice could have caused that total loss of individuality—practice and a deathly need to be obscure.

These weren't men like I had ever known.

This was primitive survival.

If you've never seen humans like this, I hope you never do.

THE LAST POWS

Inside the prison, more than two dozen American POWs stood nervously, seemingly unsure whether it was okay to acknowledge the nearly equal number of U.S. reporters, photographers, and television camera crews that suddenly filled the small space.

One POW vigorously refused the cigarette I offered, while a nearby colleague eagerly palmed a fistful of Winstons, checking first to make sure no one was watching.

Most stood mute. Their own rules allowed only the U.S. officer they recognized as their prison commander to speak on their behalf. Whoever that was for this group was indistinguishable among the shapeless gray and washed-out red prison uniforms.

Suddenly a familiar profile passed the barred window overlooking the yard outside.

A young prisoner looked. And looked again in disbelief.

"Is that *really* Walter Cronkite?"

In the strange world of prisoner releases, this moment was one of the most extraordinary.

Cronkite, the Most Trusted Man in America according to a national poll, strolling among prisoners who, in some cases, hadn't seen U.S. TV in four or five years—years spent in part under torture or in solitary confinement. Now the CBS News anchor was on assignment, covering the POWs, quietly, professionally, and politely. The same qualities in person that he projected nightly into millions of homes.

Three weeks after my first visit to Hanoi, I was back on a one-day visa that allowed me to bring in about thirty other journalists for the final POW release.

Getting here had been another experience. I'd asked the North Vietnamese during my previous trip for permission to return. When it was granted, a serious condition was attached.

The once-a-week Aeroflot trips were the only commercial flights into Hanoi. During my first stay, we were accompanied at all times by two government officials, someone from the Foreign Ministry and a translator—although the translator and I did slip away one afternoon to a highly recommended soup shop.

We saw all the tourists' spots, the open market, Ho Chi Minh's tomb, peaceful Hoan Kiem Lake in the heart of the city, and the former red light district, the center of sin during the French colonial era that now was rubble. Officials said a large number of civilians died when the neighborhood was struck by a B–52. Later, U.S. officials told us the B–52 didn't drop its bombs on the houses, it crashed there.

Whatever the truth, there was nothing but ruins for several blocks. And having shown us all of this, the North Vietnamese didn't want to waste their time trying to entertain me for another week.

"You can come," they said. "One day only. Hire a plane."

To their credit, UPI officials in New York actually considered the idea.

Then they learned it would cost $7,000.

Which is how everyone else got to go.

I asked the North Vietnamese if I could bring reporters from other U.S. news agencies to help offset the cost.

"Yes," came the answer. But they needed names and other identifying information to screen them. As I recall, only one name was rejected, a South Korean journalist working for a U.S. news organization. The North Vietnamese wanted Western press only.

At the same time, we needed a plane, only to learn there wasn't a single aircraft available to rent anywhere within reasonable flying range of Hanoi. CBS had reserved every large plane south of Hong Kong.

"Walter Cronkite is in Vientiane, waiting for his visa to be approved," a UPI colleague phoned with the news. "They've tied up all of the planes to keep the other networks out."

The competition among networks was every bit as fierce as the UPI-AP rivalry, only they had more money.

And there the stalemate remained for days. I had the visa. Cronkite had the planes.

Out in the world, the North Vietnamese and U.S. governments argued over the final release terms, the United States insisting that prisoners held in Laos also be returned. The final release was on again and off again. U.S. military personnel in South Vietnam were supposed to leave by March 28, the deadline to exchange all POWs. While anxious families waited for the results of those negotiations, UPI and CBS held their own discussions.

Why, CBS asked, should it provide transportation for its rivals ABC and NBC?

Because, UPI replied, we've already promised them they can go. Not a persuasive argument.

Personal collection

In the end, the North Vietnamese refused to give Cronkite his own visa. If he wanted to go, he had to come with me. But if I wanted to go—as well as the others UPI had invited—we still needed a plane, Cronkite's plane.

True to his reputation, he was courteous.

It was UPI, on its own, that suggested the final compromise.

"No!" I wailed. But it was useless.

In a bow to the greater needs of serving the public, UPI executives shattered the rules of competition and agreed that two AP reporters and a photographer could ride on my visa.

In Vientiane, Cronkite, his producer, and I met with the North Vietnamese, sipped coffee, and worked out final details for the flight.

"The plane will have to keep one engine running the whole time we're on the ground," the producer explained. Gia Lam airport lacked the equipment to restart the heavy airliner if it shut down all four engines.

The meeting room was bare of decoration, little more than a coffee table and green-and-cream vinyl-covered chairs. As soon as the flight discussions ended, Cronkite and his producer were asked to leave.

Alone with the two officials, we talked about the final conditions for coverage. Fearful of making a mistake that could sabotage the trip in its final stages, I considered my words carefully.

The North Vietnamese discussed the members of the press corps—and how they wanted them to behave.

"You must all stay together," one official warned. "No wandering off."

"I can't promise that," I replied honestly. Some of the world's top journalists were making that trip, and there was no way I or anyone else could guarantee what they would do once the plane's doors opened.

A few, like Keyes Beech of the *Chicago Daily News*, had been based in Hanoi during the days of French colonialism and were anxious to catalog damage to the graceful capital they had known in their youth.

"They must obey the rules."

"I'll tell them."

It sounded lame even to my own ears.

Would a last minute hitch put an end to the trip?

"Listen to your name called and step out from your line," the voice over the loudspeaker instructed the POWs.

Television cameras from all three networks whirred, the shutters on the still cameras clicked, and I scribbled as fast as I could in my notebook.

One by one, the last American POWs of the Vietnam War came forward, were greeted by a U.S. military escort, and boarded the white C-141 Starlifter for Clark Air Base—and home.

Laura Palmer

Mystery Is the Precinct
Where I Found Peace

I never expected to go to Vietnam, but I did. I never expected to become a journalist, but I did. I never expected that a wretched war's greatest legacy to me would finally be one of love, but that's what it has been.

Saigon feels like my hometown, because it's where the rest of my life began. It's where I met friends I will cherish forever and loved with intensity that has few parallels. It's where I began to understand life in a way I never had before.

Vietnam defined my generation and shaped the woman I became in distinct ways, but in the end, Vietnam made me more of who I already was. Like a jealous lover, Vietnam could be relentlessly demanding. But the mystery is that like the heart of love itself, Vietnam gave back far more than it ever took from me.

Vietnam destroyed my fear of death, and ultimately, Vietnam brought me closer to God, although that did not happen until a decade after I left Vietnam in a helicopter as part of the U.S. evacuation of Saigon.

I hitchhiked to Vietnam the first time. I had spent the weekend in Oregon with a former college roommate, who had dropped out and

LAURA PALMER is the author of three books and is an independent television producer in New York City.

was living off the land. I was hitchhiking back to Berkeley and summer school.

The July heat was wicked. My fifteen-year-old sister, Annie, was with me. We had a frightening ride in a red Mustang with a man who drove too fast while shifting gears haphazardly with the hook on his artificial arm. He left us on the interstate, and moments later, the Highway Patrol stopped and threatened to arrest us if we didn't leave immediately.

The next car had to be it.

A beat-up green Chevy appeared in the distance, slipping through the rippling mirage of creased heat. As it drew closer, I saw fishing poles and panting dogs. A hippie car. I stuck out my thumb. The car stopped. The driver had a ponytail, beard, and beads. His friend looked as if he had rarely been separated from his surfboard. They were headed all the way to San Francisco.

Thirteen months later, I left for Saigon with the driver of that dilapidated Chevrolet. He was a pediatrician with a specialty in neonatology. We fell in love that summer before my senior year in college.

I graduated in 1972 from Oberlin College as a government major. I was home working as a cocktail waitress when the pediatrician called me in the middle of the night from Morocco. He had been offered a job in Vietnam for six months. Did I want to go? Without a moment's hesitation I said yes. We went for six months, and I stayed for two years.

There was a time when I believed in virginity and the domino theory. Had I been born a few years earlier, I would have gone to college to find a husband or something to do until I did.

But Vietnam changed all of that. The war became a premise, a catalyst for political and cultural change. The change may have been inevitable, but the speed with which it happened was not. I grew up in the glass house of idealism that Camelot built, and when it was shattered, ran into the streets.

My senior year in high school, 1968, was defined by killing and death. The Tet offensive in Vietnam in January was followed by the assassinations of Martin Luther King, Jr., in April and Bobby Kennedy in June. It was a strange way to enter the world.

I started Oberlin College the following September. Oberlin was an extremely political campus. I was deeply opposed to the war in Vietnam and went to every major antiwar demonstration in Washington, D.C. We were teargassed in front of the Justice Department, with the same gas that was being used in Vietnam, which created a perverse feeling of solidarity among us with the Vietnamese.

> *HO HO HO CHI MINH, NLF IS GONNA WIN.*
> *1-2-3-4 WE DON'T WANT YOUR FUCKING WAR.*
> *5-6-7-8 WE DON'T WANT YOUR FASCIST STATE.*

There was no middle ground. While I was vehemently against the war, violent revolutionary tactics were abhorrent to me. I had neither sympathy nor respect for the radical wing of the antiwar movement. I opposed U.S. foreign policy in Vietnam, not democracy.

But beneath my furor about the war, I was still a very good girl who wore mascara through the revolution. Growing up with a retarded brother made me highly motivated. He did not have choices, but I did. I planned to go to law school and get Black Panthers out of jail. But I went to Vietnam instead.

The night before we left for Saigon, the pediatrician and I went to dinner in San Francisco at a Vietnamese restaurant. We ordered roasted crab. I began sipping my chilled soup. A thin slice of lemon skimmed the surface. It tasted refreshingly delicate until someone pointed out I was drinking the finger bowl.

My naïveté was wide and deep. The exotic smell I first noticed along Saigon's sidewalks turned out to be urine. The pungent Chinese parsley I floated in great gobs on bowls of noodle soup turned out to be cilantro, something I thought I'd never taste again but now buy in bunches at the grocery store. Night after night, I thought I was being lulled to sleep by the sound of tropical thunder rumbling in the distance. When someone casually mentioned that the B-52s were hitting closer to Saigon than ever before, I realized I was hearing air strikes.

In August 1972, during my first few weeks in Saigon, I'd seen soldiers and machine guns and endless coils of concertina wire snaking over walls and buildings. Vietnam was excruciatingly real. But for me it was also simultaneously unreal. I felt as invisible and disconnected as a ghost, that nuisance of an ancestor who never had a proper burial.

Saigon captivated me with her outlaw spirit. The sweep of history blew through her wide boulevards choked with exhaust fumes and animated by motorcycles, pedicabs, midget blue-and-yellow taxis and show-off Citroëns. Sidewalks were alive with panhandlers, pickpockets, prostitutes, and GIs. Vietnamese women glided through the chaos like floating feathers, ethereal in long tunic tops that fell over full black pants.

Barefooted children in tattered clothes tagged after U.S. soldiers, pestering and pleading, "You number one GI, you give me ti ti money!" Mangled amputees and lepers whose flesh had been gnawed away asked for change. Soup stands straddled the sidewalks alongside impromptu sellers of almost everything. Women in black pajamas sold cigarettes from suitcaselike stands. Some had marijuana already rolled into joints and packaged as cigarettes.

Amid the chaos and penetrating despair was a sense of defiance, an irresistible all-or-nothing mentality. But at another level, Saigon was completely unknowable, with trapdoors at every turn. She was wanton and provocative, the bad girl with a Buddhist soul. The sacred and profane were never at war in Vietnam.

The city's elegance was confined to late at night or early in the morning, when she pulled thin breezes around her like decaying lace. There was so much in Saigon that was ugly, repugnant, and cheap that by the time I sensed I was being swept away, it was too late; the shoreline had already disappeared into the distance and there was no way back. I was dangerously and thrillingly in love. I missed the sign that said "Stay away or be prepared to stay forever."

Some women went to Vietnam for the adventure, others to be pioneers in journalism. Not me. I simply landed there as a doctor's girlfriend. I had confidence in my abilities but doubted any of them had relevance in Vietnam. I was in over my head and I knew it. I was scared and I hid it. But I was broke and had to get on with it.

I needed to repay my college loans. The only jobs that paid a decent salary were with the media or the American embassy, which was not an option for a former antiwar protester. I opted for the news bureaus instead.

At each one, I was forced to answer "No" to nearly every question I was asked. The moment I explained I had followed a doctor to Vietnam, I knew no one expected me to have any experience in the military or speak Vietnamese or Chinese. French would have been a plus, but I had studied Spanish. I had neither majored in journalism nor worked on my college newspaper, although I had been a gofer for NBC News at the 1968 Democratic National Convention in Chicago. The following summer, I was the first girl copyboy at NBC News in Washington, D.C. Pulling wire copy for Chappaquiddick didn't count for much in Vietnam.

But the ABC News bureau in Saigon had an opening for a radio stringer. After Phil Starck, the deputy bureau chief, explained that it was a freelance reporting position, I told him I wanted to apply. I read through some old scripts in the bureau and then spent several days writing three 35-second radio spots.

The decision to hire me was made in New York over the objections of the bureau chiefs in Hong Kong and Saigon. During the summer of 1972, *The New York Times* was in the midst of a major sex discrimination suit, and news organizations were getting the message. Having a woman on the air from Saigon was a quick way to look good. The courage behind my work in Vietnam belongs solely to a heroic band of women at *The New York Times* who filed a landmark sexual discrimination suit against the paper at great professional sacrifice to themselves. They took a stand that benefited women for years to come.

Six weeks after I applied for the job at ABC News, I was hired.

But my elation was short-lived. On my very first day, Kevin Delany, the bureau chief whose shirts never wrinkled and poise never snapped, asked me to sit beside him. He was blunt. "I just want you to know that, of all the applicants, you were the least qualified."

Exhaling was not an option. The euphoria I felt about finally having my own job vanished. I had plenty to prove.

I began by filing several radio spots on the daily military developments, which were often broadcast during drive-time radio back in the States. "Waves of B-52 bombers pounded enemy troop concentrations along the Cambodian border" or "Renewed fighting was reported today in the rice-rich Mekong Delta." Most of my early reporting was based on the daily military briefings in Saigon, which had become known as the "five o'clock follies."

My first assignment ever as a reporter was to interview GIs at the USO in Saigon about being away from home on Thanksgiving. The Sony tape recorder slung from my shoulder felt as big as Nebraska. I felt like a neon sign flashing "scared, scared, scared."

The USO had pool tables, chocolate-chip cookies from church ladies, and buckets of letters on flowery tablet stationery from young girls seeking pen pals. "It sure is funny to write to someone you don't know. Well, I'll tell you about myself. I'm 5′4″ and weigh 130 pounds. I have brown hair and brown eyes. My favorite album is *Parsley, Sage, Rosemary and Thyme.*"

I always began the same way. "Could you please tell me your

name, rank, and where you're from in the States?" The GIs were always eager to talk. But everything they said was completely predictable—not a bad thing when you're as inexperienced as I was.

The first story I covered of any consequence was the Christmas bombing of Hanoi in 1972. I had been working for ABC for less than two months but was sent to Vientiane because everyone else in the bureau wanted to spend Christmas with their families. The Laotian capital was the closest American reporters could get to Hanoi. Covering the bombing meant covering the arrival of flights from Hanoi. We virtually tackled the disembarking passengers, scrambling for bits of information and detail.

Back in Vietnam a month later, I did some of the most disturbing interviews I have ever done. I was assigned to interview some of the last combat soldiers in-country. They were stationed just east of Da Nang on Tan My Island. As I was boarding a chopper in Da Nang, my army escort told me that Nixon would be speaking to the nation that morning. We were sure this was going to be the announcement that a cease-fire had been reached and a peace agreement was about to be signed.

The flight to Tan My Island was my first chopper ride in Vietnam. The rotors roared like a racing heart and I loved being swallowed by the sound. The mountains between Da Nang and Hue had a jagged majesty that generations of war could not defile. Death was bloodred in Vietnam. But the mountains were defiantly green. It was as if all the life sucked out by the war had been hurled back into the mountains.

Tan My Island looked like a summer camp, with small bungalows and screened-in porches set back from wide, sandy beaches. The company based there was nicknamed "Fox of the Fourth," which stood for F Troop, 4th Cavalry. "We'll talk to anything with round eyes." I arrived just after Nixon's speech. My army chaperon disappeared, and I was alone with about a dozen men in their small clubhouse. One wall of the tiny room had row after row of four lines with the fifth slashed through it—a total of 135—the kill count of a man they called "the Pervert." The other walls were plastered with pin-ups.

These men didn't want to go home.

"Ain't no reason to go home. We lost too many people. We gotta even the score."

"Aren't you afraid you might die?"

"I'm afraid, but what's the difference? You go out there to kill them. They've got as much chance as you have. That's the way it is. Kill 'em."

"How many people have you killed?"

"One."

He laughed. Others did, too.

Turning to another man, I asked him why he wanted to stay in Vietnam.

"I've been having a blast, killing dinks, chasing them. Getting shot at. It's fun. It's exciting. If you ever do it sometime, you'll like it."

"How many people have you killed?" I asked, turning to another man.

"Seven, by mistake." Again, more laughter.

"How does it feel to kill someone?"

"First, when they start shooting at you, it feels good. You know, but I never really got a chance to saw somebody in half while he was running down a path or nothing. Fill 'em full of holes. I don't know. It's fun chasing 'em. You go flying over a fighting position or something else and a *2001* space odyssey comes flying up at you, tracers and everything. It's neat. Looks like the Fourth of July. We let 'em shoot at us first. Then we kill 'em. You know, we're all fair. We're not masochists or nothing."

"Are you afraid you might get killed yourself?"

"Nah, who's going to miss me? Shit. No, everybody's scared of dying. Shit. I mean, you could die walking across the street or something."

Someone lit my cigarette with a Zippo lighter that was inscribed "The only thing I feel when I kill is the recoil of my M-16."

These men were chopper pilots who had reenlisted for their second or third tours of duty in Vietnam. Their war had been reduced to gooks, dinks, slant-eyes, and gooners.

Those interviews plunged me into the coldest chambers of war's sadistic heart. Until that afternoon I never knew there was more than one way to die in Vietnam. You could die fast, or you could die slow. After endless nights, who can be blamed for finally befriending the dark?

I had been in Vietnam only a few months when I took a baby from a Saigon orphanage. At five months, she weighed only five pounds. It was hard to look at her and not gasp. The women who ran the orphanage tried hard but simply did not have the resources to deal with the shallow tide of human misery that washed ashore daily.

The baby had a cleft lip and palate and an ugly, infected head. I was sure her brain was exposed. My ignorance probably saved her life. I gave one of the women at the orphanage a few hundred piastres and said in three of the seven words I knew in Vietnamese, *"Bac si My,"* which meant "American doctor," and waving my arms, I conveyed the rest. After swaddling her in a filthy brown blanket, I took her to the hospital.

She had an abscessed wound. The infection had chewed through her scalp and into her skull, but her brain was not exposed. The pediatrician admitted her to his hospital. She gained weight rapidly and began to smile and laugh. Skin was grafted over her head wound, and surgery closed her palate.

An American agency determined her eligibility for adoption. When she was about eighteen months old, she left for Indiana, where a waiting family planned to name her Misty Dawn. Over the years, I've thought, we seemed like opposite faces of the same coin, thrown together in a random toss. I landed in Vietnam, she in Indiana.

Going from the antiwar movement to Vietnam in less than a year was a sudden about-face that became surreal when I met General Nguyen Van Minh at a cocktail party in Saigon. He was one of Thieu's prominent commanders who controlled the military region that included Saigon. While chatting over drinks, he offered to take me to An Loc, a town in Binh Long province that the South Vietnamese had wrested from Communist control on May 3, 1972, after weeks of intense combat during what was known as the Communist Easter offensive.

The North Vietnamese army managed to occupy half of An Loc on April 13 after fierce hand-to-hand combat. President Thieu sent in one thousand parachute troops the next day with orders to "fight to the last man." The North Vietnamese were driven out but fought their way back a few days later and then kept up a massive artillery bombardment. In the kind of idiotic statistics the war was famous for, it's noted that 2,260 shells fell on An Loc on the night of April 27. American B-52s were dropping five hundred tons of bombs a night on and around An Loc but still failed to dislodge the North Vietnamese until May 3, when South Vietnamese relief forces finally broke through and the siege of An Loc was lifted. After being cut off for twenty-two days, An Loc received supplies and five hundred wounded were brought out.

During the spring of my senior year at Oberlin College in 1972, the fall of An Loc inspired a symbolic protest. A thriving town had been completely reduced to ruin and rubble. To us, the carnage and devastation of An Loc symbolized the utter futility of the war.

A tall funeral pyre was built on Tappan Square, and students brought something they valued to be burned as a way of symbolizing the destruction of An Loc. I put nothing in the pyre but watched as it was lit and flames chased one another into a bonfire devouring an antique shawl with long fringe. The college choir sang "Once to Every Man and Nation Comes a Moment to Decide." The chapel bells tolled mournfully.

Ten months later, because of a chance encounter at a cocktail party in Saigon, I flew to An Loc with General Minh, the South Vietnamese general who had led the battle. We traveled in the general's private helicopter with four F-5 fighter jets providing security.

General Minh guided me around shattered tanks and through the rubble. Flowers were blooming amid the desolation. I thought of

Personal collection

the pyre and stared at the general. I thought of the shawl and the privileged students who chose what to destroy. I thought of the villagers of An Loc whose world was in ruins. I was seeing what had been invisible to us then.

Back at the air base, we went for lunch in one of the trailers at the general's headquarters. Like a fat tick, General Minh had grown rich from the war. I was prepared for pretension and formality, but not the mammoth bed beside a small table set lavishly for two.

Presents appeared. The general gave me a sleek black cigarette case and a fake gold cigarette lighter. This meal would never have enough courses. As we approached the inevitable, the general and I began talking about music. I liked the Rolling Stones, he liked the Carpenters. He asked me if I liked to dance. I said I did. Pause. "Miss Laura, would you go-go for me?"

I declined with basic politeness, explaining that I danced only very late at night, at very large parties, and with many of my friends—conditions that could obviously not be met that afternoon in his trailer. Much to his chagrin, I left after a few more sips of tea.

A cease-fire agreement went into effect on January 23, 1973, and shortly thereafter, a Communist delegation was allowed to take up residence on Saigon's Tan Son Nhut air base. It was the first time the Communists had an official presence in the capital, and reporters were desperately eager to have access to them, naively thinking we might be able to tell the other side of the story. Ha!

It soon became clear that the Vietcong were determined to beat boredom into the best of us by holding weekly news conferences on Saturday mornings. Propaganda is inherently clumsy, and what it lost in translation from Vietnamese to English, it gained in tediousness. The party line that we heard over and over and over was that the Communists were scrupulously adhering to the provisions of the Paris peace agreement and strictly implementing its protocols.

At a break during the first news conference, I was asked if I wanted to meet two women who were soldiers in the National Liberation Front.

Moments later, I was shaking hands with two Vietcong women in pith helmets, fatigues, and combat boots. I was wearing jeans, a tight black top, and platform sandals. The contrast was striking. Soon every camera was pointed in our direction. One of the women put her pith helmet on my blond head.

Gavin Scott

The two asked me to extend their greetings to women in the United States. They hoped that American women who had supported their revolutionary efforts would now join them in the struggle for peace. A circle of reporters closed around us. Snapping camera shutters created a wheezing hum.

I had no way of knowing I was sabotaging myself. Nor could I imagine that a UPI photo editor would beam a picture around the world captioned "East meets west in Saigon as a Viet Cong woman soldier admires the bra-less look of ABC correspondent Laura Palmer, and Miss Palmer tries on the girl soldier's pith helmet. The two met during a Viet Cong press conference at Camp Davis."

The CEO of ABC News, Elmer J. Lower, clipped the photo from the *Miami Herald* and sent it to the bureau chief in Saigon with a terse note: "Passed without comment." ABC News, while pleased to have a woman broadcasting from Saigon, was not looking for its own Jane Fonda.

I'd become respected in the bureau and was doing solid work. But a few months after the cease-fire, I was told the bureau was cutting back and that someone would be hired with a wider range of experience than I had at the time. After a year at ABC, I left and was hired by NBC News in late 1973 as a radio reporter. I also began freelancing for *Time* and wrote on topics like Pentecostalism in South Vietnam, Thieu's national police, and the orphan crisis. I published my first magazine article in *Rolling Stone*. It was an impressionistic piece about Saigon. Seeing my first byline was a thrill.

The doctor and I came to an unhappy end. I moved into an apartment of my own.

In the intervening months, there was other love. Like night-blooming jasmine, it had a fragrance unto itself. Words, then and now, threaten to unravel the mystery. Live too close to war and you yearn for that naked, sweet revenge. A joint on a rooftop terrace overlooking rue Phan Than Gian. A fingertip tracing the curve from waist to hip in the echo of opal moonlight. The curfew-scoured streets of Saigon. Soup *chinois* and a chocolate soufflé. Joy was more than a perfume I bought at the PX.

One night at a small dinner party, I met a French correspondent for Agence France-Presse. Philippe was based in Saigon but spent many months in Cambodia. In commuting regularly to Phnom Penh to see him, I saw another war.

In Cambodia's national museum, there is a small rock in a glass case that was brought back from the moon by an Apollo mission. The card explaining the gift to the people of Cambodia from America quotes Richard Nixon as saying, "Cambodia is the Nixon doctrine in its purest form."

In its purest form, the Nixon doctrine was war and savagery. Vietnam was never a pathetic war. It was tragic and relentlessly sad, but a civil war had raged in Vietnam for years. American involvement prolonged and sustained the war but did not create it. There were issues the Vietnamese were willing to sacrifice and die for.

Not so in Cambodia, where the secret U.S. bombing of the countryside helped radicalize the Khmer Rouge and sustain a guerrilla war that lasted for five years. In 1975, the Khmer Rouge triumphed. Pol Pot unleashed an era of pure genocide during which as many as 1.5 million Cambodians were butchered, which the world largely ignored.

I remember interviewing Prince Sihanouk's former economic minister in 1973. He asked me if I'd ever been there before. "Last month," I said. He smiled. He meant before the war. "We used to be the most smiling people in Southeast Asia. But the smile is gone. To know it, you must look at the Buddhas."

Artillery and rockets routinely attacked Phnom Penh. Philippe and I would lie in bed at night and count the artillery rounds being fired into the city. Love made us feel invulnerable. Cambodia was where you went to the war in a Mercedes, the only car available to lease, and came back at night and ate smoked salmon and drank St. Émilion in the garden restaurant at the Hotel Le Phnom. I had never eaten baked Alaska until I went to Cambodia. It was incomprehensibly strange to be served a concoction of meringue, ice cream, and flames in the midst of a war.

There was a Spanish woman in white who had been sitting by the hotel swimming pool for twenty-eight years. Legend had it she'd once loved a French soldier who'd gone off to war one day and never returned. Grand, silent, and waiting, she had never moved from the place where her life stopped.

For the last thirty years, I've kept close to my desk a photograph of a small Cambodian girl with dog tags around her neck. A solitary tear falls across her face. One day I looked at her and understood why I do what I do. What caught my heart in Vietnam and Cambodia were the invisible and the forgotten, all of whom are, in one way or another, my retarded brother, the ones who walk beside me whispering, "Pay attention, pay attention."

Like some of the other foreign correspondents and many of the diplomats, Philippe and I were habitués at the opium den. Chantal's was a small house not far from the center of town. We drove there after curfew, when Phnom Penh looked like a back lot in Hollywood.

The hope was to get to Chantal's before the old French planter who, after years of addiction, smoked at least seventy pipes a night. Legend has it that his Vietnamese wife apparently got him hooked on opium to curb his infidelity. Opium is many things, but it is definitely not an aphrodisiac.

We'd arrive at Chantal's, slip into sarongs, and wait our turn for the pipe in a tiny room with bamboo mats and pillows. The cloak of silence around us was ripped only by the thundering sounds of American B-52 bombers pummeling the perimeter of Phnom Penh. After smoking a few pipes, we'd sip Scotch and soda by candlelight and saunter past midnight in blissful conversation somewhere on the outskirts of time.

I began to think about leaving Vietnam in mid-1974. I was living at 6 Thi Sach on a street lined with soup stands. It was a block-long buffet of noisy and cheerful clatter. As I walked back to my apartment one afternoon, I saw a Vietnamese woman squatting on the curb, clubbing a puppy to death. After a few whacks, the small dog went limp, an instant of swift cruelty within a completely ordinary scene.

For reasons I can't explain, that was the turning point. I knew I had to get out of Vietnam, and several months later, I did. My departure was delayed by Nixon's resignation. I was alone in the NBC bureau and needed to coordinate its coverage. My last radio reports began, "Although the public reaction was optimistic, privately the Thieu government is worried. . . ." "The critical question for South Vietnam now is whether Hanoi will change its military strategy in the wake of Nixon's resignation. . . ."

The next morning, on August 9, 1974, I boarded a plane for Paris.

I had no regrets. I knew how easy it would have been for me to become a war follower, because danger is exciting and most of life is not. After Saigon would have come Beirut, Somalia, Riyadh, Rwanda, Kosovo, Afghanistan, and Ramallah. Soon I'd have my own names to slap down like face cards in the boozy, late night verbal poker games journalists play in hotel bars.

Somehow I knew I had to create a life from love and not from war. I wanted roots that went down to the source of water.

Hitchhiking got me to Vietnam the first time, and Aristotle Onassis, the second. He died in Paris when I was working for NBC News as a radio reporter nine months after I'd left Vietnam. By reporting the facts of his death over and over that day, I made several hundred dollars in radio fees. I quit my job at NBC and with my Onassis money bought my last youth-fare ticket, Paris-Saigon-Paris, for $600. I was twenty-five years old.

I was wary about returning to Vietnam until Da Nang fell to the Communists on Easter Sunday and I was asked to file radio spots on the French reaction. I told the New York assignment desk there wasn't any. The French were going to church and then to dinner with their mothers-in-law.

The assignment desk didn't care. Thus, the artful dodge: "There's been no official reaction yet to the fall of Da Nang in Paris because it's Easter Sunday, but in recent weeks, the French position has been . . ." and I summed up the view from the Quai d'Orsay.

Then I got a letter from Bich Dao, my closest Vietnamese friend, telling me good-bye. "If this is the last letter you ever get from me, know that I loved you as a sister . . . the bottom of our world has fallen out and we are floating, floating, but I don't know where."

Her letter catapulted me past my self-centeredness. I stopped wondering whom I'd work for if I went back. It was enough to go and see my friends.

Before I left Paris, I called Paul Scanlon, my editor at *Rolling Stone,* and told him of my plans. I asked if Frankie FitzGerald and Hunter Thompson were on their way. He promised me they weren't and said he wanted to see anything I wrote.

When I changed planes in Bangkok, I saw the blaring headline: two hundred Vietnamese orphans killed when the huge C–5A transport plane carrying them to America plunged into a rice paddy shortly after taking off from Tan Son Nhut. Only one of the forty-three adults accompanying them survived. I felt a sense of doom.

But I was jolted out of my gloominess during the cab ride into the city. Everything looked the same. There was no visible sense of panic. Shops were open, markets full, restaurants busy. The streets were jammed with traffic, the sidewalks with squalor; the centrifugal force that held Saigon together was still spinning.

I called Bich Dao shortly after I arrived. She was finishing her second year of medical school. Getting in to medical school was exceedingly competitive because the rich and powerful bought places for their sons to keep them out of the army. Dao was one of a few who got in on merit. She wanted to see a fortune-teller we'd visited before to ask about the fate of her brother, a soldier in the South Vietnamese army who was missing.

The fortune-teller welcomed us into her small living room. She said Dao's brother was safe and finding his way back home. Days later, he did.

But the fortune-teller's friendly matter-of-factness dissolved when we began to talk about the current situation. She said if the Communists came to power, she and her husband would poison their five children and themselves. Was her clairvoyance the source of her pessimism? She shrugged. "There are some events that overwhelm destiny." It's the best explanation of the Vietnam War I've ever heard.

I'd been in Saigon about a week when Hunter Thompson arrived at the Continental Hotel. His presence sent sparks through the mostly male members of the press corps. Hunter was their alter ego, the person many fantasized they would be if they didn't have wives, children, and mortgages. He was the harmonic convergence of sex, drugs, and rock and roll. A rebel without a cause but with plenty of charisma.

I watched the late night frenzy around him in the hotel garden, sure his arrival meant I'd publish nothing in *Rolling Stone*. It took me a week to work up the courage to introduce myself, but once I did, we began working together. I knew how to cover the story and helped Hunter get organized enough to work. The surprise was how astute his journalistic instincts were. Behind the outlaw mask were the contours of a southern gentleman, a bit courtly and old-fashioned. He's a fine writer and a terrific reporter until he trips over the persona he's created. Although often self-absorbed and obnoxious, Hunter's mordantly funny and recklessly imaginative.

I did a companion piece to the only story Hunter filed from Saigon. I'd gone out to Tan Son Nhut to check on the unofficial airlift that had begun evacuating thousands of Vietnamese out of the country. Dozens of cargo flights were coming into Saigon daily. By the second week in April, some renegade employees of the CIA and defense attaché's office started filling up the empty cargo transport planes with people they were determined to help and protect. Others in the first wave of departures were American civilian contractors and their Vietnamese dependents, some of whom were common-law wives or girlfriends—all of whom tried to bring as many Vietnamese relatives with them as they could. What began with at least a semblance of order soon disintegrated into chaos. Hardly any of the Vietnamese had passports or immigration papers. Americans could sponsor someone's departure, and that, in turn, led to bribery, corruption, and mayhem. I came spinning back to the Continental Hotel with anecdotes and images. Hunter told me to stop talking and start writing. My impressionistic piece ran alongside his longer one on the mood in Saigon.

The obstacle to a more orderly and responsible evacuation was Graham Martin, the U.S. ambassador to South Vietnam whose son had been killed in the war. Martin refused to accept that Vietnam was a lost cause and that a total Communist victory was imminent. He either ignored or doctored the intelligence reports from his own CIA station chief. Martin still believed there was a way to head off defeat, which was something that President Gerald Ford and Secretary of State Henry Kissinger wanted to hear. They helped perpetuate the myth that there was still time.

Martin felt that launching a major evacuation would be tantamount to raising a white flag. His intransigence in refusing to sanction an official evacuation until the eleventh hour and fifty-ninth minute had catastrophic consequences for tens of thousands of Vietnamese who had knowingly put themselves in jeopardy by working for the American embassy, USAID, or the U.S. military and by trusting in the integrity of their American allies. Most had been promised protection and evacuation for themselves and their families if and when the end ever came. When it did, many were cruelly and shamefully abandoned.

Almost immediately after returning to Saigon in April 1975, I began freelancing again for *Time*. Each of us in the bureau filed daily on whatever aspect of the day's developments we'd covered. One night I was writing late in the bureau, on deadline, and tense. When I looked up, my friend Bich Dao was standing in front of my desk. She asked if we could speak. She could not have come at a worse time.

Dao began quietly. Her family had good intelligence. The Communists were going to sweep into Saigon. A negotiated settlement was not possible. She spoke with a start-stop quality that made me suspicious. Would I stay in touch with her family even if she was not around?

"Are you trying to tell me you've decided to commit suicide?" She looked down. As a medical student, she would know exactly how to do it. I was scared.

"Dao, listen to me. Promise me it won't be tonight. Promise me you'll meet me here tomorrow in the bureau at five-thirty. Okay?" I had not convinced her. "If you don't," I said severely, "I will never see your family. I will never talk to them, and I will never, ever help them. Promise me you'll come tomorrow." She did. But when she walked away, I was not sure if I would ever see her again.

When I came into the office the next day, I found a note on my desk. "Laura, something comes up suddenly I left. Bich Dao." Her sister, who was living in Washington, D.C., had married an American who had an American contact in Saigon who was to get the family out on one of the unofficial evacuation flights.

Instead of ending her life, Dao began it again. She got another undergraduate degree, borrowed the money to go to medical school, and became a kidney specialist and then a trauma doctor.

The following week, Hunter Thompson left for Hong Kong. *Rolling Stone* publisher Jann Wenner had sent him to Vietnam to write about the U.S. evacuation of Saigon. But as Hunter left the Continental Hotel, he told me that if anything happened, it was my story. He was going to Hong Kong to get his head together.

On Sunday, I sent a telex to San Francisco, asking *Rolling Stone* if I should cover the evacuation if it happened while Hunter was in Hong Kong. On Monday, a telex came from my editor at *Rolling Stone* telling me that if there was an evacuation, I should go. On Tuesday, I was gone.

Early in the morning of April 29, 1975, someone knocked on the door at room 20 at the Continental Hotel and said, "Come on, we're all getting out of here."

I was struck by what little thoughts you can feel in big times. How ordinary a day can feel even if it's a day on which you might easily die. How silly a French blouse can suddenly seem. How curious my own sense of calm.

The Americans were leaving Vietnam, this time for good. After $150 billion and eight million tons of bombs, the final climactic moment to a decade of U.S. involvement was to be triggered by an announcement on American Forces Radio: "The temperature is 115 degrees and rising," followed by the first eight bars of "I'm Dreaming of a White Christmas."

It was six in the morning as I walked across the square to the Caravelle Hotel. Dawn was when I loved Saigon best, and this day did not disappoint. The streets were quiet but not empty, despite the twenty-four-hour curfew. Like weary extras in hot costumes, sleepy policemen slouched on folding chairs in front of the National Assembly, rifles by their side. Most had no sense that this would be one of the most dramatic days in the war.

A few hours later, it was time for good-byes.

The first was with Slappy, a teenage boy with laughing eyes and an energetic spirit who had cerebral palsy. I never knew his real name. Nor did I know who first began calling him Slappy, which was the sound his sandals made against the pavement as he spastically lurched along. He was usually waiting outside the Caravelle Hotel, where the ABC bureau was located. When I left, he'd follow me along Tu Do Street, chasing the beggars away. In the hierarchy of the streets, Slappy had claimed his authority. We were friends but couldn't communicate in language since Slappy could only grunt.

On April 29, I saw him for the last time. He was wearing lavender pants and a print shirt. I was disappearing from the landscape of his life and felt trapped by my inability to tell him good-bye. Claustrophobia came in many ways in Vietnam. Slappy was one of the ways it came for me.

Saying good-bye with words was no easier than saying good-bye without. Pham Xuan An was the Vietnamese reporter at *Time*, and we had become good friends during the year I freelanced for the magazine. He was one of the best-informed sources in Saigon, and scores of correspondents had relied on his wisdom.

But An was also an unabashed romantic, a Confucian at heart, who still dreamed of walking down Tu Do Street in a white suit with a tiger cub on a leash. I could barely speak when it came time to say good-bye to him on the steps of the Continental Hotel. I walked away with a group of journalists toward our evacuation pickup point. I could not look back.

Robert Shaplen, the legendary correspondent for *The New Yorker* magazine, and I decided to stay together. He was an Indochina hand who started covering the war in 1946, four years before I was born. At twenty-five, I was one of the youngest reporters in Vietnam.

What did we talk about? His broken fly. Bob was dismayed that the zipper had jammed on his trousers and he was going through this momentous day with only a safety pin between him and complete embarrassment.

We proceeded to a designated spot and eventually got on a black CIA bus with grated windows. A patrol car escorted us, its red light flashing. All we lacked was a sign saying "Shoot Here." We were living in the bull's-eye. One of the enduring mysteries of that final day for me is why none of the South Vietnamese turned on us as we cruelly abandoned them. We knew that the North Vietnamese army had Saigon cut off and the air base surrounded. But the prevailing logic, which seemed to prove true, was that the Communists were so close to victory that they would not taint their final triumph in a bloodbath.

We were herded into the defense attaché compound, a sprawling complex known as Pentagon East, and were told to sit down along the wall. Someone walked along with a big cardboard box, demanding that all weapons be placed inside. When I saw the pistols, knives, ammunition, and explosives, I knew I was on a small reef in an ocean of danger. I also met my own violent heart for the first time.

Nothing was going to prevent me from getting on a helicopter. If people started fighting, I would fight, too. If people started killing, so would I. I was prepared to do anything, except die.

"You fifteen people on that chopper! Run. Now. Go. Run." Someone was screaming at us, and we ran across the tarmac. I threw my bag into the chopper. The tailgate was already up. I tried to jump in but couldn't make it. Someone grabbed my hand and pulled me on board. Moments later, in a howl of rotors, we lifted up into the sky. Bob Shaplen and I held hands and stared at the city that was slipping away. We looked at each other once with tears in our eyes, then looked away. There were no words.

We flew to an aircraft carrier. Throughout the afternoon, I remember watching South Vietnamese helicopters being pushed overboard after they landed on the aircraft carrier with fleeing military personnel. Helicopters were icons of the war, and seeing them sink into the sea was striking. An all-consuming war was finally being consumed.

I ended up on the same aircraft carrier with General Nguyen Van Minh, who had once asked me to go-go for him. He was stubbing out Kools and drinking grape juice from a plastic carton in an air-conditioned officer's suite. He seemed as lost as the war until I reminded him of his fondness for American music. His eyes brightened. "Yes, I like the Carpenters very much. They're very, very good, and also Tom Jones and Elton Johns."

During the six days it took to reach the Philippines, I wrote my article for *Rolling Stone*. It was one of only two lengthy first-person accounts of the evacuation. I remember staring in amazement as five thousand words were telexed across an ocean to San Francisco from Clark Air Base on a noisy, lurching machine.

I had just gotten out of the shower in a Manila hotel room when the phone call I had placed to the United States went through. Dripping wet, I heard my mother's voice on the line. "I was watching those pictures on CBS of people trying to get over the embassy wall.

I didn't know how you were going to get out of there. You couldn't even make it up the apple tree." It is hard to think of anything that my mother has ever said to me that's mattered more.

I went to Laos for a few days via Hong Kong, then took a twenty-hour flight back to Paris. For the next eleven years, I had nothing whatsoever to do with Vietnam.

New Year's Day 1986 was when everything changed. I left my daughter and husband at home in New York City and went to the Vietnam Veterans Memorial by myself for the first time.

The sorrow I felt at the Wall on that barren day stopped me cold. As the mother of a five-year-old daughter, I knew what it meant to cherish a child, and each of the fifty-eight thousand names had become part of me.

People had been leaving letters, poems, and personal memorabilia at the Wall ever since the memorial was dedicated in 1982. I was struck by such intimate gestures being made in a public place. A park ranger told me that everything left at the Wall was being stored in a warehouse in Maryland, and with permission, it was possible to see the collection.

Bing. I knew I was going to that warehouse. Two months later, I had a magazine assignment and spent three days alone in a huge, chilly warehouse reading through everything that had been left at the Vietnam Veterans Memorial.

It was like listening to silent screams. How could there be this much pain from that war? Who were these people? Why wasn't anyone paying attention to them?

"Dearest Eddie Lynn, I'd give anything to have you shell just one more pecan on Grandma's porch. All my love, your cousin, Anne."

My magazine piece suddenly became something bigger when a friend with tenure in my heart said, "This is your Vietnam book."

The next day I began making notes for a book, and the title came to me: *Shrapnel in the Heart*. When those four words appeared, sudden and unbidden, I sensed the book was meant to be.

During the last six months of 1986, I traced people who left letters to the dead at the Vietnam Veterans Memorial. Traversing the country several times, I showed up on strangers' doorsteps, asking about the most brutal loss of their lives.

I began to wonder if I had spent two years in Vietnam to earn the right to enter this landscape of tragedy and sorrow, where grief stood like an implacable sentry. Like Vietnam, this terrible terrain was a place I never expected to go, but one where once I arrived, I knew I belonged.

Writing *Shrapnel in the Heart* mattered more to me than any thirty-five-second radio spots I broadcast from Saigon, writing I did for *Time* magazine, or byline I had in *Rolling Stone*.

But the first interview I did for the book made me question even continuing. I was talking with a mother whose son was killed in Vietnam and assumed that this was the defining war in her life. I was half right. She told me her husband came home from World War II and began drinking heavily and beating her. With neither money nor skills, she took her baby and fled. Shortly after our interview began, she broke down. She'd recently learned that one of her grandchildren was being sexually abused. The interview ended. But what began that day was my understanding that if there were parades for people who survived their lives, the marching would never stop.

I remember sitting with the family of Bob Kalsu, the only pro football player to die in the Vietnam War. He had played for a season with the Buffalo Bills and was killed on the day his wife was due to give birth to their second child. Sixteen years later, in their living room in Oklahoma City, I watched the home movie made when the family was together in Hawaii for R&R. Jan Kalsu was very pregnant. Jill, their two-year-old daughter, held her daddy's hand as she wobbled at the ocean's edge.

Bob Kalsu was with the 101st Airborne Division and in fierce fighting on Firebase Ripcord. After six months, he met his family in Hawaii. The army instructed wives not to ask their husbands about the war.

Watching the home movie's shaky black-and-white footage, knowing that in a few weeks Bob Kalsu would be killed and a son born he would never see, affected me as deeply as anything I did in Vietnam.

Wars don't end. Every bullet in Vietnam left an exit wound as it soared back into unsuspecting hearts. Lives stopped, dreams collapsed, futures imploded. "I was supposed to marry Joey Sintoni. I didn't find it easy to progress to plan B," said Angela Prete. "Marriage was killed in action."

No one ever "gets over it," because love is never an "it." Love is the baby you brought to your breast, the son you showed how to shave. It's the brother who taught you to drive, the sweetheart who always remembered, and the lies you told over and over to your wounded buddy as you slid his intestines back inside him.

Shrapnel in the Heart forced me to bear witness, which felt sacramental and humbling. I began to sense how much larger this life is than any of us can really comprehend. I finally understood, for the first time, that love is greater than death.

I had been showing up on Easter Sundays for years. But it never connected at any deep level until I saw how those who died in Vietnam lived in the hearts and lives of those who loved them. I began *Shrapnel in the Heart* thinking I was writing about dead soldiers. But as I listened, they came alive. I could see their breath on grief's frigid morning. They lived in a love that said you were connected to me and I to you. You made my small world shine and my life count for something good.

I learned that the legacies of our lives are written in the hearts of those we love. If we love well, we never die. My fear of death was erased.

Vietnam has always blown like an unexpected wind in my life, pushing me into deeper waters than I would have ventured into on my own. Fourteen years after I first arrived in Saigon, Vietnam forced me to peer into the awfulness of death until I saw the tenacity of the love that binds the living to the dead. The war became personal for me in a way it had never been before.

During my first two years in Vietnam, I learned the history and politics of the war. I could debate the finer points of the Paris peace agreement and understand the perils of a cease-fire in place. Generals gave me quotes, and ambassadors returned my calls. I could distinguish between incoming and outgoing artillery rounds and knew the difference between a Huey and a Chinook.

But I didn't know anyone who died in Vietnam. I went to college with boys who knew how to beat the draft. As I did the reporting for *Shrapnel in the Heart,* the stories of twenty-nine soldiers slipped inside me like smoke through a screen door.

I knew who liked pinto beans and cornbread and who named his rabbits Cuddles and Midnight. I knew who played the tuba in the marching band and who bought his mother a Sunbeam electric fry-ing pan with the money from his first paper route. I knew who wore English Leather aftershave and who loved lemon meringue pie.

What I did not know was how much these lives had become part of my own until I went to see *Platoon* the day it opened in New York City in December 1986. I had just finished writing *Shrapnel in the Heart.*

The movie begins with the arrival of a platoon of soldiers in Vietnam. They jump from the back of a C-130 into choking dust as a body bag drops on the tarmac. There were my boys: Eddie Lynn Lancaster, Joey Sintoni, Dan Neely, Rick Ewald, David Stoll, Eddie Zimmerman. . . . They were alive. I knew they were going to die. I wanted to save them. I knew I could not. That was the moment I cried for Vietnam.

When I finished *Shrapnel in the Heart,* Vietnam felt completed But it wasn't. One night as I was on the verge of sleep, I had an idea. A newspaper column. Vietnam.

Within several months, "Welcome Home" was launched in the Sunday *New York Daily News,* beneath Ann Landers and beside the horoscopes. It was soon syndicated in about two dozen newspapers nationwide and ran from 1988 to 1990.

The first column began, "If you still look up in the sky when you hear a helicopter, this column is for you." America was struggling to come to terms with the Vietnam War, and my column was intended to be a log of the journey. I wanted to reach people who were afraid to venture into a Vietnam Veterans Outreach Center for help and find family members and children of those who died in Vietnam. For two years, I also wrote about issues like Agent Orange, Dan Quayle, MIAs, and Jane Fonda.

Failure and courage, heroism and despair, are not usually in lock-step with each other unless you were a nurse in Vietnam. In 1993, working on a cover story for *The New York Times Magazine,* I spent several months interviewing women who had been combat nurses in Vietnam.

The myth is that women weren't in combat. In an official sense, that's true. But Vietnam had a way of making truth lies and lies truth. Sharon Ann Lane, one of the eight nurses whose name is on the Wall, died when a mortar round hit her hospital.

Nurses in Vietnam saw more trauma because of the widespread use of helicopters, which got to hospitals soldiers who would have died in previous wars. Doctors were older and more emotionally anchored by careers and families. Nurses were often only a year or two older than their patients. They saw the war from the inside out, from the rotting wounds infested with maggots to the stink of burned flesh, the mangled limbs, and the sucking chest wounds. The grotesque images of war were punctuated by moments of unparalleled tenderness. Dana Shuster, a nurse whose nickname was Dusty, remembers a patient who asked her to unpin her hair as he was being wheeled into the OR and another who said quietly, "You're the first white woman ever to touch me."

The nurses wanted, willed, hoped, believed, prayed, and yearned for their patients to live so much that each death felt like a defeat. Nearly every nurse came home with a debilitating and corrosive sense of failure embedded in her soul. If only she had been a better nurse, more would have survived.

No other message countered the negative ones. No one said thank you. No one honored the courage it took to make a dying man feel loved. Their stateside counterparts in the veterans' hospitals confronted similar trauma over extended periods of time. Nurses in Vietnam often never had time to learn their patients' names. It was just the opposite in the VA hospitals, creating tremendous burdens. Armies have no medals for that kind of courage.

If you interview nurses and veterans extensively, a common theme emerges: "I never loved the way I did in Vietnam." When soldiers talk about their buddies and nurses talk about their patients, they describe an uncommon intensity in their feelings for one another. I became so used to hearing this, I missed its significance entirely.

But that changed in 1993, when I was interviewing a nurse for *The New York Times* piece. Lynda Van Devanter was an army nurse in Pleiku from 1969 to 1970 at the 71st Evacuation Hospital. We were talking about the love Lynda felt for her patients when she said simply, "And that love for me was where God was in Vietnam."

The love, the love, the love that I'd been listening to for years suddenly took on new meaning. In its power and radiance was, and is, the presence of God.

There are still moments, nearly thirty years later, when Vietnam catches me unawares. I produced an ABC News *Nightline* broadcast on Steve Tice, a Vietnam veteran whose determination to heal has been extraordinary. A rocket-propelled grenade ripped into the right side of his body during the battle for Hamburger Hill in 1969. Before we met, I knew he'd lost an arm and that one side of his body was maimed.

But I wasn't prepared to see him. When Steve Tice came outside to greet me in the bold California sunshine, I wanted to cry. Sheer willpower held me together. He isn't hard to look at. But seeing him made me want to cry for all of them.

The tears that didn't run down my face run through my soul. They define Vietnam for me, as surely as a soldier's dog tags lay claim to him. Vietnam is a river of pain, as mighty as the Mekong. Tears, like nightmares, tell the truth about the war.

The truth is that Steve Tice has rarely had a pain-free day in three decades. His body is a war memorial, a long shadow cast behind those sculpted in marble and bronze. Maimed, scarred, twisted, and torn, his body is the breathing ruin and wreckage of Vietnam.

If I had been a reporter in Vietnam in 1969 instead of a sophomore in college, I might have covered Hamburger Hill. I might have been humping the boonies on May 18 and seen the rocket-propelled grenade blow Steve Tice into a before and after.

But I wasn't a witness to that war.

As a reporter, I've covered the war that starts when the shooting stops. The war that is fought to hold a spoon and tie a shoe. The war that is fought in a mind loaded with trip wires and a soul so strangled with guilt that laughter and love can feel like sin, and booze and drugs like sacraments.

Steve Tice won those wars a blink at a time. Ravaged by rage, he ruined his marriage and killed off a part of himself he finally realized he was not ready to let die. He began therapy and reconciled with his wife. He then became a therapist with the Veterans Administration, specializing in trauma. For the next twenty years, he helped veterans negotiate cease-fires with themselves until he was overtaken by physical pain and forced into early retirement at fifty.

As the late afternoon sun glided through a winter's day, I watched Steve Tice watching his three sons shoot hoops in the family's driveway. A few years ago he could play basketball with them. Now he can't. A few months ago he could still open the refrigerator door. Now he can't. A few weeks from now he might not be able to drive his car. Someday he might not be able to walk.

With every coordinate for bitterness and pain, Steve Tice could have mapped out a life of anger. But he persevered until he found peace and forged a life from love. The army gave him medals for being blown up. But hardly anyone noticed that his real heroism is in healing.

In 1989, I returned to Vietnam for three weeks. Hanoi was mesmerizing, but Saigon was momentous. I had sent word to Pham Xuan An, the former Vietnamese reporter for *Time* magazine, that I was staying at the Majestic Hotel. I was eager to see my old friend who had revealed after the fall of Saigon that he had been a colonel in the Vietcong.

No one who knew An felt betrayed. He was too romantic to ever be a successful Communist and was sent to reeducation camp after the fall of Saigon. He was a nationalist who opposed all foreign intervention in Vietnam. But his friends were the treasures of his heart; when in April 1970 the Khmer Rouge captured Robert Sam Anson, a *Time* correspondent in Cambodia, Anson was a prisoner for twelve days and would likely have faced execution had An not intervened, working through back channels to secure his release. After An's double life was revealed, Anson asked him why he'd done what he had.

"We were on different sides, you and I," said Anson.

"No, we were friends," said An.

I returned to the Majestic Hotel late one afternoon after a god-awful day at the tunnels of Cu Chi. In a sweaty stupor and sour mood, I stumbled back into the lobby of the hotel. An was there, waiting. It had been more than a decade since I'd last seen him on April 29, 1975, on the steps of the Continental Hotel.

He smiled and came toward me, carrying a tiny bouquet of miniature red roses held together in a lace doily. Never will a bouquet of flowers mean more to me. "I wanted to tell you the day you left that it would be okay to stay behind. I could guarantee your safety. But what if a rocket hit or something unexpected happened? You were a young woman. I wanted you to go on in life and have a family."

And I had. A week later, I was walking back to my old apartment on 6 Thi Sach, the place where Vietnam had finally felt like home. But I knew I didn't belong there anymore. I wanted to go back to New York. I suddenly missed Sabrina, my eight-year-old daughter, with a love so fierce that it made everything else in my life seem incidental. I was overwhelmed by gratitude. I had made a life that I missed. A life that mattered was finally mine.

During the war, my best friend, Tad Bartimus, and I would drink red wine and talk late into the night on my trellised terrace, wondering if life could ever be this good again. Would we ever again live, love, and work with the passionate intensity that we had in Vietnam? Fourteen years later, I knew the answer, for me, was yes. As I stood there missing my daughter on that hazy, indolent afternoon, I knew I had finally found in life all I would ever need to make it worthwhile. I wanted to go home.

Thirty years ago, I went to Vietnam with all the answers and left with only questions. I no longer look for explanations. Mystery is the precinct where I found peace.

As I write, a small helicopter sits on my desk, as it always has. It was created from medical refuse: IV tubing, syringe holders, needles, and thin strips of aluminum. A paralyzed Vietnamese boy made it. He was shot in the spine from an American helicopter while he was walking along a rice paddy with his water buffalo. Who could take aim at a child? When I understand the helicopter, I'll understand Vietnam. But I don't expect that to be anytime soon.

Con Thien, Vietnam, 20, 134–35, 139, 151
Continental Hotel, Saigon, 68, 95, 133,
161, 163, 266, 268, 269, 277
Cook, Freda, 76
Copple, Cynthia, 42, 50
CORDS (Civilian Operations and Rev-
olutionary Development Support),
115, 227, 230
Corpora, Tom, 8
correspondents, female. *See* women, as
correspondents
Cronkite, Walter, 93, 190, 225, 246, 247,
248
Crossette, Barbara, 88
Cu Chi, Vietnam, 4, 10, 19, 101–3, 277

Da Nang, Vietnam, 28, 116, 147–48,
175, 177, 264–65
Dai Loc, Vietnam, 28
Daily Express, 46, 95
Dak To, Vietnam, 139–41
Dalat, Vietnam, 22, 52, 115
Dang Van Phuoc, 199
Darbininkas (Lithuanian-language
newspaper), 127
Darion, Sid, 92
Davis, Angela, 157
Davis, James Thomas, 242
Davis, Neil, 216
Davison, Michael, 21, 26, 28
de Marco, Joe, 63
Deepe, Beverly, 83
Delany, Kevin, 255
Desdame, Jacqueline, 43
Dien Bien Phu, 63
Dispatch News Service, 42
Dispatches (book), 133
Dith Pran, 82
Do Van Kien, 47–48
Dong Ha, Vietnam, 122, 147
d'Ornano, Pierre, 211
Duc Duc district, 28
Duc Ky, Vietnam, 15–16
Duc Pho, Vietnam, 135

East Timor, 88
Eden Building, 159, 196
Eisenhower, Dwight, 108
Elliott, Jerry, 169
Ellison, Robert, 143

Eskimo restaurant, 97
Esper, George, 160, 168, 179, 196, 209,
216, 218, 220
Ewald, Rick, 274

Faas, Horst, 21, 139, 178–79, 185, 197,
198–99, 211, 212–13, 218, 241, 244
Fackler, Martin, 148
Fall, Bernard, 61–62, 70
Fallon, Jack, 70
Fawcett, Denby, 3–31, 83, 104, 105, 170
Faye, Sam Kai, 97
Feldman, Ed, 146, 152
Finch, Robert, 242
Finnegan, James, 146, 152
Firebase Ripcord, 272
First Hotel, Saigon, 168
FitzGerald, Frankie, 265
Five O'Clock Follies, 63, 132, 167, 255
Flynn, Sean, 20, 22, 133
Follett, Dwight, 6–7
Ford, Gerald, 267
Franklin, Aretha, 18, 19
From Here to Eternity, 178
Frosch, Frank, 71, 72
Fuller, Keith, 195

Gallagher, Wes, 157, 158–59, 185, 194,
195, 197, 198, 205, 207, 216
Galloway, Joe, 88
Gay, William, 145
Geneva Accords, 210
Gia Lam airport, 245, 248
Goebner, Nancy, 156
Golf Club of Saigon, 118
Goulding, Phil, 105–6
Grall hospital, Saigon, 30–31
Green Berets, 227
Green Eyes, 220
Greene, Graham, 93
Grey, Dennis, 82
Grimsby, Roger, 95–96
Guam, 86
Guin, Lucy, 163
Gulf of Siam, 205
Gulf War, 88, 112
Gunther, Fred, 16

Hai Van pass, Vietnam, 55, 175, 177, 236
Halberstam, David, 198

Hamburger Hill, 276
Hanoi
    Army Museum, 55–56
    Tad Bartimus in, 215
    Christmas bombing, 256
    Ho Chi Minh mausoleum, 55, 246
    Tracy Wood in, 241–42, 245, 246–47
Hanoi Radio, 160, 167
Harris, Sam, 27
Harrity, Chick, 175, 176
Hawaii
    1st Battalion, 8th Infantry, 11
    2nd Batalion, 27th Infantry, 10
    25th Infantry Division, 4, 9, 19, 66, 102
    R&R in, 193
    Tripler Army Medical Center, 29, 30
health issues, 29–30, 208, 211, 215–18
helicopters, 97–98, 101, 131, 157, 194,
    228–30
Herr, Michael, 19, 133
Hersh, Seymour, 42
Higbee, Arthur, 226, 228, 230, 231
Higgins, Marguerite, 194, 216
Highpockets, 66
Hirashiki, Tony, 96, 115
Hirst, Don, 42, 44
Hmong people, 208–9
Ho Chi Minh, 55, 201, 246
Ho Chi Minh Trail, 183, 204
Hoa Hao sect, 70
Hodgson, James, 172
Hong Kong, 39, 40, 46, 47, 61, 62, 80,
    89, 106, 108, 112, 117, 180, 192,
    205, 226, 271
Honolulu Advertiser, 4, 5, 6, 7, 23, 24,
    30, 83, 105
Honolulu Star-Bulletin, 4–5
Hope, Bob, 167
Hotel de La Post, Phnom Penh, 71
Hotel Le Phnom, Phnom Penh, 180,
    181, 204, 263
Hotel Monoram, Phnom Penh, 181–82
Hotel Royale, Phnom Penh, 71, 81, 204.
    See also Hotel Le Phnom
Hotel Royale, Saigon, 178, 212
hotels
    Caravelle Hotel, Saigon, 23, 24, 68,
        95, 106, 108, 109, 132, 159, 268, 269
    Continental Hotel, Saigon, 68, 95,
        133, 161, 163, 266, 268, 269, 277

First Hotel, Saigon, 168
Hotel de La Post, Phnom Penh, 71
Hotel Le Phnom, Phnom Penh, 180,
    181, 204, 263
Hotel Monoram, Phnom Penh,
    181–82
Hotel Royale, Phnom Penh, 71, 81, 204
Hotel Royale, Saigon, 178, 212
Majestic Hotel, Saigon, 6, 95, 277
Miramar Hotel, Saigon, 156, 168
Rex Hotel, Saigon, 151
Hue, Vietnam, 26, 86, 116, 175, 177,
    209, 227–28, 231, 232, 236
Huet, Henri, 194, 195
Huyen family, 53
Huynh Minh Trinh, 199

I Corps, 67, 69, 105, 116, 122, 142, 148
ICCS (International Commission of
    Control and Supervision), 170,
    174, 175, 176, 207
India, 86, 88
India Company, 152
Indonesia, 82, 86, 87, 88
Insider's Newsletter, 127
International Commission of Control
    and Supervision (ICCS), 170, 174,
    175, 176, 207
Iron Triangle, 98

Jackson, Bill, 66
Jasmine Girl, 202–3
Jensen, Holger, 160
Johnson, Les, 122, 124, 127, 130–32
Johnson, Lyndon, 169
Joint U.S. Public Affairs Office
    (JUSPAO), 105, 109, 127
Jones, Bob, 4, 6, 30
Jones, Brett, 30
Jones, James, 178
journalists, female. *See* women, as
    correspondents
Junction City combat operation, 9
JUSPAO (Joint U.S. Public Affairs
    Office), 105, 109, 127

Kalb, Bernie, 169
Kalsu, Bob, 272
Kalsu, Jan, 272
Kampot, Cambodia, 180–81